Critical Public Archaeology

Critical Public Archaeology

Confronting Social Challenges in the 21st Century

Edited by
V. Camille Westmont

berghahn
NEW YORK · OXFORD
www.berghahnbooks.com

First published in 2022 by
Berghahn Books
www.berghahnbooks.com

© 2022 V. Camille Westmont

Library of Congress Cataloging-in-Publication Data

A C.I.P. cataloging record is available from the Library of Congress
Library of Congress Cataloging in Publication Control Number: 2022016735

British Library Cataloguing in Publication Data

A catalogue record for this book is available from the British Library

ISBN 978-1-80073-615-3 hardback
ISBN 978-1-80073-616-0 ebook

https://doi.org/10.3167/9781800736153

Contents

Part III. Situating Critical Archaeology

Illustrations

Figures

Tables

INTRODUCTION

In Pursuit of a
Critical Public Archaeology

V. Camille Westmont

Introduction

In the early 2000s, concerns grew about the role archaeology serves in society. Discussions centered on questions such as "is archaeology useful?" and "*should* archaeology be useful?" (Dawdy 2009: 131, emphasis in original). Others took a more personal tack, puzzling, "Can we make our voices heard? Should we make our voices heard? Do we have anything worthwhile to contribute to current debates?" (Tarlow and Stutz 2013: 3). Still others raised the stakes of this discussion by entreating readers with questions such as "Can Archaeology Save the World?" (Dawdy 2009; Stottman 2010). Although this anxiety was nearly universally answered in the affirmative, this exercise in self-doubt also brought to the fore several key observations about archaeologists' relationships with the public. In the midst of a major reevaluation of who public archaeology should serve and in what ways, an old perspective gained renewed interest: approaches based in critical theory.

Critical theory in archaeology is, by this point, a widely accepted form of praxis. New research projects, articles, books, and even a journal dedicated to the subject—*Forum Kritische Archäologie*—attest to its versatility, longevity, and popularity. However, a review of the literature published over the last forty years indicates that how critical archaeology is conceived of and carried out continues to be debated. While these largely theoretical treatises do at times identify applied projects that have enacted one or another forms of critical theory—including Carol McDavid's work on the Levi Jordan Plantation (2002, 2004), Mark Leone's Archaeology in Annapolis program (Leone 2005; Leone, Potter, and Shackel 1987; Palus, Leone, and Cochran 2006; Potter and Leone 1986; Shackel, Mullins, and Warner 1998), Randy McGuire and the Ludlow Collective's work in Colorado (Ludlow Collective 2001; Larkin and McGuire 2009;

Saitta 2007; Walker 2000; McGuire and Reckner 2003), and Paul Shackel's Anthracite Heritage Program in northeastern Pennsylvania (Shackel 2019; Shackel and Roller 2012; Westmont 2020)—published examples of applied critical archaeology projects are still heavily outnumbered by theoretical examinations of what critical archaeological praxis could be. This volume aims to expand these conversations by bringing together a variety of projects with a diversity of perspectives in order to examine how critical theory is currently being mobilized in pursuit of emancipatory public archaeologies that confront modern-day social and economic ideologies.

The concept for this book emerged from a public archaeology session at the 2019 Society for Historical Archaeology Conference in St. Charles, Missouri. The papers and discussions inevitably diverted from discussions about archaeological findings to concerns about the modern communities taking part in this research. These concerns about communities are not new: in the last two decades, public archaeologists have increasingly pushed for archaeologists to work collaboratively with communities through power-sharing arrangements (Atalay 2012; Franklin and Lee 2020; Nassaney 2020), or even potentially through the complete transfer of control to communities, a model in which archaeologists act solely as "technicians" within community-based projects that pursue community-set research agendas (La Salle 2010: 416; Biolsi and Zimmerman 1997; McNiven and Russell 2005). What is new is the growing interest in not just sharing power and resources, but in using archaeology and archaeological findings to create social change in modern communities by exposing the ideological roots of modern inequities. I refer to this type of archaeology as critical public archaeology to clearly and forthrightly situate this work and these approaches within the tradition of critical theory. Undoubtedly, a number of public archaeology projects in the "activist" and "transformative" camps could easily be categorized as being grounded in critical theory; the goal of introducing this category to an already terminologically crowded field (see Stottman, this volume) is to explicitly communicate the liberatory aims of this type of project.

Critical theory in archaeology has enjoyed a rich tradition in many international contexts, and this book aims to capture some of the diversity of the practice. Authors were invited to contribute chapters on the critically engaged public archaeology projects taking place in their communities. This opportunity to examine how ideas on public archaeology, critical theory, and public engagement praxis come together in different cultural and legal contexts provides new opportunities for the future of the field. I believe these differences to be both a strength of their independent development and an opportunity to grow and reflect on our own individual practices.

This introduction aims to provide a brief theoretical and literature review on critical public archaeology in order to situate the chapters in the volume that follow. It begins with a background on critical theory and its previous uses within archaeology. The chapter then briefly introduces public archaeology and discusses how these two concepts—public archaeology and critical theory—can be brought together as part of a coherent archaeological praxis. Some of the challenges of implementing a critical public archaeology are then explored, with particular attention paid to the relationship between critical public archaeology and multivocality in archaeology. Finally, I explain the organization of the book and introduce the chapters in this volume.

Critical Theory as Praxis

Critical theory differentiates itself from traditional philosophical perspectives in that it aims not to simply increase knowledge, but instead to act as a "liberating and stimulating influence" with the goal of achieving "man's emancipation from slavery" (Horkheimer 1972: 246). Achieving this requires two acknowledgments: first, one's own theorizing is embedded within a socio-political context; and second, ignoring the socio-political contexts of one's work enables the reproduction of power structures of society (MacDonald 2017). Key within these considerations were the roles that social and cultural institutions played in maintaining and reproducing the dominant social structure (Gramsci 1971). Implementing a critical perspective is, therefore, not a neutral or apolitical act. A properly implemented critically informed project should aim to both dismantle the status quo and to confront the structures that create and perpetuate social inequalities.

Others have previously examined the contributions of Marx and later theorists to the formulation of critical theory (see Leone et al. 1987; Palus et al. 2006; McGuire 2008). In the interest of brevity, I will not repeat those outlines here; however, it is important to note that the constellation of scholastic influences on the topic of critical inquiry means that there can be variation in the specific intellectual tradition that underpins critical praxis (see McGuire 2008). In some instances, archaeologists took their inspiration from the writing of Marx (see Kohl 1975; Gassiot, Palomar, and Ruiz 1999; Gassiot and Palomar 2000; Vila-Mitjá et al. 2010), V. Gordon Childe (see Vargas and Sanoja 1999; Trigger 1984, 1985; Muller 1997), and/or Louis Althusser and the Frankfurt School (see Leone 1986; Leone, Potter, and Shackel 1987).

Critical theory has also been adapted outside of Marx's traditional class-centered remit, including in feminist archaeology, Indigenous archaeology, and through the application of Critical Race Theory to archaeological contexts. These non-class-based applications of critical theory within archaeology have advanced the field in vital and creative ways. Work pursued by feminist and gender archaeologists since the 1980s has employed a gender-critical approach to highlight the androcentric biases that shape fieldwork, interpretations, and permeate the discipline as a whole (Conkey and Spector 1984; Conkey and Tringham 1995; Conkey 2003). This work has exposed the taken-for-granted assumptions, particularly those related to gendered activities, embedded within archaeological interpretations and knowledge formation processes. The introduction of critical feminist approaches has laid bare the ways modern gender biases have been normalized and maintained within the discipline of archaeology (Wylie 2007; Fryer and Raczek 2020; Heath-Stout 2020).

More recently, members of the Society for Black Archaeologists (SBA) have been spearheading a movement aimed at confronting and dismantling the everyday racism and anti-blackness that pervade archaeological thought and practice (see Flewellen et al. 2022; Franklin and Lee 2020). Through the application of Black feminist and critical race theories, this work draws on critically based praxis, including reflexivity, acknowledging the political power of one's work, and exposing the biases within our current systems, to advocate and work toward a more just and equitable future archaeology (see Battle-Baptiste 2011).

Efforts to challenge the inherent colonial and Western biases of archaeology have been a long-running focus of many Indigenous archaeology projects. Beginning in the 1960s, Indigenous activists have fought for the right to control their own cultural heritage (see Deloria 1969; Echo-Hawk and Echo-Hawk 1994). Activism aimed at decolonizing archaeology has led many archaeologists to "think critically about their right to control the material culture of the Indigenous past" and to reconceptualize their relationships with Indigenous stakeholder communities (Atalay 2006: 289; La Salle and Hutchings 2016). Instead of traditional frameworks, collaborative and community-oriented approaches have emerged as means of enabling research that is "politically aware of, sensitive to, and harmonious with, the goals of Indigenous peoples" (C. Smith and Wobst 2005: 5; Supernant and Warrick 2014; Watkins 2005; Hennessey et al. 2013). These approaches exemplify the ways critical engagement with the past can lead to new, more equitable relations in the present.

Other forms of grass-roots resistance to the status quo have also emerged, such as the punk archaeology movement, which foregrounds political actions within archaeology while embracing fictive kinship, integrity, and community (see Morgan 2014; Caraher 2014; Richardson 2017; however, some have explicitly distanced punk archaeology from Marxist approaches, see Morgan 2015).

In the context of archaeology, the application of critical theory enabled the realization that archaeology is a site of ideological struggle both in the past and in the present (Tilley 1989).[1] Critical theory posits that knowledge does not exist apart from the social context in which that knowledge was created (Rowlands 1998). Therefore, the reconstructions of the past that archaeologists create are both culturally constituted and serve a social function within the culture that created them. The social functions that non-critical archaeologies serve are based in ideologies. Under this idea, archaeology does not produce objective and universal perspectives on history; rather, our interpretations are "always guided by contemporary interest" and serve as a "mirror image of the present" that is used to conceal current-day structures of domination that are actuated through ideologies (Rowlands 1998: 26).

Although critical theory in archaeology is frequently discussed as a singular approach, in practice critical theory as it relates to archaeology has been envisaged in an assortment of ways. In general, however, a critical approach to archaeology seeks greater emancipation and less alienation (McGuire 2008). Once alienated, individuals feel disconnected from their labor, their colleagues, and even potentially aspects of themselves. Emancipation solves the issue of alienation by revealing the ideological structures that cause alienation by challenging the dominant ideologies that otherwise obscure the social tensions.

Understanding the connections between archaeologically derived knowledge, the social context of that knowledge, and the ideologies perpetuated by that knowledge illuminates why archaeology matters, particularly to the very people subjugated by ideologies who might otherwise disregard archaeology as being irrelevant to their everyday life and lived experience (McGuire 2012). Archaeologists cannot expect those groups to seek out archaeology; rather, archaeologists need to identify methods that will enable greater collaboration and understanding, particularly within communities not already in the process of managing their heritage resources (see Two Bears 2008; Hunter 2008; Chirikure and Pwiti 2008).

Public Archaeology

Public archaeology brings together archaeological practice and archaeological scholarship to make the field relevant for a non-professional audience (Moshenska 2017; Matsuda and Okamura 2011); however, approaches to creating relevancy vary greatly. Over the past two decades, conceptions of public archaeology have become more refined as demand for archaeological experiences grows (Thomas 2017). This trend has not diminished, with multiple new volumes on the topic continuing to demonstrate public archaeology's increasingly international profile and wide-ranging methodologies (see Barton 2021; Gürsu 2019; Williams, Pudney, and Ezzeldin 2019). Nick Merriman's (2004) delineation of the "deficit" and the "multiple perspective" models represents one of the early attempts to categorize specific modes of practice within public archaeology, followed shortly by Cornelius J. Holtorf's (2007) "education," "public relations," and "democratic" models of public archaeology. Akira Matsuda (2016) expanded on Holtorf and Merriman's categories with a fourth approach: the critical category. The critical approach to public archaeology diverges from these earlier categories through its focus on upending modern inequalities based in ideologies.

Although public archaeology had made major advances, both theoretically and methodologically, since it was formalized in the late twentieth century, our understanding of its goals continues to develop. Increased activism around Black and Indigenous cultural resources in the early 1990s saw the relationships between archaeologists and descendant communities shift in fundamental and important ways. Public anger around the excavations at the African Burial Ground in New York City revealed the deep tensions and asymmetries that had arisen between those conducting the excavations and the area's African American community (La Roche and Blakey 1997). Since that time, the public archaeology of the African diaspora—including projects that promote critical engagement with the past—has steadily grown (see McDavid 2002; Minkoff, Brock, and Reeves, this volume).

Arguments over the central premise of public archaeology intensified at the turn of the century with Francis McManamon and Holtorf's debate in *Public Archaeology* (Holtorf 2000; McManamon 2000); disagreements arose yet again just a few years later, this time between Holtorf (2005) and Garrett Fagan and Kenneth Feder (2006) in *World Archaeology*, over the role public-generated interpretations labeled as alternative archaeologies should play in the field. Akira Matsuda (2016) identifies both of these arguments as stemming from disagreements in the conceptualization of the role public archaeology should serve in society; however, all of these arguments, in one way or another, connect back to questions about the roles of non-professionals should serve—considerations that are based in ideologies about the field and reflexivity (debates over the role of the public in archaeology continue today, see Thomas and Pitblado 2020; Watkins 2020; Pitblado and Thomas 2020).

Defining a Critical Approach to Public Archaeology

The fact that archaeology and archaeological interpretations of the past are political has largely been accepted (Shanks and Tilley 1987; Trigger 1984; Habu, Fawcett, and Matsunaga 2008; McGuire 2008; Borck 2019); what is more uncertain is what archaeology should do about those politics. For many, this political awareness has led to greater ethical engagement. To this end, recent trends in the field include working with descendant groups and promoting greater reflexivity (Hodder 2000; Hamilakis 2004; Meskell 2012; Silliman 2008; Simpson and Williams 2008). Others, however, are explicitly engaging with the politics of archaeology as a form of social justice activism (Zimmerman, Singleton, and Welch 2010; Shackel 2011; Shackel and Westmont 2016; Stottman 2010; Atalay et al. 2014; Barton 2021). This final form of political engagement takes many forms, including as critical archaeology praxis.

In many ways, the connection of critical archaeology to public archaeology is a natural one: both acknowledge the socio-political importance of the past, and both are interventions in the present into that past (Tilley 1989; Dalglish 2013). A critical approach to archaeology focuses on revealing and challenging the social and political ideologies unquestioningly maintained and reproduced through archaeological interpretations and practices. It does this in part by asking simply: who today benefits from this particular interpretation of the past (Matsuda and Okamura 2011; Hodder 2002)? Through this line of inquiry, archaeologists aim to disrupt the cycles of social subjugation and marginalization of minority groups by confronting at least one method of domination: historical narratives.

As archaeology has become a more formal, professionalized undertaking, archaeologists have recognized the importance of incorporating the public into their work (see Fritz and Plog 1970) and of considering the political implications of their work on the public. Politically engaged work often means focusing on those communities that have been traditionally ignored by or excluded from archaeology. Understanding how these groups became oppressed and marginalized by the field, however, requires self-reflection on the social and political dimensions of the field as well as on archaeologists' positionality within those dimensions (McGuire 2008). In some instances, pressure to adopt critical perspectives can also come from communities themselves. Thomas Patterson (2008: 73–74) finds that descendant and diasporic communities that suffer the injustices of hegemonic standards are often the groups to begin broader political and intellectual debates around the legitimacy of the status quo; in these instances, archaeologists have the opportunity to participate in meaningful and productive ways as they struggle alongside communities to enact change.

Challenges to a Truly Critical Public Archaeology

This discussion of the possibilities of critical public archaeology ultimately raises a new question: how can archaeology, with its purview in the past, liberate anyone from modern ideological structures? As Gavin Lucas (2001) observes, while the introduction of New Archaeology brought with it fundamental changes to the way archaeology was done, post-processualism has not similarly changed the way archaeologists carry out fieldwork. While some have identified means of integrating reflexive practice into fieldwork (see Hodder 2000, 2003), much of the critical evaluations central to a critical theory-informed practice continue to take place away from the "trowel's edge" (Berggren and Hodder 2003). If ideologies permeate everything from the sites archaeologists choose to excavate to the field approaches employed to the interpretations made back at the lab (Hodder 1999), a truly critical archaeology will ultimately require a re-building of the discipline and its methodology from the ground up (see Atalay et al. 2014).

While addressing embedded ideologies within archaeological practice is one challenge, archaeologists' positionality poses another major challenge. As people who have subscribed to and benefited from the current system of archaeology, how can archaeologists be the ones expected to change it (Castañeda 2014)? Considering that most archaeologists are employed within some form of a neo-liberal market economy, calling for change through a critical theory approach might not just be untenable, it might be career suicide (Nakamura 2012; Durrans 1987).

These problem with implementing a fully critical approach—one that critiques the very systems that employ the archaeologists launching the critiques—are also felt within the field of public archaeology. Akira Matsuda (2016) astutely posits that it is critical theory's arguments against ideology that render it ill-suited for an increasingly neo-liberal market economy, one in which private funders increasingly have control over the products of intellectual and academic research. Cornelius Holtorf (2009) even suggests that the questions presented in the opening of this introduction—questions about the usefulness of archaeology—are themselves entangled within a Western neo-liberal mindset that determines value based on profitability and revenue.

Further complications come from working with communities. Community identity is fluid, complex, and heterogenous (Pyburn 2011). When working with communities they are not personally part of, archaeologists risk overlooking or ignoring existing social relations in pursuit of community cohesion (Waterton 2005). Additionally, studies have indicated that for many volunteers and enthusiasts, archaeology is a leisure activity; if archaeologists intend to take up social issues through their public practice, they also need ensure that the demographics they are working with are truly representative of the broader community and not simply reflective of those groups who have the time and resources to engage in these forms of leisure (Richardson and Almansa-Sánchez 2015).

Other challenges also confront critical public archaeology efforts. As Durrans (1987: 294) highlights, critical interpretations that focus on liberating public audiences by revealing their naturalized ideologies "are feeble [in] comparison [to] the dominant media through which ideological views of the past are promoted." Indeed, subsequent analyses of the public archaeology tours and interpretations associated with the Archaeology in Annapolis project found that visitors often situated the liberatory narratives within their pre-existing ideological frameworks, thereby rendering archaeologists' attempts to emancipate the public futile (Potter 1994; Leone 1995).

Additionally, implementing aspects of critical practice in limited ways might actually entrench archaeological ideologies and power dynamics. Although projects seek to incorporate power-sharing and community collaborations as part of their critically informed praxis, these actions do little to address the systemic, power-based disparities inherent in the field. Even when communities are involved in research, archaeological fieldwork still often requires governmental permits or external funding, access to which continues to be heavily dependent on positionality and disciplinary ideologies (Westmont and Clay 2021). While community collaborations are important for building relationships and trust, ultimately "these worthwhile pursuits are not tantamount to any true transformation or radical redistribution of archaeological power and capital" (Nakamura 2012: 124).

Additionally, archaeologists' interpretations continue to shape understandings of the site in subtle or less overt ways throughout the entire archaeological process—including during field work (Hodder 1999)—which further obscures the power dynamics within collaborative projects. In short, archaeologists still act as gatekeepers with control over official narratives of the past; archaeologists allowing communities to direct research questions or participate in projects opens the gate but does not remove it. At worst, conducting collaborations under these circumstances—circumstances that appear on the surface to be equal but actually engage and perpetuate power disparities—can be seen as its own form of ideological obfuscation; in this light, power-sharing structures can be seen as the type of practice that presents a veneer of social change while it reproduces inequalities. While many have outlined processes for achieving a truly ethical, power-balanced, collaborative public archaeology practice (see Colwell-Chanthaponh and Ferguson 2008; L. Smith 1999), actuating methods that achieve true systemic change in a widespread way continues to be a challenge.

Multivocality and Critical Archaeology

Tenets of critical theory are deeply ingrained in all sorts of public archaeology projects today. Chief among these are projects that incorporate reflexivity and critical appraisals of assumptions, ideologies, and power dynamics into their public praxis. These types of considerations often result in projects dedicated to correcting power imbalances between archaeologists and communities (Atalay 2007; Colwell-Chanthaphonh and Ferguson 2008); in practice, these values manifest as multivocality, descendant collaborations, and/or community-based research, among other power-sharing models (McDavid 2002; La Salle 2010; McAnany and Rowe 2015; Flewellen et al. 2022).

However, others have pointed out that while these reflexive methods reflect engagement with the concepts espoused by critical archaeology, multivocal interpretations alone do not constitute a fully critical archaeology. Akira Matsuda and Katsuyuki Okamura (2011) separate multivocal approaches from critical approaches in their characterization of different forms of public archaeology. While the two forms appear similar in many respects, Matsuda and Okamura suggest that "the divide between the critical and multivocal approaches . . . could be compared to the differences between two positions on the intellectual left: the traditional left and the postmodern liberal left" (2011: 6). A multivocal approach is ultimately grounded in a hermeneutic epistemology that acknowledges and incorporates multiple perspectives on the past as a means of exploring the diversity of perspectives on the past. Oftentimes this approach is used to achieve socio-political aims, such as to counter dominant narratives of the past (Faulkner 2000) or to achieve recognition (Bender 1998). In these instances, the diversity of perspectives is the key goal, with socio-political changes then emerging from that diversity of perspectives. In critical approaches, however, the opposite is true: the key goal from the outset is to identify the social and political ideologies upheld by archaeology by first questioning the situatedness of the project and the positionality of the stakeholders. It is only though confronting those ideologies and dismantling dominating structures that communities benefit.

While this might seem like an inconsequential difference (multivocality leading to social change versus critical inquiry and reflection leading to social change), these differences have real consequences. Central among these is the role of non-expert voices in interpretations. Multivocality in archaeology has been invaluable for decolonizing archaeological practices and continues to play a major role in restorative justice for many marginalized and oppressed communities around the globe (R. Smith 2018). However, within a critical archaeological praxis, multivocality is limited by necessity. Controlling narratives and interpretations is an essential aspect of a critical archaeology framework—after all, it is through precisely these channels that dominating and hegemonic ideologies are supported, legitimized, and perpetuated. McGuire (2012: 79–80) writes that "archaeologists should practice their craft in the service of multiple communities," but archaeologists must also remain cognizant that "archaeologists need to retain some authority over the production of knowledge in order to assess [how our interpretations fit the observations we can make of the world]." These precautions are required to prevent archaeological interpretations from being misappropriated in service of the very forces critical archaeology aims to critique and dismantle. Most pressingly, unchecked archaeological interpretation can be used as an entry for pernicious and malicious nationalism (Atalay et al. 2014; Holtorf 2009; McGhee 2008), to promote populism (González-Ruibal, Alonso Gaonzález, and Criado Boado 2018), or to perpetuate convenient falsehoods (McGuire 2008). Although some have dismissed concerns about nationalism by saying that it is "problematic to take this power away from *people* in locales in which it is already utilized by their governments" (Atalay et al. 2014: 12), I believe that the goal here should be an emancipatory archaeology, not shifting ideologies.

How, then, can public archaeology bridge the gap between ethical requirements to do no harm and critical requirements to maintain a degree of control over the production of knowledge? I suggest that Carolyn Nakamura (2012: 124) proposes the best—although admittedly among the most difficult to implement—answer: that critical archaeology should focus on "how we might facilitate impoverished communities affected by archaeology gaining more direct access to those structures, resources, and capacities with which they can express their voice and get results skewed towards their own welfare." In other words, archaeologists should stop trying to act as mediators in the self-appointed role of implementing critical archaeology and focus instead on building communities' capacities so that they themselves have the tool at their disposal to challenge the ideologies that oppress them. This shift in the disciplinary "status quo" is likely to spur new conceptions and perspectives on the past and open the field to new innovations. Archaeologists must abandon our vested interest in the field as we know it—as a field of study, a discipline, a profession, an institution, and a cultural apparatus—in order to enable new methodologies, theories, and perspectives to drive the future of the discipline (Castañeda 2014). As economic and social disparities continue to grow, critical archaeologies can offer necessary and appropriate tools for navigating the future of the field (C. Smith 2012).

Structure of Book

Critical perspectives on archaeology are not new, and neither are critical perspectives on public archaeology (see Potter 1994). So what, then, does this volume add to an already well-trodden path? First, this volume aims to specifically highlight instances where critical perspectives of the past are being integrated into public archaeology and community engagement. While these examples engage with critical theory to varying extents, this volume provides a starting place to begin addressing concerns that critical public archaeology cannot function in our current economic and socio-political contexts (e.g., Kristiansen 2008; Matsuda 2016).

Second, the volume aims to introduce new ways of conceiving of the intersections between critical theory and public archaeology. Public tours, interpretations, and collaborative excavations have demonstrated utility, but what about other facets of public archaeology? This volume encourages archaeologists to think beyond traditional modes of engagement to examine where critical approaches can be implemented within a broader definition of public archaeology. Recognizing the full scale and diversity of public archaeological practice (see Moshenska 2017) can highlight areas for archaeologists to develop and implement critical praxis that extend outside of the traditional critical public archaeology remit.

Finally, this book hopes to encourage archaeologists to more explicitly and openly engage with the politics of their field. Although scholars have repeatedly emphasized the political nature of archaeology, many do not extend that acknowledgment to their fieldwork or their public engagement. A full acknowledgment that a project's public outreach is aware of and in reaction to its political and social circumstances would advance theoretical perspectives within public archaeology and make our political engagements clearer for professional and lay audiences. While undoubtedly some will say that using the phrase "critical archaeology" is jargon-y, and indeed others have cautioned against the pitfalls of jargon in public interactions (see C. Smith 2012), I believe that the terminology also provides a teaching opportunity for archaeologists to familiarize members of the public with a term that, in many ways, affects them, too. Ultimately, archaeologists need to be honest with members of the public about the politics of our work, and starting that process by using the correct terminology (and instructing members of the public on what those terms mean) is a step toward a more open and direct practice.

This book is organized into three sections. The opening section explores the ways an explicitly critical perspective can be used to advance work within communities. Mary Furlong Minkoff, Terry Brock, and Matthew Reeves open the section with their examination of the ways anti-racism can be pursued through public archaeology at Montpelier, a historic home in Orange, Virginia. Anti-racist praxis follows Critical Race Theory's acknowledgment that policy is where structures become racist or anti-racist, so to combat racism, institutions must create or sustain anti-racist policies. At Montpelier, the Archaeology Department has used critical self-reflections to implement anti-racist policies that address and confront racism in both representations of the past and in the present. These efforts have since become a defining force of the public archaeology practice, particularly with reference to descendant communities, internships, and public archaeology programming. These efforts outline how a critically informed praxis can be used to identify and dismantle the policies that create racial inequalities, particularly within public engagement and interpretation of archaeological sites.

The second chapter in the section explores how public engagement and public archaeology are working to change harmful and ingrained notions around racism and civil rights as it relates to the mass incarceration of Japanese Americans during World War II. Jeffery Burton and Mary M. Farrell demonstrate how they have used community archaeology at Manzanar, a Japanese Relocation Center in California, to challenge damaging and untrue modern narratives about the site that seek to downplay and justify the events that took place there. In challenging these narratives, Burton and Farrell are challenging modern ideologies centered in nationalism and racism while they engage the public in a critical reflection on governmental power and the rights of citizens.

The final chapter in the section on archaeologists working with communities profiles a different way public archaeology can highlight ideologies of inequality. M. Jay Stottman's work at Portland Wharf in Louisville, Kentucky, uses public archaeology not just as a means of confronting misconceptions about communities and their history, but as a form of activism in itself. Stottman investigates the possibilities of using archaeological performance to reinvest in Portland Wharf Park and, by extension, the people who live there. Portland Wharf, once a thriving independent community, was progressively annexed by the city of Louisville during the late nineteenth and early twentieth centuries until eventually the physical remains of the community itself vanished. Now an economically depressed area, archaeologists are using public archaeology programming methods to raise the profile of the former community and draw attention back to the area's working-class heritage. Exit surveys from the project indicate that archaeology itself is a political action—one the connotes worth, value, and investment. Stottman's findings suggest that rather than relying on interpretations, archaeologists can also illuminate ideologies around whose history is remembered and whose is not by using the public popularity of the discipline to draw attention to forgotten communities.

While communities will always remain at the heart of critically engaged work, deeper investigations into the means by which critically engaged work is carried out can point to new directions for innovation and collaboration. The second section of the volume explores how critical perspectives can advance other areas of archaeology, including museums, websites, narratives, and performances. The section begins with Monika Stobiecka's investigations into the possibility of a critical archaeological museum. Following the work of Piotr Piotrowski, Stobiecka examines how museums can be spaces for social critique, where anachronistic displays of the past are re-interpreted as venues for addressing modern-day social questions, as a response to recent calls for museums to reconsider their public role. Specifically, Stobiecka identifies three requirements from a critical archaeology museum: that it must feature strong bonds to other institutions such as universities; that it must focus on "big picture" problems or problems of global importance; and that it must engage visitors in ways that promote archaeological imagination and encourage them to personally reflect on the various meanings of the past. Stobiecka's observations on the roles museums have to play in promoting greater critical evaluations of archaeology thoughtfully demonstrate the important roles that archaeological institutions can play in confronting social challenges.

While Stobiecka introduces readers to the opportunities for critical engagement that exist within museum contexts, Kerry Massheder-Rigby demonstrates that public archaeology can still be carried out in places where the past's physical presence has been largely erased. The *Our Humble Abodes* project explores the viability of a joint archaeology and oral history approach to public archaeology and ultimately finds that oral history can be a powerful tool for combating essentialized mainstream narratives. Ultimately, the project succeeded in complicating narratives about working-class life in Liverpool's court houses and captured a range of emotions—from attachment to happy childhoods to nostalgia—that are often not included in official remembrances of working-class life. Massheder-Rigby suggests that incorporating oral history more thoroughly into archaeological investigations not only provides a fuller and richer perspective on the past, but it also enables members of the public to make meaningful contributions to archaeological research. These new perspectives can help to combat negative stereotypes about marginalized communities while empowering those communities to take more active roles in the interpretation of their history.

The applicability of new methods of critical public archaeology continues with Camille Westmont's chapter on the potential for narratives to ground critical reevaluations of the past and connect past injustices to modern circumstances. Westmont inserts narratives derived from archival documents into her archaeological site tours of the Lone Rock Stockade, a private prison used to house forced laborers in nineteenth-century Tennessee. Over the course of the tour, Westmont transitions from narratives about historical prison labor abuses to narratives based on modern prison labor abuses. Through these stories, Westmont attempts to build empathy for prisoners that can then be translated into political action in the present. Westmont points out that while narratives are not a new strategy within archaeology or within public archaeology, their potential as a form of critical scholarship is currently underdeveloped within the field of public archaeology.

Moving away from traditional approaches to public engagement, Adam Fracchia turns to digital means of reaching broader audiences. Fracchia provides an update on one of the United States' early critical public archaeology projects—Archaeology in Annapolis. Forty years into the project, however, Fracchia highlights a major absence: the inclusion of diverse and non-expert perspectives in the project's production of knowledge. Fracchia acknowledges that while that omission cannot be corrected, a critical approach to Archaeology in Annapolis's forthcoming digital humanities aims to move in a new direction—one that pursues the democratization of knowledge and the inclusion of non-expert voices. To achieve this, Archaeology in Annapolis explores the possibilities of new data frameworks, expanded access, and online collaborations. While the application of digital humanities concepts to archaeology is not new, Fracchia's aims to seek an explicitly critical digital archaeology that offers new directions for the field.

While the first two sections of the book explore how critical approaches to public archaeology are currently deployed, chapters by Torgrim Sneve Guttormsen and Chiara Zuanni offer important critiques and identify areas of further evaluation for a critical public archaeology praxis. Guttormsen uses the Norwegian Museum of Technology as a foil for examining the way public historiography can be used to explain the relationship between archaeology and the public. Using Bakhtin's concepts of dialogism and chronotopes, Guttormsen explains how museums can become real-life chronotopes where spatial and temporal aspects of history are fused according to popular conceptions of the past. The chapter suggests that archaeology itself can end up being negotiated by publics, and that the relationship between archaeology and the public can only truly be understood retrospectively as the findings of archaeologists become discursively linked with those created by society. Guttormsen advocates a nuanced understanding of the interconnections between various stakeholders' perspectives on the past, and calls for critical reflexivity in understanding these relational aspects of public archaeological interpretation.

The second chapter in this section explores similar concerns about the efficacy of critical interpretations, although this time from the visitors' perspective rather than from the museum's. Zuanni recounts the role that museums play in shaping visitors' experiences and understandings of the past, and analyzes those sentiments in light of visitors' preconceived ideas, interests, and beliefs about the past. Zuanni finds that museums continue to be viewed as a source of authoritative knowledge, with recent efforts to promote participatory practices potentially being overlooked by the public. These observations are crucial for critical public archaeologies because they echo warnings outlined in the 1990s: the balancing of archaeologists' interpretations with the publics' own embedded understandings of history was a major obstacle identified by Parker Potter (1992) in the Archaeology in Annapolis public tours in the 1980s, demonstrating that the interplay between old and new knowledge can potentially continue to create obstacles for critically engaged projects.

The book closes with a thoughtful consideration on public archaeology in the context of critical theory. Suzie Thomas presents the historical origins and current trajectories of public archaeology, particularly in a rapidly changing post-COVID world. Thomas connects each chapter in turn to the broader public archaeology movement and demonstrates the opportunities that critical approaches hold for the future of the practice and the future of archaeologically engaged communities.

Conclusion

This volume provides a view to the intersections between critical theory and public archaeology in American and European contexts. The diversity of communities involved, approaches used, definitions, and conceptualizations of critical approaches to archaeology demonstrates the current growth and future potential for these forms of outreach and inquiry.

In particular the range of practitioners and situations in which critical public archaeology is being applied is promising. From small, socially disadvantaged communities in the Midwestern United States to museum goers in Poland, the range of groups to which critical approaches can be applied is extraordinary. Given the various legal and regulatory restrictions on public involvement in archaeological research across different countries, the fact that critical approaches can be implemented to a plethora of types of public archaeology lends the approach even more value. The wide application and high adaptability of critical approaches shine through in the range of circumstances presented in these chapters.

Another pattern across the chapters is the diversity of definitions archaeologists use when discussing their approaches to critical theory. Some projects seek a critical perspective that incorporates those voices that have been marginalized historically by making space for those voices to play leading roles in current and future research; other projects define critical approaches as those that raise awareness about pressing social issues by connecting the past and the present into a single continuous narrative; still others see critical approaches as means to restore historical voices and correct misinformation through direct conversation with descendant groups and interested interlocutors. The core tenets of critical theory—reflexivity, liberatory aims, and positionality—all come through to various degrees in these chapters.

While far from comprehensive, the chapters in this book provide a starting point from which I hope future critically engaged public archaeology projects will emerge. The range of approaches, methodologies, communities, and perspectives captured by the chapters in this volume offer potential directions for future innovations in the field. As the world continues to struggle with constant and growing social, economic, environmental, and political conundrums, these chapters demonstrate that the past can still be a resource for creating change for the future.

V. Camille Westmont is the Andrew Mellon Foundation Postdoctoral Fellow in Historical Archaeology at the University of the South in Sewanee, Tennessee. She received her PhD in anthropology from the University of Maryland. Her work focuses on labor archaeology, industrial cultural heritage, landscape analyses, and public engagement. She currently serves as the co-chair of the Public Archaeology Community in the European Association of Archaeologists.

Notes

1. Ideology has long been a subject of study within archaeology (see Kristiansen 1984; Paynter 1985; Handsman 1980, 1981, 1982). In this context, ideology refers to the aspects of cultural systems that prevent social conflict by obscuring or masking contradictions in society (Barnett and Silverman 1979; Leone 1986).

References

Atalay, Sonya. 2006. "Indigenous Archaeology as Decolonizing Practice." *American Indian Quarterly* 30(3/4): 280–310.

———. 2007. "Global Application of Indigenous Archaeology: Community Based Participatory Research in Turkey." *Archaeologies* 3: 249–70.

———. 2012. *Community-Based Archaeology: Research with, by, and for Indigenous and Local Communities.* Berkeley: University of California Press

Atalay, Sonya, Lee Rains Clauss, Randall H. McGuire, and John R. Welch, eds. 2014. *Transforming Archaeology: Activist Practices and Prospects.* London: Routledge.

Barnett, Steve, and Martin G. Silverman. 1979. *Ideology and Everyday Life.* Ann Arbor: University of Michigan Press.

Barton, Christopher P., ed. 2021. *Trowels in the Trenches: Archaeology as Social Activism.* Gainesville: University Press of Florida.

Battle-Baptiste, Whitney. 2011. *Black Feminist Archaeology.* Walnut Creek, CA: Left Coast Press.

Bender, Barbara. 1998. *Stonehenge: Making Space.* Oxford: Berg.

Berggren, Åsa, and Ian Hodder. 2003. "Social Practice, Method, and Some Problems of Field Archaeology." *American Antiquity* 68(3): 421–34.

Biolsi, Thomas, and Larry J. Zimmerman, ed. 1997. *Indians and Anthropologists: Vine Deloria Jr. and the Critique of Anthropology.* Tucson: University of Arizona Press.

Borck, Lewis. 2019. "Constructing the Future History: Prefiguration as Historical Epistemology and the Chronopolitics of Archaeology." *Journal of Contemporary Archaeology* 5(2): 229–38.

Caraher, William. 2014. "Introduction." In *Punk Archaeology*, ed. William Caraher, Kostis Kourelis, and Andrew Reinhard, 9–13. Grand Forks, ND: Digital Press.

Castañeda, Quetzil E. 2014. "Situating Activism in Archaeology: The Mission of Science the Activist Affect, and the Archaeological Record." In *Transforming Archaeology: Activist Practices and Prospects*, ed. Sonya Atalay, Lee Rains Clauss, Randall H. McGuire, and John R. Welch, 61–90. London: Routledge.

Chikikure, Shadreck, and Gilbert Pwiti. 2008. "Community Involvement in Archaeology and Cultural Heritage Management: An Assessment from Case Studies in Southern Africa and Elsewhere." *Current Anthropology* 49(3): 467–85.

Colwell-Chanthaphonh, Chip, and T. J. Ferguson, eds. 2008. *Collaboration in Archaeological Practice: Engaging Descendant Communities.* Lanham, MD: AltaMira Press.

Conkey, Margaret W. 2003. "Has Feminism Changed Archaeology?" *Signs: Journal of Women in Culture and Society* 28(3): 867–79.

Conkey, Margaret, and Janet Spector. 1984. "Archaeology and the Study of Gender." Advances in Archeological Method and Theory, 11 vols., ed. Michael B. Schiffer, 5:1–38. New York: Academic Press.

Conkey, Margaret, and Ruth Tringham. 1995. "Archaeology and the Goddess: Exploring the Contours of Feminist Archaeology." In *Feminisms in the Academy*, ed. Domna Stanton and Abigail Stewart, 199–247. Ann Arbor: University of Michigan Press

Dalglish, Chris, ed. 2013. *Archaeology, the Public, and the Recent Past.* Woodbridge: Boydell Press.

Dawdy, Shannon Lee. 2009. "Millennial Archaeology: Locating the Discipline in the Age of Insecurity." *Archaeological Dialogues* 16(2): 131–42.

Deloria, Vine, Jr. 1969. *Custer Died for Your Sins: An Indian Manifesto.* London: Macmillan.

Durrans, Brian. 1987. "Response to: Toward a Critical Archaeology." *Current Anthropology* 28(3): 293–94.

Echo-Hawk, Roger C., and Walter R. Echo-Hawk. 1994. *Battlefields and Burial Grounds: The Indian Struggle to Protect Ancestral Graves in the United States.* Minneapolis, MN: Lerner.

Fagan, Garrett G., and Kenneth L. Feder. 2006. "Crusading against Straw Men: An Alternative View of Alternative Archaeologies: Response to Holtorf (2005)." *World Archaeology* 38(4): 718–29.

Faulkner, Neil. 2000. "Archaeology from Below." *Public Archaeology* 1(1): 21–33.

Flewellen, Ayana, Alicia Odewale, Justin Dunnavant, Alexandra Jones, and William White III. (2022). "Creating Community and Engaging Community: The Foundations of the Estate Little Princess Archaeology Project in St. Croix, United States Virgin Islands." *International Journal of Historical Archaeology* 26: 147–76. https://doi.org/10.1007/s10761-021-00600-z.

Franklin, Maria, and Nedra Lee. 2020. "African American Descendants, Community Outreach, and the Ransom and Sarah Williams Farmstead Project." *Journal of Community Archaeology and Heritage* 7(2): 135–48.

Fritz, John, and Fred Plog. 1970. "The Nature of Archaeological Explanation." *American Antiquity* 35(4): 405–12. https://doi.org/10.2307/278113.

Fryer, Tiffany C., and Teresa P. Raczek. 2020. "Introduction: Toward an Engaged Feminist Heritage Praxis." *Archaeological Papers of the American Anthropological Association* 31(1): 7–25.

Gassiot, Ermengol, and Beatriz Palomar. 2000. "Arqueología de la Praxis: Información Histórica de la Acción Social." *Complutum* 11: 87–99.

Gassiot, Ermengol, Beatriz Palomar, and Gustavo Ruiz. 1999. "Brief Outline of the Marxist Archeology in the Spanish State." *European Journal of Archaeology* 2(3): 234–36.

González-Ruibal, Alfredo, Pablo Alonso González, and Felipe Criado Boado. 2018. "Against Reactionary Populism: Towards a New Public Archaeology." *Antiquity* 92(362): 507–15.

Gramsci, Antonio. 1971. *Selections from the Prison Notebooks of Antonio Gramsci*, trans. Quintin Hoare and Geoffrey Nowell Smith. New York: International Publishers.

Gürsu, Isilay, ed. 2019. *Public Archaeology: Theoretical Approaches and Current Practices*. Oxford: Oxbow Books.

Habu, Junko, Clare Fawcett, and John M. Matsunaga, eds. 2008. *Evaluating Multiple Narratives: Beyond Nationalist, Colonialist, Imperialist Archaeologies*. New York: Springer.

Hamilakis, Yannis. 2004. "Archaeology and the Politics of Pedagogy." *World Archaeology* 36(2): 287–309.

Handsman, Russell G. 1980. "The Domains of Kinship and Settlement in Historic Goshen: Signs of a Past Cultural Order." *Artifacts* 9(1): 2–7.

———. 1981. "Early Capitalism and the Center Village of Canaan, Connecticut: A Study of Transformations and Separations." *Artifacts* 9(3): 1–21.

———. 1982. "The Hot and Cold of Goshen's History." *Artifacts* 10(3): 10–20.

Heath-Stout, Laura E. 2020. "Who Write about Archaeology? An Intersection Study of Authorship in Archaeological Journals." *American Antiquity* 85(3): 407–26.

Hennessey, Kate, Natasha Lyons, Stephen Loring, Charles Arnold, Mervin Joe, Albert Elias, and James Pokiak. 2013. "The Inuvialuit Living History Project: Digital Return as the Forging of Relationships Between Institutions, People, and Data." *Museum Anthropology* 7(1/2): 44–73.

Hodder, Ian. 1999. *The Archaeological Process: An Introduction*. Hoboken, NJ: Wiley-Blackwell.

———. 2000. "Developing a Reflexive Method in Archaeology." In *Towards Reflexive Method in Archaeology: The Example of Çatalhöyük*, ed. Ian Hodder, 3–15. British Institute of Archaeology at Ankara Monograph No. 28. Cambridge: McDonald Institute for Archaeological Research.

———. 2002. "Archaeological Theory." In *Archaeology: The Widening Debate*, ed. Barry Cunliffe, Wendy Davies, and Colin Renfrew, 77–90. Oxford: British Academy.

———. 2003. "Archaeological Reflexivity and the 'Local' Voice." *Anthropological Quarterly* 76(1): 55–69.

Holtorf, Cornelius J. 2000. "Engaging with Multiple Pasts: Reply to Francis McManamon." *Public Archaeology* 1(3): 214–15.

———. 2005. "Beyond Crusades: How (Not) to Engage with Alternative Archaeologies." *World Archaeology* 37(4): 544–51.

———. 2007. *Archaeology is a Brand!: The Meaning of Archaeology in Contemporary Popular Culture*. Oxford: Archaeopress.

———. 2009. "Archaeology: From Usefulness to Value." *Archaeological Dialogues* 16(2): 182–86.

Horkheimer, Max. 1972. *Critical Theory: Selected Essays*, trans. Matthew J. O'Connell et al. New York: Herder and Herder.

Hunter, Andrea A. 2008. "A Critical Change in Pedagogy: Indigenous Cultural Resource Management." In *Collaborating at the Trowel's Edge: Teaching and Learning in Indigenous Archaeology*, ed. Stephen Silliman, 165–87. Tucson: University of Arizona Press.

Kohl, Phil. 1975. "The Archaeology of Trade." *Dialectical Anthropology* 1(1): 43–50.

Kristiansen, Kristian. 1984. "Ideology and Material Culture: An Archaeological Perspective." In *Marxist Perspectives in Archaeology*, ed. Matthew Spriggs, 72–100. Cambridge: Cambridge University Press.

———. 2008. "Should Archaeology Be in the Service of 'Popular Culture'? A Theoretical and Political Critique of Cornelius Holtorf's Vision of Archaeology." *Antiquity* 82(316): 488–90.

Larkin, Karin, and Randall McGuire, eds. 2009. *The Archaeology of Class War: The Colorado Coalfield Strike of 1913–1914*. Boulder: University Press of Colorado.

La Roche, Cheryl J., and Michael L. Blakey. 1997. "Seizing Intellectual Power: The Dialogue at the New York African Burial Ground." *Historical Archaeology* 31(3): 84–106.

La Salle, Marina. 2010. "Community Collaboration and Other Good Intentions." *Archaeologies: Journal of the World Archaeological Congress* 6(3): 401–22.

La Salle, Marina, and Rich Hutchings. 2016. "What Makes Us Squirm—A Critical Assessment of Community-Oriented Archaeology." *Canadian Journal of Archaeology* 40: 164–80.

Leone, Mark P. 1986. "Symbolic, Structural, and Critical Archaeology." In *American Archaeology Past, Present, and Future*, ed. David Meltzer, Donald Fowler, and Jeremy Sabloff, 415–38. Washington, DC: Smithsonian Institution Press.

———. 1995. "A Historical Archaeology of Capitalism." *American Anthropologist* 97(2): 251–68.

———. 2005. *The Archaeology of Liberty in an American Capital: Excavations in Annapolis*. Berkeley: University of California Press.

Leone, Mark P., Parker B. Potter, Jr., and Paul A. Shackel. 1987. "Toward a Critical Archaeology." *Current Anthropology* 28(3): 283–92.

Lucas, Gavin. 2001. *Critical Approaches to Fieldwork*. London: Routledge.

Ludlow Collective. 2001. "Archaeology of the Colorado Coal Field War 1913–1914." In *Archaeologies of the Contemporary Past*, eds. Victor Buchli, Gavin Lucas, and Margaret Cox, 94–107. London: Routledge.

MacDonald, Bradley J. 2017. "Traditional and Critical Theory Today: Toward a Critical Political Science." *New Political Science* 39(4): 511–22.

Matsuda, Akira. 2016. "A Consideration of Public Archaeology Theories." *Public Archaeology* 15(1): 40–49.

Matsuda, Akira, and Katsuyuki Okamura. 2011. "Introduction: New Perspectives in Global Public Archaeology." In *New Perspectives in Global Public Archaeology*, ed. Katsuyuki Okamura and Akira Matsuda, 1–18. New York: Springer.

McAnany, Patricia A., and Sarah M. Rowe. 2015. "Re-visiting the Field: Collaborative Archaeology as Paradigm Shift." *Journal of Field Archaeology* 40(5): 499–507.

McDavid, Carol. 2002. "Archaeologies that Hurt; Descendants that Matter: A Pragmatic Approach to Collaboration in the Public Interpretation of African-American Archaeology." *World Archaeology* 34(2): 303–14.

———. 2004. "From 'Traditional' Archaeology to Public Archaeology to Community Action." In *Places in Mind: Public Archaeology as Applied Anthropology*, ed. Paul A. Shackel and Erve J. Chambers, 35–56. New York: Routledge.

McGhee, Robert. 2008. "Aboriginalism and the Problems of Indigenous Archaeology." *American Antiquity* 73(4): 579–97.

McGuire, Randall H. 2008. *Archaeology as Political Action*. Berkeley: University of California Press.

———. 2012. "Critical Archaeology and Praxis." *Forum Kritische Archäologie* 1: 77–89.

McGuire, Randall, and Paul Reckner. 2003. "Building a Working-Class Archaeology: The Colorado Coal Field War Project." *Industrial Archaeology Review* 25(2): 83–95.

McManamon, Francis P. 2000. "Archaeological Messages and Messengers." *Public Archaeology* 1(1): 5–20.

McNiven, Ian, and Lynette Russell. 2005. *Appropriated Pasts: Indigenous Peoples and the Colonial Culture of Archaeology*. Oxford: Altamira Press.

Merriman, Nick. 2004. "Introduction." In *Public Archaeology*, ed. Nick Merriman, 1–18. London: Routledge.

Meskell, Lynn. 2012. "The Social Life of Heritage." In *Archaeological Theory Today*, 2nd edn, ed. Ian Hodder, 229–50. Cambridge: Polity.

Morgan, Colleen. 2014. "The Young Lions of Archaeology." In *Punk Archaeology*, ed. William Caraher, Kostis Kourelis, and Andrew Reinhard, 63–70. Grand Forks, ND: Digital Press.

———. 2015. "Punk, DIY, and Anarchy in Archaeological Thought and Practice." *AP: Online Journal in Public Archaeology* 5: 123–46.

Moshenska, Gabriel. 2017. "Introduction: Public Archaeology as Practice and Scholarship Where Archaeology Meets the World." In *Key Concepts in Public Archaeology*, ed. Gabriel Moshenska, 1–13. London: UCL Press.

Muller, Jon. 1997. *Mississippian Political Economy*. New York: Plenum Press.

Nakamura, Carolyn. 2012. "Archaeology and the Capacity to Aspire." *Forum Kritische Archäologie* 1: 123–33.

Nassaney, Michael S. 2020. "Archaeology, Heritage, and Public Participation: Fulfilling the Promise of Authentic Collaboration." *Advances in Archaeological Practice* 9(2): 119–131. https://doi .org/10.1017/aap.2020.40.

Palus, Matthew M., Mark P. Leone, and Matthew D. Cochran. 2006. "Critical Archaeology: Politics Past and Present." In *Historical Archaeology*, ed. Martin Hall and Stephen W. Silliman, 84–104. Malden, MA: Blackwell.

Patterson, Thomas, C. 2008. "Social Archaeology and Marxist Social Thought." In *Companion to Social Archaeology*, ed. Lynn Meskell and Robert W. Preucel, 66–81. Malden, MA: Blackwell.

Paynter, R. 1985. "Surplus Flow between Frontiers and Homelands." In *The Archeology of Frontiers and Boundaries*, Stanton W. Green and Stephen Perlman, 163–211. Orlando, FL: Academic Press.

Pitblado, Bonnie L., and Suzie Thomas. 2020. "Unravelling the Spectra of Stewards and Collectors." *Antiquity* 94(376): 1077–79.

Potter, Parker B., Jr. 1992. "Critical Archaeology: In the Ground and on the Street." *Historical Archaeology* 26(3): 117–29.

———. 1994. *Public Archaeology in Annapolis: A Critical Approach to History in Maryland's Ancient City*. Washington, DC: Smithsonian Institution Press.

Potter, Parker B., Jr., and Mark P. Leone. 1986. "Liberation not Replication: 'Archaeology in Annapolis' Analyzed." *Journal of the Washington Academy of Sciences* 76(2): 97–105.

Pyburn, K. Anne. 2011. "Engaged Archaeology: Whose Community? Which Public?" In *Global Public Archaeology*, ed. Akira Matsuda and Katsu Okamura, 29–41. New York: Springer.

Richardson, Lorna-Jane. 2017. "I'll Give You 'Punk Archaeology', Sunshine." *World Archaeology* 49(3): 306–17

Richardson, Lorna-Jane, and Jaime Almansa-Sánchez. 2015. "Do You Even Know What Public Archaeology Is? Trends, Theory, Practice, Ethics." *World Archaeology* 47(2): 194–211.

Rowlands, Michael. 1998. "Objectivity and Subjectivity in Archaeology." In *Social Transformations in Archaeology: Global and Local Perspectives,* ed. Kristian Kristiansen and Michael Rowlands, 26–35. London: Routledge.

Saitta, Dean J. 2007. *The Archaeology of Collective Action*. Gainesville: University Press of Florida.

Shackel, Paul A. 2011. "Pursuing Heritage, Engaging Communities." *Historical Archaeology* 45(1): 1–9.
———. 2019. *An Archaeology of Unchecked Capitalism: From the American Rust Belt to the Developing World*. New York: Berghahn.
Shackel, Paul A., Paul R. Mullins, and Mark S. Warner, eds. 1998. *Annapolis Pasts: Historical Archaeology in Annapolis*. Knoxville: University of Tennessee Press.
Shackel, Paul, and Michael Roller. 2012. "The Gilded Age Wasn't So Gilded in the Anthracite Region of Pennsylvania." *International Journal of Historical Archaeology* 16(4): 761–75.
Shackel, Paul A., and V. Camille Westmont. 2016. "When the Mines Closed: Heritage Building in Northeastern Pennsylvania." *General Anthropology* 23(1): 1–10.
Shanks, Michael, and Christopher Tilley. 1987. *Social Theory and Archaeology*. Oxford: Polity Press.
Silliman, Stephen, ed. 2008. *Collaborating at the Trowel's Edge: Teaching and Learning in Indigenous Archaeology*. Tucson: University of Arizona Press.
Simpson, Faye, and Howard Williams. 2008. "Evaluating Community Archaeology in the UK." *Public Archaeology* 7(2): 69–90.
Smith, Claire. 2012. "The Benefits and Risks of Critical Archaeology." *Forum Kritische Archäologie* 1: 90–99.
Smith, Claire, and H. Martin Wobst. 2005. *Indigenous Archaeologies: Decolonizing Theory and Practice*. New York: Taylor and Francis.
Smith, Linda T. 1999. *Decolonizing Methodologies: Research and Indigenous Peoples*. New York: St Martin's Press.
Smith, Rhianedd. 2018. "Plurality and Multivocality." In *The Encyclopedia of Archaeological Sciences*, ed. Sandra L. Lopéz Varela. Retrieved 4 April 2021 from https://onlinelibrary.wiley.com/doi/abs/10.1002/9781119188230.saseas0466.
Stottman, M. Jay, ed. 2010. *Archaeologists as Activists: Can Archaeology Save the World?* Tuscaloosa: University of Alabama Press.
Supernant, Kisha, and Gary Warrick. 2014. "Challenges to Critical Community-Based Archaeological Practice in Canada." *Canadian Journal of Archaeology* 38(2): 563–91.
Tarlow, Sarah, and Liv Nilsson Stutz. 2013. "Can an Archaeologist Be a Public Intellectual?" *Archaeological Dialogues* 20(1): 1–5.
Thomas, Suzie. 2017. "Community Archaeology." In *Key Concepts in Public Archaeology*, ed. Gabriel Moshenska, 14–30. London: UCL Press.
Thomas, Suzie, and Bonnie L. Pitblado. 2020. "The Dangers of Conflating Responsible and Responsive Artefact Stewardship with Illicit and Illegal Collecting." *Antiquity* 94(376): 1060–67.
Tilley, Christopher. 1989. "Archaeology as Socio-Political Action in the Present." In *Critical Traditions in Contemporary Archaeology*, ed. Valery Pinksy and Alison Wylie, 104–16. Cambridge: Cambridge University Press.
Trigger, Bruce. 1984. "Marxism and Archaeology." In *On Marxian Perspectives in Anthropology: Essays in Honor of Harry Hoijer*, ed. Sidney Mintz, M. Godelier, and Bruce Trigger, 59–99. Malibu, CA: Undena Publications.
———. 1985. "Marxism in Archaeology: Real or Spurious." *Reviews in Anthropology* 12: 114–23.
Two Bears, Davina R. 2008. "Íhoosh'aah, Learning by Doing: The Navajo Nation Archaeology Department Student Training Program." In *Collaborating at the Trowel's Edge: Teaching and Learning in Indigenous Archaeology*, ed. Stephen Silliman, 188–209. Tucson: University of Arizona Press.
Vargas, Irada, and Mario Sanoja. 1999. "Archaeology as Social Science: Its Expression in Latin America." In *Archaeology in Latin America*, ed. Gustavo G. Politis and Benjamin Alberti, 59–75. London: Routledge.
Vila-Mitjá, Assumpcio, Jordi Estévez, Daniel Villatoro, and Jordi Sabater-Mir. 2010. "Archaeological Materiality of Social Inequality among Hunter-Gatherer Societies." In *Archaeological Invisibility and Forgotten Knowledge*, ed. Karen Hardy, 200–10. Oxford: BAR International Series.

Walker, Mark. 2000. "Labor History at the Ground Level: Colorado Coalfield War Archaeology Project." *Labor's Heritage* 11(1): 58–75.

Waterton, Emma. 2005. "Whose Sense of Place? Reconciling Archaeological Perspectives with Community Values: Cultural Landscapes in England." *International Journal of Heritage Studies* 11(4): 309–25.

Watkins, Joe. 2005. "Through Wary Eyes: Indigenous Perspectives on Archaeology." *Annual Review of Anthropology* 34: 429–49.

———. 2020. "Not with the Same Brush." *Antiquity* 94(376): 1071–73.

Westmont V. Camille. 2022. "Working-class Intangible Heritage from the Pennsylvania Coal Fields." *Forum Journal* 32(4): 54-63.

Westmont V. Camille, and Elizabeth Clay. 2021. "Introduction: Current Directions in the Community Archaeology of the African Diaspora." *International Journal of Historical Archaeology* 26(1): 195–210. https://doi.org/10.1007/s10761-021-00631-6.

Williams, Howard, Carolina Pudney, and Afnan Ezzeldin, eds. 2019. *Public Archaeology: Arts of Engagement*. Oxford: Archaeopress Publishing.

Wylie, Alison. 2007. "Doing Archaeology as a Feminist: An Introduction." *Journal of Archaeological Method and Theory* 14(3): 209–16.

Zimmerman, Larry, Courtney Singleton, and Jessica Welch. 2010. "Activism and Creating a Translational Archaeology of Homelessness." *World Archaeology* 42(3): 443–54.

Part I

Work with Communities

CHAPTER 1

Aiming for Anti-Racism
Policies and Practices of a
Publicly Engaged Archaeology Department

Mary Furlong Minkoff, Terry P. Brock, and Matthew B. Reeves

Archaeologists who study African American experiences have a responsibility to examine not only the complicated relationships and emergence of race and racism in the past, but also their legacy in the present. This is particularly true when this research is part of a public archaeology program, especially one that seeks to engage with African Americans. As part of that legacy, archaeologists must examine our own personal and institutional biases and relationships with race and racism. This critical approach helps move archaeological research and interpretations beyond a simple recognition of racial biases, and toward efforts to make real change in how the discipline is practiced and how the past is understood. By working to truly engage with a broader constituency of people, particularly African Americans who are descendants, local residents, or archaeological practitioners, we are able to do archaeology in a way that draws on a wide variety of experiences and viewpoints. The Archaeology Department at the Montpelier Foundation has committed to adopting anti-racist policies in our approach to collaborative archaeological research, staffing and training, and public interpretation. This chapter will present the various policies and procedures that we have taken to try to combat racist archaeological practice and move toward an anti-racist archaeology.

This chapter will address three main points. First, we will discuss definitions of racism and anti-racism, as discussed within the context of policy. Second, we will look at how critical public archaeology and Critical Race Theory call for archaeologists to examine their racial biases, and how those biases are manifest in their practice. Next, we will discuss ways that racial bias is present in our discipline, institution, and departmental practice. And fourth, we will discuss the ways we have enacted anti-racist policies to more effectively combat the biases that are present at disciplinary, institutional, and departmental levels.

Defining Racism and Anti-Racism

This chapter adopts the definitions of racism and anti-racism presented in Ibram X. Kendi's book, *How to Be an Antiracist*. Kendi defines racism as the "marriage of racist policies and racist ideas that produces and normalizes racial inequities" (Kendi 2019: 18). He argues that "racial inequity is when two or more racial groups are not standing on approximately equal footing," and that a racist policy is a policy that "produces or sustains" racial inequality (18). These policies are often discussed as institutional, structural, or systemic racism.

Furthermore, Kendi describes anti-racism as the creation of policies and ideas that "produces or sustains racial equity between racial groups" (Kendi 2019: 18). When he describes policy, Kendi means "written or unwritten laws, rules, procedures, processes, regulations, and guidelines that govern people," and he notes that there is no such thing as "nonracist or race-neutral policy . . . every policy in every institution in every community in every nation is producing or sustaining either racial inequity or equity between racial groups" (18). This means that anyone who has the power to create policy has the ability to do so in a racist or anti-racist capacity.

Kendi's approach to understanding race and racism follows the tradition of Critical Race Theory, which "acknowledges, analyzes and challenges the fundamental role of the law in the construction of racial difference and the perpetuation of racial oppression in American society" (Epperson 2004). Kendi argues that it is through the creation of policy that racist or anti-racist ideas are developed, not the other way around. He defines anti-racism as the "powerful collection of antiracist policies that lead to racial equity and are substantiated by antiracist ideas" (Kendi 2019: 20). Racist policy leads to racial inequity, which leads to racist ideas that further support and create more racist policies. Anti-racist policy works in the opposite direction. As such, creating anti-racist policy is a first step in creating anti-racist practice. Fostering ideas and values that support anti-racist thought sustains those policies. Centering the definitions of racism and anti-racism on policy is particularly useful for institutions and departments such as ours who are seeking to adopt anti-racist practice.

In 2004, archaeologist Terrence W. Epperson used Critical Race Theory to critique the superficial incorporation of African Americans into the archaeological process and to suggest ways in which archaeologists can apply Critical Race Theory to their work in order to avoid the pitfalls of their predecessors. Drawing on both Kendi (2019) and Terrence Epperson (2004), we as leaders of Montpelier's Archaeology Department, have embraced our role as policymakers in the field of archaeology and our power to create and sustain anti-racist policy. Within this purview, we have control over our research methodology, hiring and training of personnel, program development, workplace culture, and collaborating with colleagues. We do not, however, have the power to directly create policies for the Montpelier Foundation as a whole, although we do have the ability to advocate for these policy changes as much as possible—an act we are able to perform due to our privileges, which among the authors includes our whiteness, gender, education level, and institutional seniority. In some cases, this advocacy has been successful, while in others it has not. These will be discussed later in the chapter.

This chapter will place our department's efforts to institute anti-racist policies within the broader field of public archaeology. Then we will examine how we have put forth these efforts in three primary phases of archaeological practice: research questions, archaeological process, and public interpretation. At each stage, we have instituted policies that we believe address areas of racial inequality, and move toward a more equitable practice. We will also discuss ways that our departmental efforts have trickled-up to influence the broader organization's efforts and the areas where this has not happened. Lastly, we will provide some best practices for implementing anti-racist policy in archaeological organizations.

Critical Public Archaeology and Racism in Archaeology

In 1987, Mark Leone, Parker Potter, and Paul Shackel called for archaeologists to adopt a critical approach to their work. In their words, "The claim of a critical archaeology is that seeing the interrelationship between archaeology and politics will allow archaeologists to achieve less contingent knowledge" (Leone, Potter, and Shackel 1987: 284). While this work, and particularly how the application of critical theory in practice, was immediately met with criticism (Blakey 1987 etc.), its effects can still be felt in the field (Leone 2010). For the next several decades, archaeologists including Laurie Wilkie and Kevin Bartoy (2000), Alfredo González-Ruibal (2012), and Randall McGuire (2008) continued to write pieces discussing the role of critical archaeology. For us, the core idea of the recognition of the relationship between archaeology and politics is essential to building an anti-racist archaeology department, because it forces us to acknowledge that our archaeological practice is not immune from its own historical or current political moment. Like González-Ruibal's (2012) argument that it is the role of critical archaeology to historicize rather than naturalize capitalism, we believe that it is our responsibility to do the same with racism and race-based slavery. With this, we follow Shackel's (2007: 247) call for archaeologists "to critically analyze and expose racism in the past and present and to dismantle the structures of oppression where we can."

However, like the early critics, we embrace the notion that adopting a critical approach does not achieve a "less contingent knowledge" but rather a "*differently* contingent knowledge" (Blakey 1987). Likewise, we find it essential that we follow Blakey's (1987) suggestion that archaeologists utilizing critical theory should aim their critical analysis at themselves. This is a key component for white archaeologists, such as ourselves, working to develop an anti-racist approach to their work. In order to address the racism built into our department and institution, we must critically examine and acknowledge the structures and biases that allow it to exist. These structures and biases exist within our discipline, in our own department, and our larger institution. They also exist in each of us as individuals. In each instance, critically examining these areas is essential to establishing an anti-racist practice.

Racism in Archaeology

The discussion of racism in archaeology is not new. This is particularly true in historical archaeology, the subdiscipline practiced by the authors. Archaeologists have cited racism in archaeology as occurring in both archaeological research methods and the discipline itself as one that is hostile to African American archaeologists and African American studies (Battle-Baptiste 2011; Blakey 2020; Carey 2019, Epperson 2004; Franklin 1997a, 1997b; Ike Miller, and Omoni Hartemann 2020; La Roche and Blakey 1997).

Historical archaeology is itself predominately white and has been engaged in conversations about its lack of racial diversity for multiple decades (Franklin 1997b; Nassaney 2018; Shackel 2007). African American archaeologists in particular have called out the racist practices embedded in the discipline, and the racism of white archaeologists for years through publications, professional organizations, conferences, talks and webinars, and the creation of projects and organizations designed to combat the racism they face (Carey 2019; Franklin 1997b; Ike et al. 2020).

Despite these efforts, racism continues. As archaeologist Mia Carey (2019: 30) writes about her experience as an African American archaeologist, "I say we are present, but we are unwanted. Our perspectives and research are not as esteemed as our white colleagues. Students of color are supported as long as they uphold existing problematic standards and ignore the inherent racism in research and professional training. The invisible rules are made clear when graduate students of color are discouraged from joining projects, when they are expected to produce work in hostile environments, and when their work, credibility, and authority is questioned in the classroom, in the canon, and in the field." Racism is embedded deeply in all aspects of our discipline, and, even though African Americans are increasingly present in our field, it does not mean that the systems that they have to navigate to succeed are not hostile.

Anti-racist practice is also not new in archaeology. Members of the Society for Historical Archaeology (SHA) and the Society for Black Archaeologists (SBA) have been vocal and active regarding the lack of diversity in the field. In response to the social unrest during the summer of 2020, an online webinar hosted by the SBA, North American Theoretical Archaeology Group (TAG) and the Columbia Center for Archaeology was attended by 1,700 people, and featured Black archaeologists making calls for the adoption of an anti-racist archaeology (Flewellen et al 2021). Yet there remains a lot of frustration with the lack of action through policy changes that could affect real change within the discipline (Nassaney 2018). Efforts within SHA stem primarily from the Gender and Minority Affairs Committee (GMAC), which has spearheaded initiatives including a number of diversity-focused awards and recognitions and providing anti-racism training to SHA members.

At Montpelier, we acknowledge that our perspectives and experiences as white people skew our research questions and interpretations. We also acknowledge that there are structural barriers to our discipline that hinder the ability of African American archaeologists to succeed. We recognize challenges in diversifying our own staff, be it through hiring full-time staff, choosing interns, and recruiting field school students, and its association with racism. Additionally, as a department focused on educating future archaeologists through our field school and internship program, and also as professionals who serve on thesis committees, we acknowledge that our efforts at recruiting, teaching, and mentoring students of color may potentially inhibit their ability to succeed due to racist practice. This is particularly true considering the context of our research and institution, a former slave plantation.

The Montpelier Foundation

At the time of this writing, white archaeologists almost entirely make up our department, which consists of full-time, paid archaeology staff and full-time, paid archaeology interns. Our efforts, discussed below, have resulted in employing four full-time, paid African American interns over the past three years. The Montpelier Foundation itself also consists of a predominantly white staff, including a white executive leadership team and president. In addition, the majority of the Board of Directors is white. Despite our efforts, as an institution we do not adequately represent the population that has historically lived and worked on the plantation—in fact, since the National Trust for Historic Preservation acquired it in 1983, the racial makeup of Montpelier is the whitest the property has ever been. Its current makeup does not reflect the historic population of the property nor the racial makeup of the county, state, or country. The lack of racial diversity at Montpelier is not unique—American museum professionals are disproportionately white (Eid 2018 and Schonfeld et al. 2015). Likewise, the field of archaeology, particularly at the senior level, is also predominantly white. This makes the work reflected in this chapter that much more important. It also means our work

Table 1.1. Percentages of African Americans at Montpelier compared to Population Data.

	Percent African Americans	Percent White (non-Latino) Americans
Montpelier 1820	92 percent	8 percent
Montpelier Employees 2019	1.8 percent	95.6 percent
Orange County 2010	13.3 percent	77.7 percent
Virginia 2010	19.9 percent	61.5 percent
United States 2010	13.4 percent	60.4 percent

comes through the lens of people who do not feel the impacts of racism on a daily basis and likely reflects the biases that come with that lived experience.

We are engaging in this work in the context of a historic plantation that currently functions as a museum. The Montpelier Foundation administers the National Trust for Historic Preservation's nearly 2,700-acre estate, Montpelier. The land was the eighteenth and nineteenth century home to more than three hundred enslaved African Americans; James Madison, the fourth president of the United States and father of the US Constitution; and Dolley Madison, the first to actively define the role of first lady. The property was also home to Confederate Civil War encampments, post-emancipation African American homes such as the Gilmore family cabin, and a 1910s segregated train station. In the twentieth century, Montpelier was the workplace of African Americans employed by the duPont family who owned the property from 1901 to 1983. Since the Montpelier Foundation's beginning in 2000, interpreting the lives of African Americans has been a component, but not the center, of the property's interpretative efforts. Over the past few years, African American life became a leading focus of interpretation at Montpelier. This has been the product of decades of research and community engagement, culminating in the award-winning exhibition *The Mere Distinction of Colour* in 2017.

Despite the interpretive effort, the Foundation has and continues to struggle with a prevalent white identity both in its staff and board makeup and the direction it takes in regard to interpretive and business practices. What underlies this whiteness is a delay in addressing racism in the workplace and enacting basic procedures, such as Foundation-wide anti-racism training. This has fostered a racist environment that has made it exceedingly difficult for hiring and retaining Black Americans in the organization. Acknowledging the context of our workplace is important because it is an already complicated racialized landscape. This informs both the perception of Montpelier by staff and visitors. Understanding how racism was inscribed into this landscape in the past, and is currently inscribed in the present, is a critical component of the process of creating an anti-racist public archaeology and museum program.

Critical self-evaluation is integral to implementing anti-racist policy. The authors of this chapter are all white. We have each engaged in decades of work examining and deconstructing our numerous privileges that are not only present in our whiteness, but in our gender, sexual orientation, economic class, social status, able-bodiedness, and education level. We acknowledge that these privileges have influenced the access we have had to education, hiring practices, personal and professional networks, and general comfort in a predominately white discipline. We also acknowledge that our privilege allows us to continue to financially benefit from studying and researching the history of African Americans. It is through this self-investigation that all three of us realize that our privilege positions us to use our power to combat racism through our research, interpretation, in our discipline and institution. We also acknowledge that the work illustrated in this chapter is entirely dependent on the decades of work by African Americans and other people of color to dismantle racism—and yet we will receive another line-item on our curricula vitae, the ultimate form of academic currency.

Engaging Descendants and the Local African American Community

Best practices in archaeology dictate that archaeological research and interpretation should be multivocal and equitable as seen in Jeffery Burton and Mary Farrell (this volume). Such an approach is critical to an anti-racist approach to research and interpretation (McDavid and Brock 2015; Laroche and Blakey 1997; Nassaney and Levine 2009; Reeves 2004; Silliman and Ferguson 2010; Battle-Baptiste 2011; Blakey 2010; Engaging 2019). The Montpelier Archaeology Department has been collaborating with descendants and the local African community since the early 2000s with the excavations at the Gilmore Farm (Reeves 2004). This project began a long relationship with the local African American community, leading to a formation and collaboration between Montpelier and the Orange County African American Historical Society (OCAAHS). Since that initial project, Montpelier's archaeology department, OCAAHS, and the Montpelier enslaved descendant community have worked together to explore Montpelier's landscape. Work with these groups has informed research, interpretation, and departmental practices. By fostering fruitful, trusting, and mutually beneficial collaboration among these groups, the departmental practice of descendant engagement began to "trickle-up," and become a part of the Foundation's museum practice and institutional policy. It has impacted the way that the Foundation conducts research, does interpretation, and even how it functions at the Board level.

The process of building engagement from a departmental to an institutional level was slow and deliberate. At the departmental level, collaboration often took the form of descendant community members participating in archaeological excavations and using this as the platform to garner further engagement. These collaborative excavations with descendants follow a similar model to those described by Burton and Farrell and Jay Stottman in this volume. Key to this process was making the knowledge of what we do as archaeologists accessible to the community. Matt Reeves, Director of Archaeology, began incorporating Montpelier colleagues outside of the archaeology department by hosting meetings and workshops at Montpelier. These meetings were an important first step in getting white museum professionals to listen to black voices, and started building the groundwork for more equitable methodologies.

The first of these projects took place at the Gilmore Farm, a post-emancipation homestead (with standing structure) built by George Gilmore, a formerly enslaved laborer at Montpelier. Archaeologists engaged with descendants from the beginning of this four-year project (2001–2005), and they played a critical role in decision-making. During the stabilization of this structure (2001), descendants took part in the excavation inside the cabin examining sealed deposits that dated to the first generation of the Gilmore family (1873–1910). For the family, this was a moving experience, as little oral history existed for this time period and no material items were passed down. The week spent at Gilmore showed the family their history was accessible through the archaeological and architectural investigations. Following the dig, family members took part in a two-day steering committee that determined the period to which Montpelier would restore the Gilmore residence. The voices of the Gilmore descendants profoundly influenced the steering committee and their decision to restore the cabin to 1880, the first generation of freed Gilmores who built the cabin. The removal of twentieth-century fabric from the Gilmore Cabin was a radical departure from National Trust for Historic Preservation policy of preservation in place. This decision to restore the structure based on its period of significance (as informed by community) set a precedent that informed the Montpelier Foundation's decision to restore the Montpelier main house, a massive undertaking that made a major impact on the entire field of historic preservation.

Following the Gilmore project, Montpelier held the most important event to facilitate collaboration between descendants and Montpelier staff in 2014. At that time, Montpelier hosted a gathering of descendants that dedicated an entire day for discussion and critique of where Montpelier was as an organization. In the round table talks, descendant advisors spoke about the need to further restore the homes and spaces of the enslaved community and to also work against the predominantly white plantocracy culture that dominated Montpelier. Descendant advisors suggested bringing voices of African Americans into the interpretive programs, printed material, staff hiring, and making Montpelier a more welcoming space for African Americans. Continuing to examine and research sites of enslavement at Montpelier were paramount in this investigation. A product of this engagement were efforts to find financial support to fully excavate and reconstruct the buildings in the South Yard domestic quarter. This effort was ultimately successful, and archaeological investigations began with the intention of understanding the architectural design of the dwellings and work buildings located in the domestic quarter. These buildings, and the other information gathered from the sites, became part of a larger permanent exhibition built through descendant collaboration, called *The Mere Distinction of Colour.*

The collaboration of the descendant community and Montpelier's research and interpretive staff on *The Mere Distinction of Colour* produced a number of new outcomes. First, in partnership with the National Trust for Historic Preservation, Montpelier hosted a summit on Interpreting Slavery. During the summit, attendees, including scholars, museum professionals, descendants, and archaeologists, created *Engaging Descendant Communities in the Interpretation of Slavery at Museums and Historic Sites: A Rubric of Best Practices Established by the National Summit on Teaching Slavery* (2018). This document outlines a series of best practices and evaluative criteria for museums to follow and to grade themselves on their effectiveness (Engaging 2018). Its three tiers are Multidisciplinary Research, Relationship Building with Descendant Communities, and Interpretation (Engaging 2018). Montpelier adopted this rubric as policy for the purposes of evaluating their future efforts at interpreting the African American experience at Montpelier. Such a document of best practices is critical as a means of instituting anti-racist policies.

Second, Montpelier and descendants agreed to pursue the memorialization of the African American Community Cemetery as their next collaborative effort—a project that is still very much in its early stages at the time of this writing. As part of this decision, descendants decided to form an official and cohesive organization as their representative body, called the Montpelier Descendant Committee. Following the formation of the Committee, the Montpelier Foundation Board decided to designate a spot on the Foundation's Board for the Chairperson of the Descendant Committee. The formation of the Committee has fundamentally changed how Montpelier engages with the descendants. Prior to its formation, Montpelier engaged with descendants through personal relationships or through partnerships with organizations that included but were not exclusively composed of descendants, such as the Orange County African American Historical Society. While these relationships produced important and meaningful work, both the Archaeology Department and the Foundation as a whole became reliant on a small group of descendants with whom we created deep personal relationships. This meant that we often left out other descendants, privileged certain descendant voices, and no one was in the position to speak for the community as a whole. It meant the descendants were not choosing their own representation. The formation of the Committee has changed this by electing representatives to speak on behalf of the descendant community as a whole and making the relationship between the Foundation and descendants one between two organizations rather than an organization and individuals. What began as a process in the archaeology department is now in the process of being institutionalized through Board policy and practice.

Finally, while early projects at Montpelier were quite successful in engaging the community, they still existed largely on the terms of the Montpelier Foundation. Montpelier staff were the ones that invited select individuals to take part in the projects. Montpelier Foundation Board and staff set and defined the larger goals, and there was no formal contract that bound the Montpelier Foundation to the needs of the community. Going forward, Montpelier Archaeology has adopted the "Clientage Model," as devised by Michael Blakey, who is a member of the Montpelier Descendant Community, for its future work with the Committee (Blakey 2010 and 2020). Using this approach, the Montpelier Descendant Committee is the ethical client, the Foundation is the business client, and our profession serves as the best practices for research, who all make equal contributions, have equal stake, equal say, and receive equal credit for the work of our research projects. It also means that the Foundation financially compensated descendants for their time, expertise, and contributions to Montpelier. While the official adoption of this practice happened in 2020, we have incorporated the spirit of this work in many of our previous projects. As we write this piece, leadership from the Foundation, the Committee, and the National Trust for Historic Preservation, are working to figure out how to navigate the relationships between these three organizations. For our part, we are pushing for the Foundation to adopt the clientage model as policy for all projects. Key to the clientage model is viewing all 2,650 acres that make up Montpelier as being the ancestral lands of the Montpelier Descendant Committee. As such, any work the Montpelier Foundation conducts reflects on the Committee's identity and makes their voice imperative in maintaining the Foundation's ethical stance.

While this will not shift the ownership of the property to the Descendant Committee, it shifts the decision-making power into the hands of descendants and those they select to represent them.

Asking Anti-Racist Questions

All archaeological research begins with research questions. As a policy, our archaeology department seeks to ask questions that address issues of race and racism in the past, and focus on understanding the lives of people impacted by slavery and its legacies. This practice is anti-racist in three ways. First, it prioritizes African American experiences in the past. Second, it examines the way racist policy was enacted in the past, and the effect it had on the United States. And third, we develop these questions through collaboration with the Montpelier Descendant Committee and the broader African American community—which includes scholarly colleagues and interested members of the public.

By asking questions about the lives of African Americans during and after slavery, we are prioritizing and addressing largely underexamined and uninterpreted areas of scholarship at historic house museums and presidential homes (Flewellen 2017). It also forces us to examine the archaeological record from multiple perspectives, and to bring new stories to plantation spaces, similar to the Black Feminist approach to archaeology developed by Whitney Battle-Baptiste (2011). By adopting this multivocal approach to investigating the past and by prioritizing these questions, we are righting inequities in the way we tell our foundational stories. This allows us to ask questions about the plantation landscape that move beyond the Madisons' intention and definition of plantation spaces and instead allows us to focus on the different ways African Americans experienced, used, and redefined these spaces. This policy—of always developing research questions that examine the African American experience—ensures that we are learning about the entire population of people who lived and worked at Montpelier.

Second, our research questions also examine the implementation and effect of racist policies created by James and Dolley Madison at Montpelier and our nation. On the plantation, James and Dolley crafted policies that dictated the ways that enslaved African Americans and white Americans lived and worked on the plantation. These policies had lasting impacts on the ways individuals, families, and communities crafted their sociocultural practices and built personal ideologies. Nationally, James Madison crafted racist policy that created and shaped our nation: he was the primary author of the United States Constitution; as a US congressman, he authored the Bill of Rights; he served as secretary of state for Thomas Jefferson; and he was the nation's fourth president. Following his political retirement, Madison continued to influence policy on his and other plantations across the South. He was a well-respected voice on agricultural science, president of the American Colonization Society, and the second rector of the University of Virginia. In all these ways, Madison was one of the most influential policymakers in our nation's founding era—a period where our newly formed government protected slavery into its foundation. These national policies directly affected the lives of the people who lived, worked, and were enslaved at Montpelier. Our research questions, therefore, not only address the policy that Madison instituted at the plantation level, but also on a national scale. Researching the people who lived and worked at Montpelier, therefore, is an investigation of how racist polices set forth in the US Constitution and the subsequent policies built through this system influenced enslaved people and how they navigated these racist policies.

Third, we have sought to build research questions in collaboration with members of the descendant community, which has begun to extend to Montpelier as a whole. Prior to the establishment of the Montpelier Descendant Committee, the Montpelier Archaeology and Research Departments set up quarterly meetings with members of the descendant community. The goal of these meetings was to work with descendants to make decisions about archaeological research phases and methods. To get as many descendants as possible involved, we live-streamed meetings and incorporated the comments from our virtual participants into the discussions. This also allowed for sharing meetings' content after they occurred. It also allowed for descendant participation, without requiring them to come to the plantation, which can be emotionally unsettling for community members.

These meetings consisted of two major components: information sharing and listening. A recent example involved the opportunity for genetic testing of human teeth recovered from non-burial deposits at several house sites. The first meeting centered on determining the types of biological analysis the descendant community was interested in for three human teeth recovered from non-burial African American contexts. For that meeting, experts in ancient-DNA analysis from the University of Oklahoma and biological anthropologists from the Institute for Historical Biology from the College of William and Mary, presented their preliminary findings and the information potential of future analysis (Wright et al. 2018). They also answered questions about how DNA analysis works, from public DNA services like Ancestry.com to university research. From this meeting, the representatives of the descendant community decided to continue with further biological analysis of the teeth and, equally important, they were more informed about the potential for both modern and archaeological biological analysis to help them learn more about their ancestors.

We codified descendant engagement into our grant proposal process. Recent federal grants received from the National Endowment for the Humanities designate funds and financial support for descendant community advisors to be a part of the research process. This ensures compensation for their expertise and time. This is increasingly vital to the process of collaborative research, because it demonstrates the descendants' expertise and contributions are valued, by paying them and not just Montpelier staff. This policy holds the archaeology department and the larger institution accountable to the anti-racist practices of descendant engagement in order to adhere to the grant requirements. Descendant community members represented within the grant itself obtain the necessary power to hold the institution accountable. Ensuring that our grants include line items for descendants is an important policy and the entire institution increasingly follows.

Anti-Racism and the Archaeological Process

We also adopted anti-racist policy to address the way we conduct archaeological excavation and analysis and who does that work. This effort rests primarily in ensuring the descendant community and Black Americans participate in excavations and analysis, making efforts to diversify our field school, internship, and staff and provide supportive work culture and training, and making efforts to collaborate with groups such as the Society for Black Archaeologists.

Providing opportunities for enslaved descendant community members to participate in archaeological excavations has been a component of our archaeological excavations since the Gilmore Farm project (2001–2005). We hold one excavation expedition program specifically for descendants each year as part of our series of LEARN Archaeology Expedition Programs as a series of one-day, three-day, and five-day residential workshops where members of the public have the opportunity to live on the property and participate in archaeological survey, excavation, lab analysis, and interpretation. These programs have been incredibly fruitful, providing opportunities for descendants to not only learn about how archaeological excavation works, but also for us to work together on the project—this type of collaboration builds trust and familiarity between the community and archaeology staff and deepens our relationships.

The success of these programs has also allowed us to institute scholarships for African Americans to participate in all the different workshops that we offer through our LEARN Archaeology Expedition Programs. Scholarships waive the fee for African Americans who want to participate in a program, further increasing the opportunity for African Americans to participate in connecting with their heritage. As a result, more than fifty African Americans from across the country, several returning multiple times, have participated in the public archaeology programs as scholarship recipients over the past decade.

African American expedition participants, whether directly descended from Montpelier's enslaved community or not, have shared with us that the process of excavation is a means of connecting with their ancestors. This is particularly significant considering so many African Americans have difficulty tracing their ancestry through historic documents into the period of enslavement. Visiting and excavating sites of slavery provide a different way of connecting with their ancestors, by uncovering the physical objects and places that their ancestors may have lived. Similar to how genealogists have discussed their research as being a social justice initiative (Twitty 2017), public archaeology also serves as a means of social justice and anti-racism, since it provides an alternative route to connecting with ancestors who have been removed or were never included in the historical record.

Recruiting and training field school students and staff is another important area for our department to institute anti-racist policy. Our efforts to diversify our professional staff have only been mildly successful, despite concerted efforts to send our job postings to a wide variety of job recruiting sites and organizations targeting African American archaeologists and students. We believe a lack of representation in our own staff is part of the problem and unfortunately reflects the lack of diversity in the discipline at large (Franklin 1997b; White and Draycott 2020). In 2016, following a call by our descendant community to diversify our staff, we instituted a scholarship for African American students to attend our archaeology field school. This scholarship covers the equipment and housing expenses, and, since students can take our field school as a no-credit option, it means that students could take the field school free of charge. Since that time, we have had seventeen applicants and provided scholarships to nine students.

The scholarship then provides immediate employment opportunities in our department, because field school students qualify for our internship position. Montpelier archaeology interns are full-time employees for summer or yearlong experiences. Interns are paid and receive benefits and free housing. Since the creation of the scholarship, we have hired three African Americans as interns, all of whom have gone on to careers or graduate programs in archaeology. We continue to have work to do, however: exit interviews and meetings with former interns and scholarship recipients continue to provide us with more feedback about how to make our field school and workplace better places for African American students and employees.

We have made efforts to improve the training and workplace culture in our department to address these concerns by working on establishing a clearly defined workplace culture. Building accountability within our department is a critical element to ensuring that we focus our archaeological practice on anti-racism. We want to build a culture of accountability and are explicit about the type of culture we strive to foster in our department for our staff, volunteers, and program participants. A departmental workshop in 2014 resulted in the creation of a set of department values that guide our behaviors and policies. These include: accountability, professionalism, mutual respect, open communication and transparency, learning, publicly focused, choose positivity, and family. Within the document, anti-racism is specifically addressed and accounted for in a number of areas, particularly within the value of mutual respect, where employees are expected to respect a diversity of experiences, adopting anti-discriminatory policies and examining and critiquing our own privileges and biases (Montpelier Archaeology 2017; Brock 2018).

This document has proven effective over the past five years for working with current staff and incorporating new hires. The Archaeology Department staff on all levels, including interns, technicians, and senior staff created the original document. This created buy-in that would not have existed if this had been solely a top-down effort. Each year the staff review and update the document. Recent updates include action steps for carrying out values and clarification of terms and explanations in the document (Montpelier Archaeology 2017). This annual review process allows staff hired after the creation of the document to feel invested in its maintenance and content and for the document to continue to be relevant and aligned with who we are and how our department is changing.

Student and staff training is also an important component of anti-racist policy. Like many archaeology departments in both museums and universities, funding is at a premium. Therefore, training that requires outside experts are often the first things to go, or not even make it to the level of consideration, when budget cuts are made on an administrative level. To counteract this, we had to think creatively and take advantage of all the opportunities that are available to us. One way has been through our quarterly staff article club. Reading material explored in the club regularly includes books and articles that address issues of racism in archaeology, museums, and society. Our article club follows efforts seen across academia to "decolonize our syllabus."

One of the biggest opportunities for our staff, however, has been the anti-racism training offered through the Society for Historical Archaeology (SHA). Since 2015, SHA's Gender and Minority Affairs Committee has partnered with Crossroads Anti-racism Organizing and Training to offer anti-racism training workshops for free or negligible costs. Members of our senior archaeology staff were part of the first group of archaeologists to participate in this training and have gone on to participate in both the level I and level II training workshops. In 2017, the senior staff in the Montpelier Archaeology Department established a policy requiring any Montpelier Archaeology staff and interns who attend the annual SHA Conference to attend the level I anti-racism training workshop. Through these means, we are able to ensure that our staff receive anti-racism training.

We are also working on addressing anti-racism in our field school. In addition to addressing the issue of systemic racism in lectures, tours, and in all aspects of the field school curriculum, we dedicate a day to discussing discrimination in archaeology due to racism, sexism, homophobia, and ableism, and have implemented anti-racism training for all students. This includes a panel discussion and small group conversations led by colleagues from other institutions. One regular panelist/discussion leader and departmental partner, Dr. Alexandra Jones, Director of Archaeology in the Community (AITC) and a Board Member of the Society for Black Archaeologists, has also served in a mentorship role for Montpelier scholarship recipients. Her partnership has been integral to the program's success, since we currently have no members of our departmental leadership who can speak on a personal level about racism in the discipline. We believe these types of conversations are integral for field school students and staff, so that they are aware of the current state of racism in archaeology, and also how they can be active participants in developing an anti-racist archaeology. Providing this training for the people who conduct our archaeological excavations and analysis ensures that the people trained by Montpelier are entering the discipline with an anti-racist perspective on our discipline.

Partnerships with African American colleagues has also been critical to how we approach our practice. However, we strive to make sure that these relationships are mutually beneficial for everyone's research, careers, and pocketbooks. We have worked to make sure we are not calling on our colleagues to do the emotional labor of explaining racism to us but collaborating with them for their expertise and paying them for their time (Ike et al. 2020). Colleagues from the Society of Black Archaeologists are critical partners and advisors to our department. In addition to working with our field school, we collaborate with Dr. Jones and AITC on a week-long teacher expedition program each year Likewise, we are working with Alexis Morris and the National Park Service to develop components of the Urban Archaeology Corps program at the Petersburg National Battlefield.

Through descendant engagement, scholarships, training, culture, and partnerships, we have enacted a number of policies that seek to influence the process of archaeology to be more anti-racist. Whether this is by ensuring people of color have more opportunities to be participants in the archaeological process, training all of our staff in anti-racist practice, or collaborating with colleagues of color, we believe these policies and practices contribute to the broader effort.

Anti-Racism and Archaeological Interpretation

Figuring out how to build anti-racist practice into our interpretation serves as one of the primary collaborative efforts with other departments at Montpelier, including Historic Preservation and Architecture, Research, and Education and Visitor Services. We strive to have our interpretation reflect the wishes of the descendant community in both our reconstruction of the landscape, exhibitions, and programming.

Understanding the entirety of the cultural landscape at Montpelier is one of the critical elements of interpretation at Montpelier, which began with the effort to restore the Madison family house but has extended to the broader landscape. This means preserving historic structures that exist and discovering and reconstructing buildings and landscape features found archaeologically. The archaeology department codified these efforts by an annual reconstruction program where participants reconstruct a structure found archaeologically as a ghost frame. This interpretive policy is particularly important when it comes to presenting the African American experience, because almost all of the buildings and spaces that African Americans lived and worked in during the eighteenth and nineteenth centuries were removed from the landscape or left to deteriorate. Likewise, it is an interpretive practice explicitly called for by members of the descendant community. During a 2007 visit to Montpelier, enslaved descendant and renowned anthropologist, Dr. Iris Ford asked, "Where are my people? You spend $24 million on the Madisons, and all my people get are dead grass and railroad ties?" (Montpelier Foundation 2019). Interpreting the landscape by preserving or reconstructing these structures and spaces is a policy grounded in anti-racism, by ensuring that lived experiences of persons of color are represented visually on the landscape.

This process is most profound in the South Yard, where descendants requested that the six structures identified through archaeological excavations and historical documents visually returned to the landscape. Initial efforts resulted in the construction of ghosted timber frame structures representing three dwellings, two smokehouses, and a detached kitchen. These frames made the African American experience visually represented on the landscape and established a working relationship with a local craftsperson company, SalvageWrights, experts in historical building techniques. This partnership soon led to the establishment of the Log Cabin Reconstruction program, which has resulted in the reconstruction of four additional log cabin slave dwellings, based on archaeological evidence. For the South Yard, the presence of the ghosted structures garnered the attention of David Rubenstein and led to a gift for excavating and rebuilding these structures and the creation of an exhibition, *The Mere Distinction of Colour*, taking a critical look at the racist policy embedded in the US Constitution.

Likewise, descendants played an essential role in the furnishing of these buildings and the creation of *The Mere Distinction of Colour* exhibition. Artifacts excavated and processed by descendants through the archaeology expedition programs, served as the primary guide for furnishing the slave quarters. In addition, all of the objects featured in the *Mere Distinction* exhibition are archaeological artifacts. While the archaeological artifacts were just one component of an exhibition co-created with descendants, they do provide a powerful connection to community members when they visit the exhibition because they not only can see their own faces and hear their own voices telling the stories of their ancestors, but they can also see objects their ancestors owned that they themselves discovered.

The reconstruction of the South Yard and installation of *Mere Distinction* created new resources to use in our public programming for discussing the issues of race and racism. The spaces, along with our research agenda, which examines the institution of slavery and impact of racist policy in the past and its effect on people, has greatly informed our interpretive process. Through tours, lectures, and hands-on program, we use archaeology to facilitate a conversation that connects the past, and particularly the institution of slavery, to issues of racism today. We do this by designing our public programs with explicit goals of addressing issues of race and racism.

The Montpelier Archaeology Department is unique in both the scale and scope of our public participant-based archaeological programming. At the core of this are our LEARN Archaeology Expedition Programs. Through these residential programs the general public work alongside our staff conducting archaeological survey, excavations, analysis, or physical reconstruction. The Archaeology Department designed and carried out these programs to follow a series of learning objectives. In addition to wanting participants to gain a basic understanding of archaeological skills and process, and the importance of historic places, we also want participants to understand how slavery and racism are part of America's cultural heritage from the past to the present. We address through the framing of our research questions, archaeology-focused tours that explore *The Mere Distinction of Colour* exhibition, Confederate encampments, the Gilmore Cabin, and the segregated train station. As a collective, examining these sites brings visitors through the entire history of our nation, connecting these different periods to each other on a single landscape. The tours designed within a dialogical methodology, which encourages conversation and engagement, and the process of building empathy and shared experience between participants and the content. As such, participants and archaeologists have conversations about the content, the past, and how they connect to the present. Discussions regarding the racist underpinnings of the Constitution and American society are a critical part of these discussions.

Making Montpelier Anti-Racist

Through our work in the Archaeology Department, we hoped to make changes across our institution as a whole. Some other staff members and institutional leadership met these early efforts with resistance and apathy. For example, several years ago a senior staff member from another department reprimanded one author for asking a potential new hire if they would be willing to adopt an anti-racist approach. Other times our suggestion to include the Montpelier descendant community in the interpretive process was met with excuses relating to the time and effort that it would require. As time went on, this began to change. New leadership in the museum division and the success of *The Mere Distinction of Colour* exhibition were the primary catalysts for this. After winning multiple awards and gaining national attention, the success of *Mere Distinction* forced the property as a whole to reexamine the role of our institution in discussing race and racism, and how we were or were not equipping our staff and board to do so. However, three years after the opening of *Mere Distinction*, the pendulum is beginning to swing back beyond apathy to strong resistance.

One of our hopes for engaging in an anti-racist archaeology was that the potential for "trickle-up" influence on the Montpelier Foundation as a whole. We have had success in some areas more than others. Of particular strength has been the impact of our research agenda and work with descendant communities on the approach that Montpelier has taken toward interpretation and community engagement. We have had less success in regard to influencing our institution's training and personnel—while for a period (2017–18) we were reaching parity between staff diversity and regional population demographics, budget cuts, attrition, and staff isolation led to a return to an almost all-white staff.

Most recently, in recognition of the formation of the Montpelier Descendant Committee, the Montpelier Executive Director and Board of Directors agreed that the Descendant Community chairperson will also serve as a member of the Executive Board. This is an unprecedented policy, and means that the descendant community will have official board-level representation. This comes along with an effort to further diversify the board membership, which has to this point has primarily consisted of white Americans. At the writing of this chapter, this is a process with an ever-shifting strategy and results.

Our work with the Montpelier Descendant Committee provides us with the most hope for the future of Montpelier. Moving toward structural parity in sharing power between the Montpelier Descendant Committee and the Montpelier Foundation offers the greatest opportunity for change. While we continue to enact change in our department, this change faces a bulwark of antipathy without recognition and support from the top of the power structure. With any organization, the call for action has the most response when made from the top of the pyramid. Until this parity is achieved, our department will still carry out anti-racist work on the departmental level and collaborate with the Montpelier Descendant Committee to effect change on all levels.

What we have learned from our work within the Montpelier Foundation is that individuals and departments can make a significant contribution within a larger organization. Others will see partnerships and collaborations build a common purpose that bear fruit. These incremental changes make available the opportunity for larger institutional changes that can happen at incremental or sometimes tectonic intervals. The importance of being ready and mindful of the opportunity for change is critical for taking advantage of such situations to avail themselves. As a department dedicated to being anti-racist, we have a long way to go. But maintaining a critical approach to work and ourselves will allow us to continue to move in this direction.

Mary Furlong Minkoff is the Assistant Director of Archaeology and Curator of Archaeological Collections at James Madison's Montpelier. There she manages over 3 million archaeological artifacts, serves as the Director of the Digital Collections Project, and has co-curated numerous exhibitions including the *Mere Distinction of Colour.* Her research focuses on utilizing material culture and community engaged archaeology to understand the inequalities created through race-based slavery in the American South. In 2019, Mary was the co-recipient of the Brennan Archaeology Award for her long term work at Fort Ward and with the Fort Ward/Seminary African American Descendant Society.

Terry Brock is the Manager for Archaeology and Research at the Wake Forest Historical Museum, and a Part Time Assistant Teaching Professor in Cultural Heritage and Preservation Program at Wake Forest University. He formerly served as Assistant Director for Archaeology at The Montpelier Foundation, and continues to conduct research at Montpelier. His research focuses on community-engaged public archaeology, digital cultural heritage, archaeological landscapes of American slavery and freedom, and the use of archaeology in cultural heritage practice. He also serves as the Chairperson of the Executive Board for Archaeology in the Community.

Matthew Reeves is the Director of Archaeology and Landscape Restoration at James Madison's Montpelier in Orange, Virginia. His specialty is sites of the African Diaspora including plantation and freedman period sites, and Civil War. In his 20 years at Montpelier and alongside his co-authors, Reeves has developed a strong public archaeology program known for its citizen science approach to research. At the heart of this program is community-based research with a heavy focus on investing descendant communities in the research and interpretation process and governance of cultural institutions.

References

Battle-Baptiste, Whitney. 2011. *Black Feminist Archaeology*. Walnut Creek, CA: Left Coast Press.

Blakey, Michael L. 1987. "Comments on "Toward a Critical Archaeology." *Current Anthropology* 28(3): 292.

———. 1997. "Past is Present: Comments on "In the Realm of Politics: Prospects for Public Participation in African American Plantation Archaeology." *Historical Archaeology* 31(3): 140–45.

———. 2010. "African Burial Ground Project: A Paradigm for Cooperation?" *Museum International* 62(1–2): 61–68.

———. 2020. "Archaeology under the Blinding Light of Race." *Current Anthropology* 61(22). https://doi.org/10.1086/710357.

Brock, Terry 2018. "Archaeology, Values, and Workplace Culture." *Terrypbrock.com*, 9 July. http://terrypbrock.com/2018/07/archaeology-values-and-workplace-culture/.

Carey, Mia. 2019. *Unpacking White Supremacy in the Black Muslim Experience: Towards an Anti-Racist Archaeology*. Unpublished manuscript.

Eid, Haitham. 2018. "Connecting the Dots: The Impact of Diversity in the Museum Workforce on Innovation, Relevance and Audience Engagement." Museums and the Web Conference Proceedings, 18–21 April 2018, Vancouver, Canada.

Engaging Descendant Communities in the Interpretation of Slavery at Museums and Historic Sites: A Rubric of Best Practices Established by the National Summit on Teaching Slavery. 2018. National Trust for Historic Preservation African American Cultural Heritage Action Fund.

Epperson, Terrence W. 2004. "Critical Race Theory and the Archaeology of the African Diaspora." *Historical Archaeology* 38(1): 101–8.

Franklin, Maria. 1997a. "'Power to the People': Sociopolitics and the Archaeology of Black Americans." *Historical Archaeology* 31(3): 36–50.

———. 1997b. "Why Are There So Few Black American Archaeologists?" *Antiquity* 71(274): 799–801.

Flewellen, Ayana O. 2017. "Locating Marginalized Historical Narratives at Kingsley Plantation." In *Challenging Theories of Racism, Diaspora, and Agency in African America*, ed. William A. White, III and Christopher C. Fennell, Special issue, *Historical Archaeology* 51(1): 71–87.

Flewellen, A., Dunnavant, J., Odewale, A., Jones, A., Wolde-Michael, T., Crossland, Z., & Franklin, M. (2021). "The Future of Archaeology Is Antiracist": Archaeology in the Time of Black Lives Matter. *American Antiquity* 86(2): 224–243.

González-Ruibal, Alfredo. 2012. "Against Post-Politics: A Critical Archaeology for the 21st Century." *Forum Kritische Archäologie* 1:157–166.

Ike, Nkem, Gabrielle Miller, and Gabby Omoni Hartemann. 2020. "Anti-Racist Archaeology YOUR TIME IS NOW." *The SAA Archaeological Record* 20(4): 12–16.

Kendi, Ibram X. 2019. *How to Be an Antiracist*. New York: One World.

La Roche, Cheryl J., and Michael L. Blakey. 1997. "Seizing Intellectual Power: The Dialogue at the New York Burial Ground." *Historical Archaeology* 31: 84–106.

Leone, Mark P. 2010. *Critical Historical Archaeology*. Walnut Creek, CA: Left Coast Press.

Leone, Mark P., Parker B. Potter, and Paul A. Shackel. 1987. "Toward a Critical Archaeology." *Current Anthropology* 28(3): 283–302.

McDavid, Carol, and Terry Brock. 2015. "The Differing Forms of Public Archaeology: Where We Have Been, Where We Are Now and Thoughts for the Future." In *Ethics and Archaeological Praxis*, ed. Cristóbal Gnecco and Dorothy Lippert, 159-183. New York: Springer.

McGuire, Randall H. 2008. *Archaeology Political Action*. Berkeley: University of California Press.

Montpelier Archaeology Department. 2017. #DigMontpelier Family: Culture and Values. Internal document.

Montpelier Foundation. 2019. "The Mere Distinction of Colour: 6 ways understanding slavery will change how you understand American freedom." *Montpelier*. Retrieved 4 March 2022 from https://www.montpelier.org/learn/6-ways-that-understanding-slavery-will-change-how-you-understand-american-freedom.

Nassaney, Michael. 2018. "Race and the Society for Historical Archaeology: Steps Toward Claiming an Anti-Racist Institutional Identity." Poster presentation. Society for Historical Archaeology. 3–6 January 2018. New Orleans, Louisiana.

Nassaney, Michael S., and Mary Ann Levine. 2009. *Archaeology and Community Service Learning*. Gainesville: University of Florida.

Reeves, Matthew B. 2004. "Asking the "Right" Questions: Archaeologists and Descendant Communities." In *Places in Mind: Public Archaeology as Applied Anthropology*, ed. Paul A. Shackel, and Erve J. Chambers, 71–81. New York: Routledge.

Schonfeld, Roger, and Mariët Westermann, with Liam Sweeney. 2015. *Art Museum Staff Demographic Survey*. New York: The Andrew W. Mellon Foundation.

Shackel, Paul A. 2007. "Civic Engagement and Social Justice: Race on the Illinois Frontier." In *Archaeology as a Tool of Civic Engagement*, ed. Barbara J. Little and Paul A. Shackel. Lanham, MD: Altamira Press.

Silliman, Stephen W., and T.J. Ferguson. 2010. "Consultation and Collaboration with Descendant Communities." In *Voices in American Archaeology*, ed. Wendy Ashmore, Dorothy T. Lippert, and Barbara J. Mills. Washington, DC: The SAA Press.

Twitty, Michael W. 2017. *The Cooking Gene: A Journey through African American Culinary History in the Old South*. New York: Amistad.

White, William, and Catherine Draycott. 2020. "Why the Whiteness of Archaeology Is a Problem." *Sapiens*, 7 July. https://www.sapiens.org/archaeology/archaeology-diversity/.

Wilkie, Laurie A., and Kevin M. Bartoy. 2000. "A Critical Archaeology Revisited." *Current Anthropology* 41(5): 747–77.

Wright, Sterling, Cara Monroe, Mary Furlong Minkoff, Matthew Reeves, Tanvi Honap, Rita Austin, and Courtney Hofman. 2018. "Exploring the Biological Heritage of Enslaved People at James Madison's Montpelier through Ancient DNA Analysis." Poster. Society of American Archeology. 11–15 April 2018. Washington, DC.

CHAPTER 2

Legacies of Shame, Legacies of Hope

Community Archaeology at a World War II Japanese American Internment Camp

Jeffery Burton and Mary M. Farrell

＋・✦✦✦・＋

Introduction

Public archaeology is immensely popular. Whether because it connects with "some of our time's most widespread fantasies, dreams, and desires" (Holtorf 2007), or because it can create "new history" (Handler and Gable 1997), or simply because humans need an excuse to play in the dirt, archaeology is one of the few professions where the public happily donates time, skills, and hard labor. Such is archaeology's appeal that some volunteers will even pay for the experience of doing manual labor, getting dirty, and working in all sorts of weather. Public archaeology projects can stretch scarce resources, increase public support and promote stewardship of cultural resources (Moyer 2015); make archaeology relevant to society (McDavid 2002); identify and engage diverse stakeholders (Betz 2007; Little and Amdur-Clark 2008); engage descendant communities (Colwell-Chanthaphonh and Ferguson 2008), and clarify and test commonly held perceptions about the past (South 1997). Community archaeology can also affirm or enhance a community's self-identity and connection with its heritage (Moyer 2015; Prybylski and Stottman 2010), and even illuminate a contested past by incorporating multiple perspectives (Colwell-Chanthaphonh and Ferguson 2006). By exploring parallels between the past and the present, critical public archaeology can even address modern social issues. In this chapter we describe how critical public archaeology projects at Manzanar National Historic Site explore issues of racism, the treatment of immigrants, the fragility of civil rights, American ideals, and the question of who, after all, is American.

Background

The United States entered World War II when the Japanese Empire attacked Pearl Harbor on 7 December 1941. The United States was immediately at war with the Axis Nations, including the Empire of Japan, the Third Reich of Germany, and the Kingdom of Italy. For the most part, immigrants and US citizens whose ancestors were from Germany or Italy were not suspected of being loyal to their country of origin and therefore potentially treacherous to the United States. But immigrants and US citizens whose ancestors were from Japan were treated as dangerous: over 120,000 Japanese Americans were forced from their homes, farms, schools, and businesses and were incarcerated in ten "Relocation Centers," most for the duration of the war. Most of those incarcerated were US citizens; they included men, women, and children, even US Army veterans. At the time, the mass incarceration was justified as a military necessity, in the name of national security. Forty years later, the US government officially acknowledged that the mass incarceration was an unnecessary and unjust abrogation of civil rights and a violation of the US Constitution. In 1992, the US Congress designated one of the former Relocation Centers, Manzanar, as a National Historic Site to protect and interpret cultural resources related to the mass incarceration and to serve as a reminder of the fragility of American civil rights. Critical public archaeology at Manzanar explores this recent past and impacts modern understanding of parallel issues that the United States continues to grapple with today.

Controversies / Different Narratives

Even today, the "Japanese American Relocation" is controversial, despite its clearly established unconstitutionality. Some politicians and commenters have claimed that the event was justified (Hawkins 2016; e.g., Malkin 2004) and cite it as support for current scapegoating based on ethnicity, national origin, or religion. In addition, there have been widely divergent narratives about details of the event, covering everything from who the prisoners were, to how they were treated, to how they reacted. Public archaeology projects undertaken since the establishment of Manzanar National Historic Site have allowed the National Park Service (NPS) to collaborate with descendant and local communities to explore and challenge these and other narratives.

Terminology

Following Roger Daniels (2008) and Yoshinonori Himel (2016), we use "Relocation" and "Relocation Center" where the historical context is clear and "incarceree" or "prisoner" to refer to individuals involuntarily confined. As Himel (2016: 801) notes, historically the term "internment camp" applied only to places where selected alien residents or the military of an enemy nation were confined during war. The term "internment" did not, and still does not, apply to mass incarceration of a country's own citizens or incarceration of immigrants who are not suspected of wanting to aid the enemy.

Historical Background

The mass incarceration of Japanese Americans was authorized by President Franklin D. Roosevelt through Executive Order 9066, signed on 19 February 1942. The Executive Order authorized the military to designate areas "from which any or all persons may be excluded." Although the Executive Order did not specify who would be excluded or from which areas they would be excluded, in practice, it was applied almost exclusively to Japanese Americans on the United States West Coast and from parts of Arizona. Most were imprisoned for the duration of the war.

By the time Roosevelt signed Executive Order 9066, the US government had already determined that the Japanese American population did not pose a military threat. However, many newspaper editors, politicians, and members of the general public did not distinguish between the Empire of Japan and Japanese American farmers, fishermen, gardeners, teachers, doctors, merchants, and students who lived in the United States. Many had immigrated to the United States decades before the Pearl Harbor attack but were denied citizenship because of anti-Asian naturalization laws. Their descendants born in the United States were American citizens.

At the beginning of the Relocation, the federal government hoped that Japanese Americans removed from the West Coast could be resettled in the interior of the country. But racism and prejudice intervened: several governors refused to let Japanese Americans into their states. For example, Wyoming Governor Nels Smith said that if the Japanese were brought into Wyoming "they would be hanging from every tree"; another governor stated that "if these people are dangerous on the Pacific coast, they will be dangerous here" (Daniels 1993: 57). As a result, the ten Relocation Centers operated for the duration of the war. The federal government constructed the Relocation Centers in remote parts of the country, most in deserts or swamps, perhaps unwittingly following newspaper columnist Henry McLemore's vitriolic "Herd 'em up, pack 'em off and give them the inside room of the Badlands. Let 'em be pinched, hurt, hungry and dead up against it" (McLemore 1942). Imprisoned Japanese Americans lost their homes, businesses, and other property estimated to have been worth, in today's currency, more than 3 billion dollars.

Physical Infrastructure of Manzanar

Located in the arid Owens Valley of eastern California, Manzanar was built in six weeks in the spring of 1942. Within three months, ten thousand people were incarcerated there. It included thirty-six blocks of barracks, an administration area, a hospital, churches, a motor pool, warehouses, and small-scale factories, in over 750 buildings within a one-square-mile area surrounded by a security fence and guard towers (Figure 2.1). Outside the security fence were the military police compound, a water reservoir, a cemetery, a landfill, sewage treatment facilities, chicken and hog farms, and farm fields.

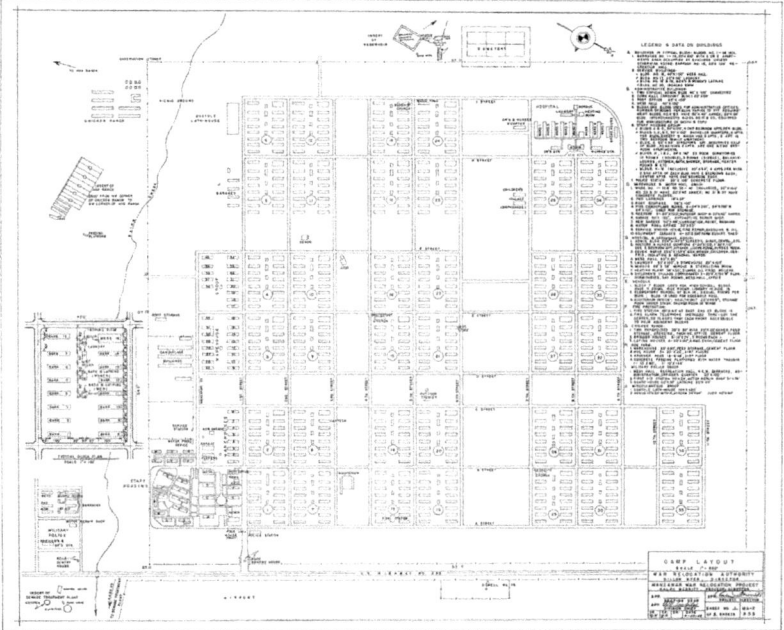

Figure 2.1. Manzanar Relocation Center, October 1944 aerial photograph and April 1945 Camp Layout blueprint. National Park Service, Manzanar National Historic Site, public domain.

When the camps closed at the end of 1945, each incarceree received a train or bus ticket to their desired location and $25 to start a new life. The story began to fade from memory. US school history books did not discuss Manzanar and Japanese Americans' mass incarceration during World War II; like the treatment of Native Americans and African Americans, it did not fit with the country's constitutional ideals of justice and equality (Adams 1945; Cahan and Williams 2016; Roosevelt 1943). Having absorbed the shame of incarceration, many Japanese Americans were reluctant to talk about it.

Redress

Inspired by the civil rights movements of the 1960s, Japanese Americans and civil rights activists lobbied Congress to establish a commission to study the episode. In 1982, the Commission on Wartime Relocation and Internment of Civilians (CWRIC), a bipartisan group, concluded that the incarceration was caused not by military necessity, but by racism, wartime hysteria, and a failure of political leadership (CWRIC 1982). Besides the enormous material losses to the incarcerees, the commission report also cited long-lasting intangible losses, including lost education and job training, loss of family structure, and prolonged racial stigma (Yamato 2013). The Manzanar Committee, a volunteer group dedicated to raising public awareness about the incarceration and violation of civil rights, lobbied Congress to preserve the former Manzanar Relocation Center as a unit of the National Park system (Nakagawa 2015). In 1992, Congress passed enabling legislation that designated Manzanar a National Historic Site, part of the National Park Service (Lyon 2015).

The Manzanar National Historic Site would be a place to tell an important story, but the common perception held by both the public and many in the National Park Service was that little remained at Manzanar when the National Historic Site was designated. After the last incarcerees had left Manzanar in November 1945, the government dismantled and removed all but three of the more than 750 original buildings (Burton 1996: 107; Wehrey 1993).

Local Opposition to Manzanar as a National Park Unit

Many in the local community did not support the National Historic Site designation; the first Manzanar NPS superintendent even received death threats from local residents (Edds 2004). The history of the camp had become muddled in two contradictory ways. For example, for years, some people who resided near Manzanar were not even aware that the former prison camp in their valley had incarcerated American citizens. They assumed that the "Jap camp" housed Japanese prisoners of war; who else would be held at a World War II prison camp? If the camp did hold civilians, they must have been dangerous, unassimilated visitors from Japan who posed a threat to national security.

Others remembered that Manzanar held Japanese American civilians but did not remember any guard towers or a security fence. Their stories told of Manzanar residents being "coddled" by the government, supplied with goods that were frugally rationed and rare for the long-term residents of Owens Valley, and provided with flush toilets and a sophisticated sewer system when many of the valley residents still used outhouses. Even some local residents who acknowledged that the government had unjustly incarcerated Japanese Americans at Manzanar were against the designation because it would highlight a negative aspect of Owens Valley history, perhaps putting the entire region in a bad light.

Community Archaeology

When Congress designated Manzanar as a historic site administered by the National Park Service, the site became subject to federal laws regarding cultural resources. The National Park Service conducted archaeological surveys and excavations at the National Historic Site in the early 1990s to provide baseline data for management (Burton 1996). The National Park Service recorded hundreds of features and thousands of artifacts dating to World War II and also found evidence of earlier occupations at the site. For the most part, the archaeological finds at confinement sites are not, in themselves, unique or particularly exciting: the most obvious are related to infrastructure, such as building foundations and sewage treatment plants. But there are also small and poignant remains such as toys, ornamental ponds, and graffiti inscriptions in concrete.

The National Park Service worked with the public to identify priorities for further archaeological investigations and restoration. Rather than being dictated by purely academic interests or management needs, the goals of the more than twenty community archaeology projects conducted at Manzanar National Historic Site since 2003 were developed in collaboration with the public. Taking advantage of the power of archaeology to foster civic engagement (Little and Shackel 2007; Little and Amdur-Clark 2008), Manzanar's archaeology projects have originated with, and been implemented with, several distinct descendant and local communities who have perspectives they believe relevant to, and important for, understanding Manzanar's history as it informs the present. The power of archaeology to address and bring light to current social issues is a key aspect of critical public archaeology, but must be done consciously and conscientiously, as explained by Camille Westmont and Andreas Antelid (2018: 10):

> When one considers the fact that archaeology is a practice that is constantly influenced by current political and social movements, it is not difficult to see it as a tool and method to influence it in a desirable direction. It is, however, crucial to do it in an open and aware manner so that the aim and purpose is apparent to all participants. In order for this tool to be successful, an open acknowledgement of the political agendas motivating

the work should be discussed, negotiated, and refined with the input and active involvement of the community.

For example, former incarcerees and their descendants wanted at least one guard tower and the security fence accurately reconstructed to convey the prison atmosphere, but others wanted some of the gardens they and their parents created excavated and restored to show how they improved their surroundings. The descendants of Caucasian staff members requested that parts of the Relocation Center's administration area be delineated. Local residents of Owens Valley wanted the pre–World War II history recognized. Working together in community archaeology projects, volunteers have explored different aspects of Manzanar's history and have been able to address some of the narratives that had developed, accurately or erroneously, about the mass incarceration. Four examples of these narrative themes where critical community archaeology came into play are discussed below.

Narrative Theme 1: The Incarcerees Were Coddled

Part of the opposition to the establishment of the Manzanar National Historic Site was born of resentment: some local residents claimed there were no guard towers or fences, and some claimed the Japanese Americans received special treatment while the nearby residents of Owens Valley suffered wartime privations. Some of the archaeological projects requested by the Japanese American community were designed to interrogate this perspective. Archaeological excavations uncovered guard tower foundations and remnants of the security fence, which provided direct evidence to contradict the first set of allegations.

One could argue that those standard prison features would be enough evidence against "coddling"—if the Japanese Americans were treated so luxuriously, why would guard towers and a security fence be necessary to keep them in? But archaeological investigations also recovered indirect evidence. The remains of the sewer plant recorded indicate that it did, indeed, employ up-to-date technology. But combined with evidence of 10,000 people living in one square mile, the sewer plant was clearly not a luxury but a necessity. Manzanar was the densest settlement in Owens Valley during World War II and in fact was more densely populated than any current settlement in the region. Fragments of gallon-sized disinfectant bottles are among the more common artifacts recovered at the site, indicating that the spread of disease from living in such close quarters was a serious concern.

Details of the plumbing also argue against coddling: those flush toilets were located at communal latrines, the slabs for which were documented during archaeological work. Each residential block had fourteen barracks and housed up to three hundred people, served by one men's latrine with eight toilets and one women's latrine with ten toilets. Toilets were placed close together in rows, without partitions; modifications to the concrete slab floors show that partitions were added later. Each barracks had four or five "apartments," which were actually single rooms to house up to eight people, without indoor plumbing. A single outside spigot, many still visible, served each barrack. In contrast, archaeological work in the administration area, where the Caucasian staff lived, exposed indoor plumbing and water heater slabs for the individual apartments, which had multiple rooms and private bathrooms (Burton 2005).

Community archaeology projects have also uncovered features at places where the incarcerees worked as part of an effort to make Manzanar self-sufficient or to contribute to the war effort. For example, volunteers found evidence of how brooding and processing facilities at the "Chicken Ranch" were modified and expanded, and uncovered the foundations of the factory where incarcerees made camouflage nets for the US military (Burton 2019a, 2019b).

Narrative Theme 2: The Incarcerees Were Truly a Threat to National Security and Were Not Really Americans

This myth was not the planned focus of any critical public archaeology project, because it could be easily discredited by examining the archival record, which documents that the majority of the incarcerees were US citizens, or by perusing the oral histories of former incarcerees, which tell of their all-American struggles to find a place in their adopted or birth country. However, not all of Manzanar's visitors or people in the nearby communities are likely to engage in this sort of research on their own. Community archaeology projects have proven to be effective at proving this point by uncovering tangible evidence of all-American sports, all-American consumer goods, and incarcerated children and babies.

Sports

Oral histories and historical photographs document the popularity of many sports at Manzanar. Incarcerees built a dozen baseball fields, a football field, and constructed basketball courts in nearly every residential block throughout the prison camp. In 2015, using donated funds, volunteers helped restore a basketball court in Block 14 where the NPS has reconstructed two new barracks to give visitors an idea of what life was like at Manzanar. Historical photographs and archaeological investigations determined the location of the backboard posts and the outline of the court itself. Volunteers cleared the area and reconstructed the backboards and the backstop fence. The court has an earthen surface, as it did originally, and the NPS provides basketballs for visitors to use.

This simple court has turned out to be a popular interactive exhibit. But it is also subtly poignant, pointing out that young Americans were part of the mass incarceration, and linking visitors who pick up the basketballs to those young people who originally built the court. This reminder that many prisoners were all-American youth may engage the all-American youth who visit today as effectively as any carefully worded museum exhibit. Soon after its reconstruction, one visitor said that seeing the basketball court brought tears to her eyes: she was moved by the fact that people "in such a lousy situation would construct something like that, trying to carry on by doing something as normal as playing basketball" (Rose Masters, personal communication, 13 July 2015).

American Consumer Goods

When the Japanese Americans were ordered to leave their communities, they were told to bring only what they could carry. Countless oral histories tell of the sadness this restriction caused: one former incarceree remembered that, as a ten-year-old, she had to forgo packing her books and dolls so that her clothes would fit in her suitcase (Yamamoto 2006). Very little was provided to the incarcerees when they first arrived at Manzanar: rooms were supplied with metal-frame beds, and incarcerees stuffed sacks with straw for mattresses. But as soon as they were able, incarcerees began ordering necessities via mail order and set up cooperative stores to provide other goods. American tastes are evident in the artifacts encountered; for example, fragments of Coca Cola and other soda bottles are common.

Children's Toys

Perhaps the most poignant artifacts found at Manzanar belonged to children. Hundreds of marbles attest to one way children spent their free time, but toy cars and pieces of games are commonly found during the community archaeology projects. One surprise was the many "war" toys found during the projects, including toy tanks, planes, ships, and soldiers, as well as full-size toy guns, all representing American forces.

Manzanar even had an orphanage: about a hundred orphans who had lived in different orphanages or foster homes before the war were brought to Manzanar's "Children's Village." During community archaeology projects, volunteers have found a wheel from a crib, a baby bottle, doll parts, and other toys at the former orphanage, and uncovered the remnants of a swing and gazebo. It would be difficult to argue that orphan babies and children posed a true threat to national security. One visitor, whose parents had been incarcerated, visited Manzanar with her Korean American husband. Possibly reflecting decades of animosity between Korea and Japan, her husband indicated that he considered the "Relocation" justified, but when he found a child's toy on site, he had second thoughts.

A Public Acknowledgment

The very fact that the archaeology of Relocation Centers often features the mundane practical aspects of everyday life can have a social benefit. One woman wrote that she did not realize her mother had been incarcerated until an archaeological overview of all the sites of World War II Japanese American incarceration was published (Burton et al. 2002). Her mother did not tell her children about the "Relocation" for fear they would become resentful and unpatriotic. Once her mother saw that the government itself was documenting the incarceration and the mess hall foundations and latrine slabs that still remain at several of the sites, she could talk about it openly.

Narrative Theme 3: *Shikata Ga Nai*

The phrase *Shikata ga nai* is sometimes used by Japanese Americans themselves to describe their attitude to imprisonment during World War II; it is a common Japanese expression meaning "it cannot be helped" or "there is nothing to be done." This gave rise to the narrative that the Japanese Americans were passive, willingly going to the Relocation Centers to prove their loyalty to the United States. This may have been true in some cases, but many members of the Japanese American community requested critical public archaeological projects that would uncover how much the incarcerees did to counter the conditions at Manzanar.

Japanese Gardens

Although they were being persecuted for their Japanese heritage, many incarcerees asserted that Japanese heritage by creating distinctively Japanese gardens. Gardens reduced dust, added beauty, and provided a more normal, less prison-like backdrop for daily activities and special occasions. After the relocation center closed, some of Manzanar's gardens had been bulldozed along with other remnants of the camp. Flood- and wind-borne sediments buried the rest, or they became overgrown with trees and brush. The Japanese American community requested that the gardens be excavated and restored as witnesses to their ethnic identity and their resistance to the bleak circumstances of their incarceration. With the help of the public, including many former incarcerees and their families, the NPS has excavated more than twenty gardens and landscaping features (Burton 2015; Figure 2.2).

The largest and most elaborate of Manzanar's Japanese gardens is Merritt Park, named after the camp director. The garden was the backdrop for hundreds of photographs and home movies, including well-known photographs by Ansel Adams (1945). Merritt Park had two connected ponds, an island in the upper, larger pond, and a waterfall that fell into the upper pond from a symbolic mountain constructed of rocks. With the help of more than 150 volunteers, the NPS archaeologically excavated and stabilized Merritt Park from 2006 to 2008. In 2011, a former incarceree, then ninety-one years old, and his family reconstructed an iconic rustic bridge that the incarceree's father had built. Restoration at Merritt Park continues and the NPS plans to someday bring water back to the ponds and replace the long-dead vegetation.

Figure 2.2. Garden excavations at Manzanar; clockwise from upper left: Water lily boxes in pond at Block 33 barracks garden, screening pond fill at Block 15 barracks garden, pond at Block 9 mess hall garden, stream at Merritt Park, pond with faux wood concrete logs at Block 17 barracks garden. National Park Service, Manzanar National Historic Site, public domain.

Community archaeology projects also uncovered a variety of other Japanese gardens. Some were built by individuals at their barracks to provide their families with a reminder of better times (Burton 2014, 2017). Some were built by block residents at mess halls to give incarcerees something pleasant to look at while they stood in line three times a day for meals. A garden was built at the hospital to give patients and staff a healing space. The gardens adhere to ancient Japanese garden design principles while making optimal use of materials found around the camp. In some cases, gardeners were allowed to collect rocks and plants from outside of the security fence, and gardeners were able to order seeds and plants from catalogs.

The camp administrators cautioned the garden builders to not make their gardens too "Japanese" as that might look bad to Caucasian visitors (Unrau 1996: 278). The most overt Japanese elements, such as rustic stone lanterns, were at barracks gardens. The larger mess hall and community gardens, which were more likely to be seen by visitors, lacked these elements. However, they often had less-recognizable Japanese elements, such as symbolic turtles, cranes, and Dragon Gate falls; incorporating these traditional symbols was certainly an assertion of Japanese heritage and may even have been a subversive form of resistance.

In fact, scholars have posited that all of Manzanar's Japanese gardens were a form of resistance, subversion, or defiance (Helphand 2006: 189; Okihiro 1984) or invoked the "re-territorialization" of space (Dusselier 2008). Others cite gardens as evidence of personal agency, cultural cohesion, creativity, and community (Embrey 2009; Horiuchi 2001; Ng 2014; Tamura 2004). Volunteers who have helped uncover the gardens see them as symbols of hope and resilience: the son of one garden builder said, "My father's heart and soul are in the garden he built at Manzanar" (quoted in Burton 2015).

Graffiti

Graffiti at the Manzanar Relocation Center also argues that the Japanese American community did not, after all, passively accept the Relocation, nor the negative self-identity promoted by the government-sanctioned racism. After the initial construction of the relocation center, incarcerees formed the work crews that did routine maintenance, modified inadequate infrastructure, and built new structures where needed. Relatively cheap and abundant, concrete was used for foundations, floors, dams, irrigation ditches, and sewer systems. Wet concrete also provided a blank slate for graffiti. Over 280 inscriptions made in wet concrete have been recorded at the Manzanar Relocation Center, proclaiming self-identity, enduring dignity, and resistance. Some of the texts include militaristic slogans, poems, individual and group names, present and former addresses, whimsical sayings, and expressions of love (Burton and Farrell 2013).

Some of Manzanar's inscriptions express anger and defiance or militant slogans. Only a few of these were found inside the camp. Two from 1942 are in Japanese: one at the traffic circle in the administration area translates roughly to "rice" or "America" and "urine" (dated June 1942, shortly after the camp opened). The character for America was the same as the character for rice; Americans were seen as rich and if you were rich, you would have lots of rice. A second, dating to October 1942, was inscribed at the fire station. It consists of three characters that translate as *Dainippon* (Great Japan). Both inscriptions are in conspicuous locations inside the camp, but it should be noted that most of the Caucasian staff could not read Japanese kanji. The third inscription inside the camp is in Roman script and dates to 1943: at the hospital morgue sidewalk is "BANZAII" (along with "Zero Boys" and an unclear Japanese inscription). Banzai can be a Japanese cheer of triumph, but Banzaii is used to mean "[let the emperor live] ten thousand years," which would be a decidedly pro-Japan sentiment.

Most of the pro-Japan inscriptions date to between February and October 1943 and are located outside the camp security fence. The expressions suggest a strong resentment against the United States as well as emotional attachment to Japan. For example, the name "Tojo," which appears near the chlorination tank's slab foundation, probably represents a subtle form of resistance: Tojo was the name of the Japanese Prime Minister and army general who ordered the attack on Pearl Harbor. There was only one "Tojo" incarcerated at Manzanar, a ten-year-old orphan boy, who when shown the inscription said it was not his doing.

Several Japanese inscriptions at the Chicken Ranch convey militant sentiments, with translations such as "Great Japanese Empire," "Beat the US," and "Unconditional US surrender." The fact that the same text is written in slightly different ways suggests that more than one person created the graffiti. Two inscriptions commemorate Japan's propaganda move of granting independence to the Philippines in October 1943. The phrase, "BANZAI NIPPON," inscribed at an irrigation ditch in the farm fields south of the central area, can be translated as "Long live Japan." Using the Romanized form of the native name of Japan, this inscription is the only one that someone who does not know Japanese would recognize as pro-Japan.

Some of the most militant graffiti occurs at the camp reservoir: "Beat Great Britain and the US," "Loyal to the emperor," and "Black Dragons." In Japan, the Black Dragon Society was a prominent paramilitary, ultra-nationalist group. At Manzanar it consisted of a dozen or so very outspoken men, most of whom had been educated in Japan. Working on repair and scavenger crews, they rode around on a trash truck with a black pirate flag. They were reportedly responsible for numerous acts of violence and intimidation, including beatings, trying to run over people, instigating unrest, and drawing up a death list (Inada 2000: 161–62).

These anti-American and pro-Japan sentiments could be seen as validating the narrative that the incarcerees were dangerous and un-American. Indeed, the graffiti illustrates some of the discontent in camp and disparate attitudes of the incarcerees. However, some factors militate against ascribing these sentiments to the majority of Manzanar's population. For one thing, pouring concrete was considered one of the worst jobs at Manzanar and was the only job offered to people considered "troublemakers." Although most young Japanese Americans at that time knew some Japanese, the kanji inscriptions were likely created by Kibei, those who had been born in the

Figure 2.3. Resistance graffiti at Manzanar; top translates as "Banzai, Great Japanese Empire, Manzanar Black Dragon Society Headquarters," left center translates as "Philippine Independence / October 14, 1943." National Park Service, Manzanar National Historic Site, public domain.

United States and educated in Japan. It would not be surprising that some of the Kibei would have felt resentful that their American citizenship counted for nothing in the mass incarceration; for that matter, it would not be surprising for any young Americans to feel resentment toward their own country if it incarcerated them without cause. Whatever resentment they felt, however, did not stop them from taking on difficult work to make the camp a better place for their fellow incarcerees. None of the incarcerees were forced to work; all received food and shelter whether they accepted a job or not, and the pay ($16 per month for over 160 hours of work) was not in itself a compelling inducement.

Barracks Basements

Building basements was another way that the incarcerees modified the prison camp to assert their independence, improve their surroundings, and in some cases, hide clandestine activities. In 2015, a community archaeology project excavated (or re-excavated) a basement that had been dug out by a teenager under his family's barracks room so that he and his friends could have a cool place to play cards in the summer when temperatures often reach 105 degrees Fahrenheit (Higa 2012). By then, the young man who had built the basement was in his eighties, and because of health issues could not return to Manzanar. But his son helped excavate the basement, updated his father on our progress, and asked him questions about some finds. The teenager and his family were transferred to Tule Lake in February 1944 and other incarcerees subsequently took over the basement, enlarging it and adding concrete steps. When he returned to volunteer at another community archaeology project, the son of the basement builder told a moving story of how he and his father had become closer through the basement project: talking about the basement allowed the father to open up about other aspects of the incarceration that he had been silent about before.

The publicity from the 2015 project generated even more stories about basements, so now there is archaeological and anecdotal evidence that there were likely hand-dug basements beneath most barracks. Some have even requested that their family basement be excavated and investigated. Indeed, additional basements were excavated during subsequent community archaeology projects and revealed other aspects of the incarcerees' lives. Basements exhibited different construction details: one built under the mess hall in Block 34 (excavated in 2007) was authorized by the administration and had substantial rock and concrete retaining walls. Basements built by the incarcerees were discouraged, and so were lined with whatever materials the excavator could scavenge. One had a concrete floor, some had wood framing and sheetrock walls, and others had only earthen walls. When the Relocation Center was closed and the buildings dismantled, the basements were filled with deconstruction debris and items left in the barracks. However, artifacts found in situ on the basement floors indicate different original uses. Bedsprings and bedding found in one and shoyu jugs in another are a reminder that mail-order shopping allowed the incarcerees to substitute better furnishings and more familiar food products for those provided by the government. Bedpans may have provided a more convenient alternative to going outside to the communal latrines. In one basement the volunteers found fragments of cement with Japanese kanji. Piecing the puzzle together, the writing could be translated to "Heaven and earth forever (Long live His Majesty the Emperor)," "Loyal to the emperor and love the country," and "Great Japan (Japanese Empire)." Although disposed of in a basement, the inscription suggests that pro-Japanese sentiments may have been more common within the security fence than the original graffiti study suggested. Finally, fragments of large jars found in some basements are likely from activities not allowed in the prison camp, such as making and storing home-brewed sake. According to the son of a Caucasian staff member, after the camp closed, his teenage buddies would search out the basements for sake left behind (Williams 2014).

Narrative Theme 4: The National Historic Site Distorts the Local History

One of the local residents' objections to the establishment of the Manzanar National Historic Site was that the site would distort local history; as the only National Park Service unit in Owens Valley, Manzanar would focus attention on one unflattering incident. But within the Historic Site boundaries, there are Indigenous sites dating back thousands of years, remnants of ranches and farms reflecting late nineteenth- and early twentieth-century European American settlements, and traces of a town initiated as an orchard community, all pre-dating the World War II relocation center. Through critical public archaeology projects, the community and the NPS have worked together to preserve evidence of other important chapters in Owens Valley history.

Shepherd Ranch

To accommodate local residents who wanted their history told, one of the first public archaeology projects that NPS undertook at Manzanar was at the Shepherd Ranch, the base of operations for both late nineteenth-century ranching activities and early twentieth-century farm and orchard developments and the original townsite of Manzanar. In 2003, volunteers, mostly recruited from the local community, helped map the site and features, conducted a metal-detector survey, and excavated test units. We found the remains of John Shepherd's original 1860s adobe house, the location of his later Victorian-style residence, a privy pit, and extensive trash deposits.

We also found children's toys such as doll parts and marbles, more than sixty different types of buttons, and seventy-seven types of beads. Some of the beads and other artifacts recovered, similar to those found at other Native American sites, were undoubtedly left by the Paiute Indians who worked for Shepherd.

Chinese artifacts were also recovered, including a coin, a spoon, a dish fragment with a China base mark, rice bowl fragments, and a medicine vial. It is likely that the Chinese cook in the Shepherd household, who was listed in US Census records, discarded or lost the items. The experience of Chinese immigrants in Owens Valley is another often-overlooked story.

The site of Shepherd Ranch is now marked by a wayside exhibit and the rock outline of the original adobe house. The archaeology spurred additional work by volunteers. Some local volunteers, who originally only wanted to work on the ranching and town archaeology, found camaraderie with the other volunteers and discovered commonality with other aspects of the site's history. These "locals" have become regular volunteers who do archaeology at Japanese American features.

Manzanar Townsite

In 1905, John Shepherd sold his ranch lands to the Chaffey brothers, who then formed the Owens Valley Improvement Company for the express purpose of developing a town. The Chaffeys founded the town of Manzanar in 1910, which converted the ranch's range land to 5,000 acres of orchards and fields. At its height, the town included twenty-five homes as well as a school, a town hall, and a general store. The town was short-lived: the City of Los Angeles bought up most of the land in Owens Valley so they could transport the water to Los Angeles. The townsite of Manzanar was completely abandoned by 1934 and soon erased from the landscape (Burton 1998). The Chaffey connection reaches all the way to Australia, where the brothers are much better known for their innovative irrigation techniques that facilitated successful farming even in drought conditions. Thwarted by the export of water from the valley, Manzanar was the Chaffey brothers' only unsuccessful development. Descendants of others who had lived at the town of Manzanar frequently return and maintain a keen interest in the site. On the surface, the townsite descendants have little in common with the Japanese Americans who were incarcerated at Manzanar, but both groups were relocated for what was considered, at different points in time, the greater good. Water issues are still relevant in the Owens Valley today as Tribal and other local groups try to reinstate their water rights.

Indigenous Sites

Paiute and Shoshone Tribal members who live in Owens Valley have asked that the Indigenous archaeological sites be preserved and protected. Although the Indigenous residents were largely displaced from most of their traditional territory in the late nineteenth century, the archaeological sites tie today's Tribal members to their ancestors and to their original homeland. Maybe ironically, the treatment of the Paiutes and Shoshones illustrates that the racism that engendered the Japanese American incarceration is not the "one unflattering episode" in Owens Valley history. The Indigenous people of the valley suffered an even greater trauma—war, genocide, and forced exile when European American immigrants wanted their land.

In fact, community archaeology projects at Manzanar reveal a long-contested landscape: European Americans violently drove the Indigenous inhabitants from their land, then farmers supplanted ranchers, then Los Angeles removed the farmers by buying up the water rights, then Japanese Americans were brought to Manzanar against their will. The legislative record for Manzanar's establishment as a NPS unit demonstrates that Congress intended for the full history of the site to be protected and interpreted. The inclusion of these stories increased local support for the Historic Site and local opposition largely ceased (Rhea 1997: 62), although the interpretation of the full history is not as flattering as some of the original opponents had hoped.

Discussion

Manzanar's community archaeology program arose from public research priorities, addresses public conceptions and misconceptions, and helps members of the public connect with each other and with the site. Community archaeology can affirm or enhance a community's self-identity and connection with their heritage. For example, the wholesale incarceration during World War II of the Japanese American community was traumatic, economically and emotionally devastating, and left a lingering sense of shame and betrayal. A former incarceree might be bitter and quiet when considering the Relocation's economic and social consequences, but will open up and tell dozens of stories when they see the foundations of their barracks or remnants of a garden their parents built. Although archaeology cannot explain the racism the Japanese Americans experienced, it can show how the incarcerees reacted: they did what they could to improve life while incarcerated and were not afraid to flaunt their Japanese heritage.

The archaeology projects have been able to identify and engage diverse communities, including former incarcerees and their descendants, the grown-up children who had lived in the administration area, townspeople and their descendants, and Paiute and Shoshone Tribal members. One former incarceree stated that volunteering for the community archaeological projects was the best way to understand what being incarcerated at the World War II Manzanar Relocation Center was like: hot and dusty, or cold and dusty, depending on the season, but always windy (Umemoto 2013). Given the site's remote location and ofttimes challenging conditions, it is notable that an average of more than a hundred people come together each year to work on all of Manzanar's history, many of the volunteers returning year after year. The community archaeology participants are actively engaged and become emotionally tied to the site and become ardent supporters of exploring the full history of the site.

It could be argued that every society and every era creates its past, or memorializes selective parts of its past, for the purposes of the present. Critical public archaeology, conceived and conducted in collaboration with Manzanar's diverse communities, gives us the opportunity to examine how well our society has lived up to its professed ideals and moral code, both in the past and today. Racism and its repercussions continue to be vital, if difficult, topics in the United States, and the community archaeology projects provide a forum for discussing racism and the treatment of immigrants and minority groups. The history of how civil rights and the US Constitution were casually and unjustly set aside during World War II is directly relevant to how civil rights can be curtailed today in the name of national security or law and order. The different descendant communities of Manzanar may have more in common than evident at first glance: what role did racism and classism play when Indigenous peoples were dispossessed for European Americans, or when rural ranchers and farmers were dispossessed to provide water to the city, or when Japanese Americans were incarcerated at Manzanar? Critical public archaeology can remind us that there are many stories, many perspectives, and the landscape itself holds memories. Through the community archaeology projects, descendant communities come together to explore and tell these stories. and discuss how the United States must work to live up to the ideals expressed in its Declaration of Independence and Constitution.

Acknowledgments

We want to acknowledge the former incarcerees, whose indomitable spirit and grace have been an inspiration, and Manzanar National Historic Site's superintendents, who have encouraged public archaeology. In addition, the Japanese American community's interest and participation in the archaeology of the World War II mass incarceration have led us to the realization that archaeology can be a force for truth and justice in the present, as well as a way to better understand the past. Finally, we thank all the volunteers without whom this work would not have been possible and there would not be much for visitors to see at Manzanar.

Jeff Burton is Cultural Resource Program Manager at Manzanar National Historic Site in California. Each year he leads volunteer projects uncovering Manzanar's history, including restoring gardens built by imprisoned Japanese Americans during WWII. His archeological overview of Japanese American internment sites was cited in the national law that created the $38 million Japanese American Confinement Sites grant program. His work has also been pivotal in the establishment of National Park Service units at three other internment sites: Minidoka (Idaho), Tule Lake (California), and Honouliuli (Hawaii). In 2017 he received an award for excellence from the Society for American Archaeology for his work at confinement sites.

Mary M. Farrell is currently director of Trans-Sierran Archaeological Research (Lone Pine, California), a senior archaeologist for TEAM Engineering and Management (Bishop, California), and for four years taught an archaeological field school for the University of Hawaii West O'ahu. Most of her career was with the US Forest Service in California and Arizona, where she had the privilege of working with volunteers,

Tribal members, and Mexico's *Instituto Nacional de Antropología e Historia* and *Universidad de Sonora* on projects exploring public archaeology, historic preservation, and traditional perspectives on land use and stewardship.

References

Adams, Ansel. 1945. *Born Free and Equal: Photographs of the Loyal Japanese-Americans at Manzanar Relocation Center, Inyo County, California.* New York: US Camera. Retrieved 21 October 2019 from http://lcweb2.loc.gov/service/gdc/scd0001/2002/20020123001bf/20020123001bf.pdf.

Betz, Barbara. 2007. "Putting the Past to Use: A Plea for Community Archaeology." Retrieved 21 May 2017 from http://savingantiquities.org/putting-the-past-to-use-a-plea-for-community-archaeology.

Burton, Jeffery F. 1996. "Three Farewells to Manzanar: The Archeology of Manzanar National Historic Site, California." *Western Archeological and Conservation Center Publications in Anthropology* 67. Tucson, AZ: National Park Service.

———. 1998. "The Archaeology of Somewhere: Archaeological Testing Along U.S. Highway 395, Manzanar National Historic Site, California." *Western Archeological and Conservation Center Publications in Anthropology* 72. Tucson, AZ: National Park Service.

———. 2005. *Archeological Investigations at the Administration Block and Entrance, Manzanar National Historic Site.* Western Archeological and Conservation Center. Tucson, AZ: National Park Service.

———. 2014. *A Place of Beauty and Serenity: Excavation and Restoration of the Arai Family Fish Pond, Block 33, Barracks 4.* Manzanar National Historic Site: National Park Service.

———. 2015. *Garden Management Plan: Gardens and Gardeners at Manzanar.* Manzanar National Historic Site: National Park Service.

———. 2017. *Uncovering Community: The Archeology of Block 15, Manzanar Relocation Center.* Manzanar National Historic Site: National Park Service.

———. 2019a. *Archeological and Preservation Work at the Camouflage Net Factory 2009–2018, Manzanar Relocation Center.* Manzanar National Historic Site: National Park Service.

———. 2019b. *Archeological and Preservation Work at the Chicken Ranch 2009–2018, Manzanar Relocation Center.* Manzanar National Historic Site: National Park Service.

Burton, Jeffery F., and Mary M. Farrell. 2013. "'Life in Manzanar, Where There Is a Spring Breeze': Graffiti at a World War II Japanese American Internment Camp." In *Prisoners of War: Archaeology, Memory, and Heritage of 19th and 20th-Century Mass Internment*, ed. Harold Mytum and Gilly Carr, 239–69. Contributions to Global Archaeology. New York: Springer Press.

Burton, Jeffery, Mary Farrell, Florence Lord, and Richard Lord. 2002. *Confinement and Ethnicity: An Overview of World War II Japanese American Relocation Sites.* Seattle: University of Washington Press.

Cahan, Richard, and Michael Williams. 2016. *Un-American: Incarceration of Japanese Americans during World War II.* Chicago: CityFile Press.

Colwell-Chanthaphonh, Chip, and T. J. Ferguson. 2006. "Memory Pieces and Footprints: Multivocality and the Meanings of Ancient Times and Ancestral Places among the Zuni and Hopi." *American Anthropologist* 108(1): 148–62.

———, eds. 2008. *Collaboration in Archaeological Practice: Engaging Descendant Communities.* Lanham, MD: AltaMira Press.

Commission on Wartime Relocation and Internment of Civilians (CWRIC). 1982. *Personal Justice Denied: Report of the Commission on Wartime Relocation and Internment of Civilians.* Washington, DC: Government Printing Office.

Daniels, Roger. 1993. *Prisoners without Trial: Japanese Americans in World War II.* New York: Hill and Wang.

———. 2008. "Words Do Matter: A Note on Inappropriate Terminology and the Incarceration of Japanese Americans." *Discover Nikkei.* Accessed 20 May 2017 from www.discovernikkei.org.

Dusselier, Jane. 2008. *Artifacts of Loss: Crafting Survival in Japanese American Concentration Camps*. New Brunswick, NJ: Rutgers University Press.

Edds, Kimberly. 2004. "New Museum Revives Painful Memories for Internees." *Washington Post*, 26 April.

Embrey, Monica. 2009. "A Place Like This: An Environmental Justice History of the Owens Valley—Water in Indigenous, Colonial, and Manzanar Stories." Bachelor's Thesis, Claremont, CA: Pomona College. Retrieved 20 May 2017 from http://scholarship.claremont.edu/pomona _theses/72/.

Handler, Richard, and Eric Gable. 1997. *The New History in an Old Museum: Creating the Past at Colonial Williamsburg*. Durham, NC: Duke University Press.

Hawkins, Derek. 2016. "Japanese American Internment Is 'Precedent' for National Muslim Registry, Prominent Trump Backer Says." *Washington Post*, 17 November.

Helphand, Kenneth. 2006. *Defiant Gardens: Making Gardens in Wartime*. San Antonio, TX: Trinity University Press.

Higa, Roy. 2010. Oral history interview by Laura Ng, July 2, 2012 (MANZ 1362). Oral History Project, Manzanar National Historic Site.

Himel, Yoshinori H. T. 2016. "Americans' Misuse of 'Internment.'" *Seattle Journal for Social Justice* 14(3): 797–837.

Holtorf, Cornelius. 2007. "Learning from Las Vegas: Archaeology in the Experience Economy." *The SAA Archaeological Record* 7(3): 6–10, 25.

Horiuchi, Lynne. 2001. "Dislocations: The Built Environments of Japanese American Internment." In *Guilt by Association: Essays on Japanese American Settlement, Internment, and Relocation in the Rocky Mountain West*, ed. Mike Mackey. Powell, WY: Western History Publications.

Inada, Lawson F. 2000. *Only What We Could Carry: The Japanese American Internment Experience*. Berkeley, CA: Heyday Books.

Little, Barbara J., and Paul A. Shackel, eds. 2007. *Archaeology as a Tool of Civil Engagement*. Lanham, MD: Altamira.

Little, Barbara, and Nathaniel Amdur-Clark. 2008. "Archeology and Civic Engagement," National Park Service Archeology Program, Technical Brief 23. Retrieved 21 May 2017 from https://www.nps.gov/archeology/pubs/techbr/tch23.htm.

Lyon, Cherstin. 2015. "Manzanar National Historic Site." *Densho Encyclopedia*. Retrieved 22 July 2020 from https://encyclopedia.densho.org/Manzanar%20National%20Historic%20Site.

Malkin, Michelle. 2004. *In Defense of Internment: The Case for Racial Profiling in World War II and the War on Terror*. Washington, DC: Regnery Publishing.

McDavid, Carol. 2002. "From Real Space to Cyberspace: The Internet and Public Archaeological Practice." PhD dissertation. Cambridge: University of Cambridge.

McLemore, Henry. 1942. "'Internment' for Enemy Aliens." *San Francisco Examiner*, 29 January.

Moyer, Teresa. 2015. "Before 1916: The Roots of National Park Service Community Archaeology Best Practices." *Journal of Community Archaeology & Heritage* 2(3): 199–207.

Nakagawa, Martha. 2015. "Manzanar Committee." *Densho Encyclopedia*. Retrieved 10 May 2017 from http://encyclopedia.densho.org/Manzanar%20Committee/.

Ng, Laura. 2014. "Altered Lives, Altered Environments: Creating Home at Manzanar Relocation Center, 1942–1945." Master's Thesis. Boston: University of Massachusetts.

Okihiro, Gary. 1984. "Religion and Resistance in America's Concentration Camps." *Phylon* 45(3): 220–33.

Prybylski, Matthew, and M. Jay Stottman. 2010. "Reconnecting Community: Archaeology and Activism at the Portland Wharf." In *Archaeologists as Activists: Can Archaeologists Change the World?*, ed. M. Jay Stottman, 126–40. Tuscaloosa: University of Alabama Press.

Rhea, Joseph Tilden. 1997. *Race Pride and the American Identity*. Cambridge, MA: Harvard University Press.

Roosevelt, Eleanor. 1943. "To Undo a Mistake Is Always Harder than Not to Create One Originally." *Collier's Magazine*, 10 October.

South, Stanley. 1997. "Generalized versus Literal Interpretation." In *Presenting Archaeology to the Public: Digging for Truths*, ed. John H. Jameson Jr., 54–62. Walnut Creek, CA: Altamira Press.

Tamura, Anna. 2004. "Gardens below the Watchtower: Gardens and Meaning in World War II Japanese American Incarceration Camps." *Landscape Journal* 23(1): 1–21.

Umemoto, Hank. 2013. *Manzanar to Mount Whitney: The Life and Times of a Lost Hiker*. Berkeley, CA: Heyday.

Unrau, Harlan D. 1996. *National Historic Site: The Evacuation and Relocation of Persons of Japanese Ancestry during World War II: A Historical Study of the Manzanar War Relocation Center, Historic Resource Study / Special History Study*. Western Regional Office, National Park Service.

Wehrey, Jane C. 1993. *Report on Manzanar Pre-camp Period: Data and Sources and Suggestions and Sources for Further Research on Attitudes of Owens Valley Townspeople during Manzanar Camp*. Tucson, AZ: Western Archeological and Conservation Center.

Westmont, V. Camille, and Andreas Antelid. 2018. "The Place to Be: Community Archaeology as a Tool for Cultural Integration." *Journal of Community Archaeology & Heritage* 5(4): 237–49.

Williams, Arthur L. 2014. *Reflecting on WWII, Manzanar, and the WRA*. Victoria, BC: Friesen Press.

Yamamoto, Madelon (Arai). 2006. Oral history interview by Erin Brasfield Rose, 12 September 2006 (MANZ 1113A). Oral History Project, Manzanar National Historic Site.

Yamato, Sharon. 2013. "Commission on Wartime Relocation and Internment of Civilians." *Densho Encyclopedia*. Retrieved 30 October 2016 from http://encyclopedia.densho.org/Commission%20on%20Wartime%20Relocation%20and%20Internment%20of%20Civilians/.

CHAPTER 3

Archaeology as Performance
Reanimating the Portland Wharf Landscape with Critical Public Archaeology

M. Jay Stottman

Introduction

There are many concepts of public archaeology, most of which are premised on the idea of interacting with the general public in any form. However, there is much more to public archaeology than just communicating with the public and creating information for them to consume. With the development of community and activist archaeology over the last twenty years, some archaeologists have used public archaeology as a means to engage communities and advocate for them. They seek to apply the critical approaches that inspire engagement with communities and activism to a public archaeology that transcends mere public interaction to an agent of change. If we think about performing archaeology with the public, we can envision a critical public archaeology that engages the public in the discovery of their own past and advocates for the development of community heritage and identity through reanimating landscapes.

In this chapter, I will explore the concept of public archaeology as a method for activist goals and as a performance that can help reanimate heritage landscapes. I also will discuss the development of critical public archaeology strategies at the Portland Wharf site that were evaluated and tested as a means to use the performance of archaeology in the creation of a Portland Wharf Park heritage landscape.

Community and Activist Archaeology

It is not my aim to describe the breadth of community archaeology being practiced around the world today, but instead to demonstrate its importance for the development of activist and other like archaeologies that seek to use archaeology to engage with, benefit, and advocate for communities. The theoretical underpinnings of community and activist archaeology, most would agree, are derived from critical theory, in particular, approaches that emphasize self-reflexivity and engagement in and with contemporary politics (Leone, Potter, and Shackel 1987; Pinsky and Wylie 1989). When we stepped back and examined our interactions with the communities where and for whom we work, we found that archaeology could have as much of a role in understanding present-day communities as it did for those in the past (LaRoche and Blakey 1997; Derry and Malloy 2003). Engaging and collaborating with present-day communities invariably involves archaeologists in the politics, causes, and struggles of these communities (Blakey 1997; Franklin 1997; McGuire 2008; Colwell-Chanthaphohn and Ferguson 2008; Silliman and Ferguson 2010). When we started doing archaeology with communities, we began to see ways to use our understanding of the past to benefit them beyond just providing information about their past (Little 2002; see Burton and Farrell this volume). Activism seeks to not only collaborate with communities but also advocate for them (see Stottman 2010a, Little and Zimmerman 2010, Barton 2021 for a more detailed discussion of activist archaeology).

Most community and activist projects privilege archaeology's obvious ability to produce knowledge as its most transformative element. As archaeologists, we all believe that the knowledge we produced as part of our traditional research objectives has profound impacts on the world. When that knowledge is used in an activist way, which is the mainstay of most activist archaeology projects, indeed it can be that (McGuire 2008, 2014; Sabloff 2008). Unfortunately, we also have found that bestowing knowledge on the world is perhaps not as impactful as we would like to believe (Potter and Leone 1987; Potter 1994). In our traditional thinking, the problem with making archaeology impactful was not our message, it was making that message consumable for the public (Stottman 2014). We really did not think that perhaps the problem was not only our ability to connect with the public, but also the message we wanted to convey. Our messages have largely been focused on site protection and preservation, and it only has been within the last twenty years that we really began to ask the public what they wanted from archaeology.

With the arrival of the twenty-first century, we really began to reexamine not only how we interacted with the public, but also how we conceptualize archaeology. The self-reflexivity of critical approaches has inspired us to examine ourselves and think about how we use and conduct archaeology. This self-examination exposes inherent problems of inequality and power based on race, sex, and class within the field of archaeology (Blakey 1987; Battle-Baptiste 2011; see Minkoff, Brock, and Reeves this volume). These institutionalized problems within archaeology have limited the concept of archaeology and its ability to engage with the public. Some archaeologists have reconceptualized archaeology beyond preservation messages to be an agent of change and to collaborate with the public. They see archaeology as a tool for civic engagement

(Little and Shackel 2007, 2014), political action (McGuire 2008), activism (Little and Zimmerman 2010; Stottman 2010a), and transformation (Atalay et al. 2014). Thus, we have shifted focus from trying to increase the public relevancy of archaeology to thinking about how we can use archaeology, all aspects of it, to benefit the public. We have become activists for changing the structure of our field and for reconceptualizing archaeology as an agent of change.

When I think about archaeology, I not only think about the interesting history we uncover, but also about how I might use archaeology to achieve activist goals. Like others, I have argued that collaboration and public archaeology are essential methods of an activist agenda, as both require a deep understanding of stakeholders and the public at large (Stottman 2010b, 2014).

Does It Matter What We Call It?

For the last twenty years as public engagement concepts in archaeology have become more prominent, we have found ourselves in a constant struggle over terminology (Stottman 2018). There are many iterations of public engagement in archaeology, and we use a variety of terms for them. It is not my intention to discuss all of these nor to attempt to define them. I am merely acknowledging that all forms of engagement have important distinctions. Because of similarities between forms of engagement, I think we tend to conflate terms. Although public, community, activist, action, civic engagement, collaborative, transformative, movement, applied, and a myriad of other archaeologies all refer to similar ideas and concepts, the idea of a critical public archaeology reminds me that this struggle is real and not merely semantic. The use of so many different terms for seemingly the same thing seems a bit unnecessary and hints at territorialism as it can appear like individuals are staking their claim in the engagement revolution currently taking place in archaeology.

Because of this issue of terminology, some have suggested that various iterations of similar archaeological concepts are niche archaeology (Atalay et al. 2014). However, I would argue that our struggle over terminology is a product of the complexity of doing activist and engagement work. When my colleagues and I began to put together the edited volume that would become *Archaeologists as Activists* (Stottman 2010a), we had difficulty finding the right word that embodied what we were doing with our archaeology. We spent more time discussing what to call it than we did defining what we do because we knew it was important to differentiate the concepts we used from traditional archaeological thinking. I believe there is a good reason why we struggle with the words we use to describe our concepts and the introduction of the term "critical public archaeology" illustrates precisely why. Terminology is often used as a means to differentiate what challenges established norms, and this is the case with critical public archaeology, as there needs to be something to differentiate it from traditional public archaeology. I would argue that the various terms used for activist and engagement archaeology is not niche, but instead nuance.

Critical Public Archaeology

For me, public archaeology is the reason that I sought to be an activist with my archaeology: to use archaeology for engagement and collaboration with and for the benefit of the public. I thought that the relationship between public outreach and engagement was obvious and that all I had to do was reconceptualize public archaeology with activist goals (Stottman 2010b). Clearly, I underestimated the power of traditional conceptions and labels when, to my surprise, some of my colleagues discounted public archaeology as a tool for activism. This view of public archaeology perplexed me at first, because I had always seen activism as an inherent extension of public archaeology. Public archaeology is a broad term that has many definitions, but the idea that it is largely associated with cultural resource management and as outreach for our stewardship messages is how many archaeologists see it. For them, public archaeology is the work that we do in the public interest, such as government mandated cultural resource management, or it is how we communicate our stewardship message to the public. Public archaeology is certainly that, but it is and can be much more by using its methods of interacting and communicating with the public for activist purposes (see Merriman 2004; Stottman 2010b; Guttormsen and Hedeager 2015 for discussions about the development of public archaeology).

Public archaeology was very much a part of introducing critical perspectives in archaeology during the 1980s and 1990s. The call for archaeology to be politically engaged, to expose underlying power structures of society, and to be self-reflexive, resonated with some who saw public archaeology as a means to practice critical archaeology (Potter 1994). At that time, concepts of public archaeology were still firmly entrenched in public interest and stewardship, which emphasizes the need to distinguish our public archaeologies. Critical public archaeology is a term that makes this distinction, as public archaeologies that are derived from or are mechanisms of critical approaches in archaeology (see Westmont, Introduction, this volume). I see a critical public archaeology as a method used in the practice of critically based archaeologies with activist and engagement goals.

Heritage Landscapes

Archaeologists have long understood that the landscape can hold clues to helping us understand culture by exploring how people experienced and used landscapes in the past (see Ashmore and Knapp 1999; Bender 2002; Delle 1998; Ingold 1993; Leone 1984; Miller 1988; Pool and Cliggett 2008; Tilley 1994 as just a few examples). The relationship of natural and cultural landscapes to public memory, identity, and heritage have been of particular interest, thus archaeologists are aware of the role that landscapes can have in their creation, erasure, maintenance, and modification. Since we are adept at examining change through time, changes in landscapes have helped us tell the story of cultural change. Archaeologists also have become interested in the concept of heritage landscapes, as we have examined how present-day people have used the past and the landscape to create heritage and public memory (Shackel 2001, 2003, 2004; Smith 2006). Heritage landscapes include those places where heritage is communicated, such as historical parks, outdoor museums, monuments, and historic districts.

There are a variety of definitions for heritage, but these all have the basic idea of the past being used for a purpose in the present in common (Shackel 2004; Little and Shackel 2014; Messenger and Bender 2019). This very nature of heritage provides a multitude of ways that archaeology can access and become intertwined with creating heritage. Archaeology inherently has a role in the development of heritage and in the landscapes created for it. The information and knowledge that we produce is invariably used by present-day people to create heritage and this connection between the past and present is conducive to activist and engagement archaeology. We as archaeologists can embrace our role in heritage development by pursuing activist agendas with the knowledge that we produce. We also can help create heritage landscapes with that knowledge as well as help reanimate or bring life to them by facilitating public memory with the information and material objects we uncover (Orange 2014). However, I also am suggesting that we also can literally reanimate landscapes with a critical public archaeology as performance (Stottman 2016).

Archaeology as Performance

I have found that the act of doing archaeology can enhance our ability to advance activist goals. It is one thing to talk to communities about social justice with the knowledge we produce and another thing entirely for them to participate in the discovery of this knowledge. The conceptualization of archaeology for activism should include the act of doing archaeology or the performance of archaeology. The performance of archaeology as critical public archaeology can transform our traditional notions of public archaeology from an archaeology stewardship commercial to a powerful tool of engagement (see also Burton and Farrell this volume).

Our efforts to interact with the public have mainly been focused on archaeology literacy. Public archaeology was largely focused on teaching the public about archaeology and demonstrating the value of the research products that we produce, but that was not always the case. The overarching intent of Mark Leone's Archaeology in Annapolis program, initiated in the 1980s, was activist in nature by trying to inform the public about their condition as a result of capitalism in hopes that they would want to change it. This program pioneered public archaeology strategies and methods and its relationship with heritage by thinking about archaeology as a performance and seeking help from theater professionals to develop methods of engaging the public (Potter and Leone 1987; Potter 1994).

Archaeology is a literal performance, especially when it is thrust into public view, as demonstrated by the Archaeology in Annapolis project. This idea of archaeology as performance is a self-reflexive examination of the practice of archaeology reminiscent of when Michael Shanks and Randall McGuire (1996) drew attention to how we practice archaeology in their Marxist critique of alienated labor. They called for archaeology to be practiced as a craft so as to better reflect the critiques of post-processual and Marxist thought. This examination of how archaeology is practiced was seen as an important element in exposing issues of labor within archaeology and it hints at the potential of the exposure of our process to be impactful. The performance of archaeology places the practice of archaeology in public view and makes it tangible to the public. Although it is not the craft that Shanks and McGuire proposed, it is most certainly a reconceptualization of how we think about archaeology and who does it.

The proximity of the public in the performance of archaeology is certainly unnerving to archaeologists resistant to the public's participation in the process and invites a number of issues that can contradict our traditional notion of preservation ethics. However, such concerns can and have been overcome, as it is the unveiling of the archaeological process that resonates with the public. The fact that they can see it and participate in it lends to a sense of authenticity and ownership of the information that is discovered and created as a result. Performance is a powerful tool that can open our process to the public, in essence democratizing archaeology. This democratization will require us to relinquish some of our power over not only the research objectives, but also the production of knowledge with the publics with whom we work. Relinquishing power does not mean that we lose our expert status, the public will always look to our expertise to interpret the past, but we have to think about public archaeology strategies as opportunities to engage the public and invite them into our process and that is what a critical public archaeology is about (Barton 2021).

If we think about the process of archaeology as performance, then what we do as archaeologists in our efforts to understand the past and engage with the public become a part of a community's heritage (Shackel 2004). As I will demonstrate below, not only is it our production of historical knowledge that can involve archaeologists into the creation of community heritage, but also our presence and performance on the landscape which can contribute to the creation of identity through heritage (Stottman 2016).

Critical public archaeology has a role in the creation, maintenance, and modification of identity and the remembrance of the past as heritage through performance. A public archaeology project conducted at the Portland Wharf site in the Portland Neighborhood of Louisville, Kentucky, provides a case study of how the performance of archaeology on the landscape can be used for activist goals regarding the creation of a community's identity and memory through heritage and thus is an example of critical public archaeology.

The Portland Wharf

The Portland Wharf site is located in the Portland Neighborhood of Louisville, Kentucky. It was once the cultural and economic heart of a flourishing independent river town during the early to mid-nineteenth century. Founded in 1811 at the base of the falls of the Ohio River, Portland was an important port along with the burgeoning City of Louisville in the lucrative portage system that bypassed the falls (Figure 3.1). During Portland's heyday in the 1840s and 1850s, it was not unusual to see dozens of steamboats lined up at Portland's Wharf, unloading and loading cargo and passengers. It was a prosperous place that featured a distinctive commercial district with many businesses, a large luxury hotel, and residences. Despite its early prosperity, the fledgling town was annexed briefly by its older and larger neighbor, Louisville, in 1837. Broken promises led to Portland again becoming independent after seceding just a few years later. However, town leaders struggled to manage the rapidly growing community and sought to be annexed by Louisville, which was approved a second time in 1852 (Prybylski and Stottman 2010).

During the late nineteenth century, Portland's fortunes changed, which greatly altered its landscape. Changes in transportation limited its economic viability, as railroads supplanted steamboats and improvements to a canal around the falls rendered the portage system obsolete. Furthermore, a series of devastating floods ravaged the

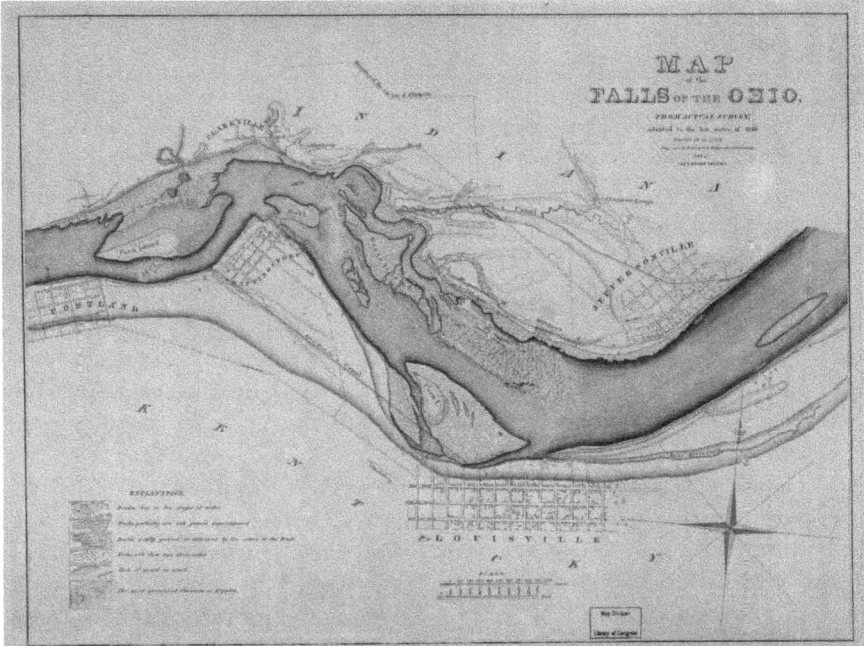

Figure 3.1. *Map of the Falls of the Ohio, from actual survey: adapted to the low water of 1819* by J. Flint, published by E.G. Gridley, Cincinnati, 1824. Library of Congress Geography and Map Division, call number G3954.L7 1824.F5.

Figure 3.2. The Town of Portland Shown in the Painting *New Albany from Silver Hills* by George W. Morrison, 1851. Courtesy of the Floyd County Library, New Albany, Indiana.

wharf area and destroyed the remnants of the once bustling economic heart of the town. Simultaneously, Louisville's suburban expansion had geographically engulfed the community and a new commercial district was created along the main road to Louisville some distance away from the wharf. By the historic flood of 1937, there was little left at the old Portland Wharf. In 1947, the remnants of the old Portland Wharf were cleared from the landscape, and a large flood levee was constructed, effectively cutting the rest of Portland off from the river and the wharf where it was founded. Adding insult to injury, Interstate 64 was constructed above the levee in the 1960s, further impeding access to the river. Since then, Portland has become one of Louisville's most economically depressed neighborhoods and fosters a negative reputation among most Louisvillians. This has helped perpetuate an identity that no longer connects to the community's prosperous history.

The landscape of the Portland Wharf today bears little resemblance to the thriving independent and prosperous river town of the 1840s. For the past fifty years, the Portland Wharf site has been a sixty-acre forest and meadow, with its historical buildings, streets, and wharf no longer evident and its illustrious past forgotten. Present-day residents do not see what used to be; they see a landscape on the other side of the levee and interstate that is much different than the Portland neighborhood today. It is a place to fish, walk, ride a bicycle, or hide nefarious activities in the dense woods. However, archaeological excavations at the site have begun to uncover the remains of the

Figure 3.3. The Portland Wharf Landscape in 2006. © M. Jay Stottman.

wharf's former landscape and Portland's birthplace. They have uncovered the remains of streets, buildings, the wharf, and artifacts from the thousands of people who used to live, work, and pass through the town (Stottman and Prybylski 2003). Archaeologists have been able to document the drastic changes that occurred in the Portland Wharf landscape throughout history and the loss of the material evidence of its independent identity (Stottman 2016).

Portland's Landscape and Identity

Even after Louisville annexed Portland for the final time, its people still maintained a strong independent identity as if Portland was still an independent town. It was generally accepted by residents of both Louisville and Portland that the community was an independent place with its own distinctive identity. This identity was reinforced by its distinctive landscape that communicated that Portland was a separate town, because at the time, it was still considered distant from Louisville and it had its own wharf and townscape (Tolbert 1999). With the drastic changes at its wharf after the nineteenth century, Portland lost much of its independent identity as the community no longer had a distinctive townscape with its own town center at the wharf. The loss of the townscape at the wharf and the subsequent creation of a neighborhood landscape in

Figure 3.4. The Portland Wharf Park Trail in 2006. © M. Jay Stottman.

the rest of Portland facilitated the forgetting of a more prosperous and independent past by current residents. These changes to the Portland Wharf landscape demonstrate the landscape's normalizing qualities, such as how the landscape can erase and replace identity. New landscapes can normalize new identities by erasing evidence of the old and providing the sense that the landscape has always been that way and that it is the way things ought to be (Schein 2003). In this case, the changes to the landscape shifted Portland's status from that of an independent town to that of a neighborhood.

In order to examine the articulation of past and present landscapes with people in the present, we must understand what the current residents of Portland know about their history and how they use it to create heritage. Archaeologists have to give as much attention to understanding present-day communities as we do those in the past (Smith 2006). As part of my dissertation research, I conducted interviews with current and former residents of Portland to further understand the community's identity and its relationship to history and the landscape (Stottman 2016). Based on this work, I found that Portland residents have a strong sense of place in what defines them as Portlanders and that they had not quite completely lost the independent attitude of their ancestors. However, they generally had a poor understanding of the facts of their community's nineteenth-century past and often conflated events and cherry-picked histories for deployment in the present. Usually, these fragments of history are used by current residents to propagate identities that are intended to fend off an influx of newcomers that threaten to change the neighborhood. I found that some of the identities deployed by residents have racial undertones, as the majority white Portland neighborhood residents fear encroachment from the surrounding majority black neighborhoods. Recently white residents have deployed an Irish immigrant identity in response to the City of Louisville's efforts to rename a street that passes thought Portland in honor of Martin Luther King, Jr., in order to differentiate themselves from their neighboring communities. Although Portland, like many other parts of Louisville, had a strong Irish immigrant community, it was a relatively minor part of its history, and Portland was not historically known as an Irish enclave. This is but one example of how current residents use the past to create identity through heritage to serve a present-day purpose. During my interviews, I found several instances of white identity deployed as heritage to distinguish Portland from its neighbors, despite the fact that historically Portland had been racially diverse (Stottman 2016). These heritage narratives hide the African American history in Portland, such as its role as a stop on the underground railroad, a historically important national network that enabled enslaved individuals to escape to the North. Portland was key in helping enslaved people escape across the Ohio River to New Albany, Indiana (Hudson 2002).

The fluidity of current identities in Portland suggests that the neighborhood's historical identities lacked a material anchor that then led to past identities being forgotten. For example, the attempts of current Portland residents to differentiate themselves from the rest of Louisville suggests that the spirit of their historical independent identity is still present, although it is latent and largely unconscious. Portlanders in general have little understanding that their independent spirit is rooted in the past when Portland was an independent town. Residents do not see evidence of that town, they see the current neighborhood landscape, which was imposed on them by Louisville to erase Portland's previous townscape.

Although the Portland Wharf landscape no longer reflects the independent identity of Portland's past townscape, many residents who know about its nineteenth-century history and the archaeological remains have, for the last thirty years, desired to create a park at the Portland Wharf dedicated to that history. They want to create a heritage landscape to anchor the memory of Portland's more prosperous, diverse, and independent days. Archaeology has an important role in this effort to reanimate the Portland Wharf landscape. As an activist, I am using archaeology to advocate for the community's desire to create this park, which will inevitably facilitate changes to identity and the many negative perceptions of the neighborhood that have become ingrained in the psyche of people in Louisville for generations. The people of Portland want to change perceptions about their neighborhood, and more than that, they want to change their economic fortunes through tourism and by portraying it as place for economic development (Prybylski and Stottman 2010). Archaeology is an important means for providing information to interpret the history of the Portland Wharf and for locating the physical remnants of Portland's former townscape. However, perhaps the practice of archaeology as performance is just as, if not more, important in that goal.

In this sense, we have to think of archaeology not just as a way to discover a forgotten landscape and provide information to interpret it but also as a part of the landscape itself. Through public archaeology, archaeology becomes a performance. It is an action that the public can see taking place and one in which they can even participate. We cannot think of the landscape just as promoting identity through its physicality; it is also what people do and experience in the landscape to create and maintain identity (Anschuetz, Wilshusen, and Scheick 2001; Ashmore and Knapp 1999; Low 2000; Tilley 1994). Archaeology as a performance can be seen in the same way. Thus, when a master plan and design was developed for the Portland Wharf Park, archaeology as a performance was featured prominently. The plan calls for ongoing public archaeological excavations at the site, thereby exposing the process of interpretation. The public, rather than just consuming the interpretive products we produce, can see and even participate in that process, which provides a sense of authenticity to those interpretations while giving the public some ownership of them.

Reanimating the Portland Wharf Landscape

The reanimation of a Portland Wharf landscape that communicates the history of a prosperous, diverse, and independent Portland could transform community identity and change the negative perceptions that outsiders have. Efforts have been made to reintroduce the former landscape of the Portland Wharf into its current landscape, such as placing history-themed markers on the park's trail and the re-establishment of the old street grid into the forested landscape through selective clearing. However, the full implementation of the park master plan would create a memorialized landscape of what Portland used to be and its independent identity. Aside from building a memorial to old Portland, archaeology was seen not only as a way to gather information to interpret this landscape, but also as a means to connect people to it. The archaeological remains buried at the Portland Wharf represent real tangible remnants of that past and the act of recovering those remains is powerful tool for the creation of identity and heritage.

In addition to placing archaeology in public view, a major part of the park's plan calls for the development of public participation programs, thus animating the landscape with the performance of archaeology. While the idea of archaeological performance shown in the plans that designers produce seems easy, those of us who are veterans of public archaeological practice know that it is no easy task. The planning, skill, and logistics needed to do large scale participatory public programs are daunting. To test the feasibility of doing such programs at Portland Wharf Park, we developed test programs during our research archaeology projects at the site. We wanted to know what the logistical challenges were for doing public programming at the site, what kinds of programs would be most effective, and, perhaps more importantly, I wanted to know if public archaeology could bring people to the site and whether they made any difference with regards to changing negative perceptions about the Portland neighborhood.

Figure 3.5. Public ArchaeologyTour at the PortlandWharf Site in 2005. © M. Jay Stottman.

Evaluating the Potential of Critical Public Archaeology at the Portland Wharf Park

Test programs were designed to assess the potential of various public archaeology strategies at the site including self-guided tours with signage, guided tours of the archaeological dig, and participatory excavation. But, like all good public archaeology programs, we also needed to understand our audience and how people used the park. Thus, a park usage survey was conducted to assess how many people visited the park and what they did there. Every day that archaeological excavations were being conducted at the site, the field crew recorded information on daily tally sheets about the people who visited. During the forty-four days that the archaeological project took place, a total of 1,542 people visited the park. Most of these people (66 percent) visited while cycling, walking, or running, which indicates that the park itself was not a destination, but that visitors were merely passing through using the trail (Prybylski and Stottman 2010:135).

The archaeological excavations also were a part of the park's landscape during that time, and some public archaeology strategies were instituted every day that the project took place. The self-guided tours and interpretive signage were always available to visitors, as were crew members designated to talk with and engage with passerby visitors. More formal public archaeology strategies such as participatory digs and guided tours were conducted primarily during advertised special events held at least once a week. The public archaeology programming conducted during the project drew nearly four hundred people to the park, representing 25 percent of the total park visitors. Many of these were people using the trail who saw the archaeological excavations and/or signage and stopped to participate in some of the public archaeology programming. Of the destination activities at the park, public archaeology drew the most participants. Other destination activities were minimally represented and included picnicking and fishing.

From the park usage survey, it can be concluded that public archaeology and what we learned about Portland's history has the potential to attract people to the park and help it become a destination. In order to assess the public archaeology strategies and better understand archaeology's and the park's role in the development of Portland's heritage, an exit survey was conducted with those that participated in public archaeology programming. The survey consisted of a series of questions that participants answered after their public archaeology experience. The surveys collected basic demographic information such as their zip code, age, and whether they were Portland residents, former residents, or non-residents. The survey asked some yes or no and rating questions regarding their knowledge and perception of the neighborhood prior to and after participating in the programs and about the potential for future programming. The survey ended with an open-ended question about their experience and comments.

Of the people that participated in the public archaeology program, most (60.8 percent) participated in the tour of the archaeological site while 31.7 percent participated in the dig program. A small percentage (7.5 percent) of people only participated in a self-guided tour that features interpretive signage. Based on the surveys, I found that most people preferred some type of interaction with the archaeologists rather than the static unguided tour of the site. Most (87.2 percent) of those that participated in the test programs were excited about the program and expressed eagerness to participate in future programs.

The exit surveys also indicate that the public archaeology programs had the ability to draw people into the neighborhood and/or expose a wide variety of people to the Portland area. Of the 134 people who completed exit surveys, most (79.2 percent) were neither residents nor former residents of Portland. They represented forty-six different zip codes and six states. Most (80 percent) of the people were from the Louisville area or Southern Indiana, representing twenty-one different neighborhoods or suburban cities. These results indicate that many of the participants (54.5 percent) were from the wealthier eastern Louisville or the eastern suburbs and were unlikely to visit Portland as a destination otherwise. The exit surveys demonstrated that a variety of people were experiencing the neighborhood and its history through the programs (Prybylski and Stottman 2010:136).

The majority (97.8 percent) of those that participated felt that the programs increased their knowledge of Portland's history and 82 percent indicated that the programs affected their perception of the neighborhood. None of the participants thought that the programs affected their perception of the neighborhood in a negative way, as nearly 80 percent thought it was positive. Of the people asked about their impression of Portland prior to participating in the program, 39.6 percent stated positive,

25 percent negative, and 35.4 percent were neutral. Participants, when elaborating on how their perception changed, indicated that they were not aware that Portland had a rich history or how important the community was. For example, one respondent said, "I was unaware of the wharf." Other comments included "I realized that this area was much more active and prosperous than I realized"; "I've worked in the area for over thirty years and had not learned much of the pre-I-64 history"; "Where the actual town was, I've biked through here and never knew"; and "As a native of Louisville, my perception of Portland was negative (crime and poverty), through this project I now see Portland as rich in history and presents a strong working-class community of families." The exit surveys indicate that the public archaeology programs had increased knowledge of Portland's history and positively affected participant's perception of Portland.

Although it is clear that the park's public archaeology programs affected the knowledge and perceptions of people from outside of the Portland neighborhood, the exit surveys also indicated that residents and former residents also gained more knowledge and/or their perceptions were affected. Most of these (88.5 percent) also reported that the programs affected their perception of the neighborhood. Comments from residents and former residents included "It is very educational and helps me learn about my heritage"; "Learned that where I played in the [19]60s was actually buildings at one time"; and "Portland was once a very important and useful community."

The exit surveys conducted during the public archaeology testing programs clearly demonstrate that active heritage programming at Portland Wharf Park could greatly affect perceptions of the Portland neighborhood, increase knowledge of its history, and increase experiences with that history for a variety of people who resided inside and outside of the neighborhood. As effective as the public archaeology programs were at connecting people to the Portland Wharf and its history, the surveys also exposed that the public archaeology as a performance on the landscape lack permanence. The archaeology programming was conducted for a limited period of time and has no permanent presence at the park. Thus, unless a permanent and regular public program is instituted, as indicated in the park master plan, public archaeology will have little lasting impact on Portland's identity and people's perceptions.

There were comments about the overall need for some physical elements of landscape, such as permanent interpretive signage, historic street signs, exposed foundations, reconstructions, or facsimiles of the historic landscape on display. Some comments included: "Make permanent exhibits of the excavations such as sections of the streets or interesting foundations"; "Maybe a memorial statue, fountain, or street signs for the original streets"; "I am looking forward to seeing historic buildings rebuilt or foundations laid out, would love to see a model of what the city looked like in the 1800s"; and "Permanent markers, maps, etc." The participants in the public archaeology programs recognized the impermanence of the activities and clearly thought that some permanence was needed on the landscape.

It also was clear from the surveys that more mundane aspects of the park's landscape, such as the lack of amenities and upkeep, detracted from the archaeology performances. Although people were excited to see something happening at the park, they realized that more is needed. There were many comments about the lack of amenities, the poor condition of the park, and limited access to the park. For example, a sample of the comments included: "It should be more accessible and more inviting"; "Landscaping is always nice!"; "[I]t should be treated as an actual park instead of a glorified pasture"; "Keep it mowed and landscaped so it looks like a park"; "Keep the grass mowed, set up grills, possibly a small shelter, and soccer goals"; "Perhaps a shelter and more permanent restrooms are in order"; and "Parking and restaurant to bring people down here and enjoy and learn about our great city and neighborhood."

Although people were happy to see activities taking place in the park, they did so with some trepidation. A resident remarked, "Being from Portland, I am glad to see that things are moving along," while another said, "There needs to be more funding to finish excavations, the dock on the river, and the total project." As part of the guided tours and the temporary signage that we installed at the park, we informed the participants about the master plan for the park and the need to fund the initiative. Although this information was not the focus of our presentations, it clearly resonated with the participants through their comments. Given the rather poor condition of the park, it was easy for even the non-residents to see the need for follow-through from the City of Louisville. There were many comments about funding the master plan, such as, "Provide project funding in order to continue to help community outreach and education"

Figure 3.6. Public Archaeology at the Portland Wharf Site in 2005. © M. Jay Stottman

and "We would love to see the master plan executed." Unfortunately, the impermanence of the public archaeology projects conducted could do more harm than good
for the residents of Portland. Without some real material changes to the landscape,
the archaeology project could be seen as just another temporary program that the city
occasionally does to make it look like something is happening at the park. Residents
could see the lack of follow-through as another example of the city abandoning and
neglecting them.

Although this small public archaeology test at the Portland Wharf Park demonstrates the potential power of archaeological performance in heritage landscapes, this
project also demonstrates that performance is not permanent. It is just a part of a much
larger effort to reanimate the Portland Wharf landscape through the creation of a heritage park. What happens when the performance is over? To fully achieve the activist
goals of archaeology at the Portland Wharf, the park needs to be built as planned and a
commitment made to ongoing public archaeology. Without it, the benefits of archaeology will become forgotten just like the history it sought to revive. Despite the promise
of elaborate park plans and the test programs, Portland Wharf Park is still a dream
and no closer to reality. As I and other activist archaeologists have discussed, activism is messy and consequential (Atalay et al. 2014; Derry and Malloy 2003; Stottman
2010b). We run the risk of favoring some stakeholders over others and inadvertently
disenfranchising those we seek to benefit. Activism is not easy and we cannot always
control or predict the consequences.

The Consequences of Critical Public Archaeology

The creation of Portland Wharf Park has the potential to have a lasting effect on the
interpretation of Portland's history and the installation of a heritage landscape that
can create, modify, and erase identity. The interpretation presented, the activities performed, the visuals and feel of the park will be cemented in this landscape. However,
the process of its creation and use becomes subject to the politics and power struggles
of the present. Who decides what the park looks like and what will be interpreted?
Was the process inclusive? Does it represent Portland? The creation of this landscape
will undoubtedly have an effect on how Portlanders learn about and understand their
history as well as helping to define Portland's identity. It may be a bit naïve to place so
much importance on the Portland Wharf Park landscape, but it does have the potential
to be very important in the creation and deployment of Portland's identity. Everyone involved in the creation of Portland Wharf Park has a responsibility to the consequences that could result. Thus, it would be disingenuous to pretend that this park
could be created without consequences because there will always be consequences,
good and bad. Those involved must think about the potential consequences and even
guide those consequences. It is easy for planners, city officials, neighborhood leaders,
and even archaeologists to create this park and let things happen without any recog-

nition of the landscape's power and ability to instigate change. The responsible thing to do is to recognize, anticipate, and control consequences. We must create a process that collaborates with a community and places responsibility for the consequences on everyone. Furthermore, such a process provides an opportunity to use the power of the park to help the community. As such, archaeologists within this process have the opportunity to be activists and advocate for the community.

I recognize that the landscape that we create and its reanimation through the performance of archaeology will have an effect on the community's perception of its history and heritage as well as foster the creation and modification of identity. This park will reinforce some existing identities and erase others. It will normalize the identities that are created while potentially neutralizing identities that the existing landscape has fostered over the last century. It is hoped that what is interpreted at the Portland Wharf Park will help create identities that will benefit the community, but I also recognize that it could just as well reinforce or foster others that will not.

Although the park landscape and interpretation will certainly affect the residents of Portland and the process of identity creation, they also could benefit the community by telling its story to those who visit from outside of the neighborhood and by encouraging outsiders to visit the neighborhood. It could also tell a more accurate and diverse story of Portland's history to provide an anchor in the landscape for that story, which will serve as the basis for identity creation and deployment.

To date, the Portland Wharf Park's fate has been a political football lacking funding and political will. Thus, my role as activist is not in the field doing archaeology, it is in politics advocating for the park. In such a context where theater is paramount, perhaps the performance of archaeology could have an effect. The performance of archaeology can generate interest in the project as it could have appeal for the public, perhaps including politicians. Regardless, my experiences at the Portland Wharf have demonstrated the power of performance and that, at the very least, archaeologists should consider that the power of archaeology is not always about what we learn, it is also about what we do.

Conclusions

My initial concept of activist archaeology in Portland was that archaeology was a way to get people to visit Portland. I felt that if people could just experience the community like I did, they would look beyond the stigmas and stereotypes, just as I did. I felt that many outsiders who had a negative perception of Portland had never actually been there or experienced it. I thought that archaeology could bring people to Portland and change perceptions, as has been done with some of our other public archaeology programs (Stahlgren and Stottman 2007). I thought that heritage tourism was an activist way that archaeology could be used to change or help Portland's fortunes (Prybylski and Stottman 2010). Critical public archaeology at the Portland Wharf certainly has the potential to do those things, as demonstrated in the exit surveys conducted during the public programming tests, but it can do much more.

Public archaeology program testing demonstrated that not only are the products of archaeological research important to the interpretation of the park but opening up the process of discovering the information produced through performance on the landscape also is important for facilitating and anchoring identity and heritage. The use of archaeology as performance in addition to the knowledge it produces within an activist agenda to me defines critical public archaeology. Admittedly, the information that archaeologists produce is a relatively weak tool for activist endeavors (McGuire 2008; Stottman 2010b). I argue that public archaeology and the public's participation in the process of archaeology can enable what we learn to have greater impacts on communities and our activist goals (Stottman 2010b).

Exit surveys from our test programs demonstrate that participation in the process of archaeology has the potential to draw people to Portland Wharf Park and experience Portland's culture and history. This experience begins the process that changes the way outsiders perceive the neighborhood and connects residents to the past from which they can create heritage and identities. It is a way to give them some ownership of the facts of history and have a role in an authorized discourse of their heritage (Smith 2006).

Because I was invited to the Portland community to help them use archaeology for their benefit, I have the role as an expert and subsequently an authorized discourse that is privileged above others. Thus, public archaeology, especially its performance, is important to our activist efforts in that it democratizes archaeology. There is much more to being an activist than just marching side by side with the community for their causes. We cannot know or even relate to the struggles and issues of that community because we do not experience their community like they do. In the end, however, we still control the archaeology and the discourse around it. In order to more collaboratively benefit or advocate for a community, archaeologists have to give up some of their control and open archaeology to the community. The performance of archaeology can do that, as it allows the public to participate in the process of archaeology and gives them ownership of the information we recover or, in other words, their history. My experience at the Portland Wharf and the activist perspective that I have taken is an example of that. There will be no end to the activism at the Portland Wharf, as it is the lifelong commitment that we make when we do this kind of work.

Although we have a plan to reanimate the Portland Wharf landscape through the materiality and performance of archaeology, it has yet to be realized. Delays can be detrimental to the neighborhood and reinforce the animosity between Portland, the city government, and its neighbors. The lack of action toward implementing the master plan legitimizes the current Portland Wharf landscape as a symbol of the City's inaction and neglect of the Portland Neighborhood. Despite all of the collaborative good intentions of the activist agenda to change Portland's identity and fortunes by reanimating the Portland Wharf as a heritage landscape, our intentions could easily turn to the opposite direction. Thus, the fate of the Portland Wharf Park project is dependent on political will and forces outside of the control of both the archaeologist and the community. Despite our collaborative approach and activist intentions, we can still be somewhat powerless to further our activist agenda. I do not know what is going to happen with the Portland Wharf Park project. I do not know if the planned heritage landscape will be created, if that landscape will change the community in the way we envisioned, or if it will benefit the community the way we intended. However, the process of identity and heritage creation will continue with or without the park. The community will continue to create, recreate, and deploy identities rooted in their past for purposes in the present. It is a matter of how those identities will be anchored in public memory, what purpose they serve, and what role archaeology plays. Our work thus far at the Portland Wharf has demonstrated that the performance of archaeology can be used to reanimate a landscape that serves as an anchor for the creation and maintenance of new identities rooted in the community's heritage. Thus, critical public archaeology will be an important element of that process whenever the new Portland Wharf Park is created.

Acknowledgments

I want to thank my colleagues at the Kentucky Archaeological Survey for their innovative work in public archaeology. I am especially indebted to the people of the Portland neighborhood and the Portland Museum for their tireless work for and insights into their community. I would also like to thank the organizers of the symposium on the value of performing archaeology at the 2016 Society for Historical Archaeology Conference for inspiring this chapter.

M. Jay Stottman is the assistant director of the Kentucky Archaeological Survey at Western Kentucky University. He directs public archaeology programming at Riverside, The Farnsley-Moremen Landing museum in Louisville, Kentucky. Stottman is the editor of the book *Archaeologists as Activists: Can Archaeologists Change the World?* (2010) and a co-author (with A. Gwynn Henderson, Linda S. Levstik, and Robin L. Jones) of the *Project Archaeology Investigating Shelter: Investigating a Shotgun House* curriculum (2016).

References

Anschuetz, Kurt F., Richard H. Wilshusen, and Cherie L. Scheick. 2001. "An Archaeology of Landscapes: Perspectives and Directions." *Journal of Archaeological Research* 9: 157–211.

Ashmore, Wendy, and A. Bernard Knapp, eds. 1999. *Archaeologies of Landscape: Contemporary Perspectives.* Malden, MA: Blackwell Publishing.

Atalay, Sonya, Lee Rains Clauss, Randall McGuire, and John R. Welch, eds. 2014. *Transforming Archaeology: Activists Practices and Prospects.* Walnut Creek, CA: Left Coast Press.

Barton, Christopher P. 2021. *Trowels in the Trenches: Archaeology as Social Activism*. Gainesville: University Press of Florida.

Battle-Baptiste, Whitney. 2011. *Black Feminist Archaeology*. Walnut Creek, CA: Left Coast Press.

Bender, Barbara. 2002. "Time and Landscape." *Current Anthropology* 43: S103–S112.

Blakey, Michael L. 1987. "Comments on 'Toward a Critical Archaeology.'" *Current Anthropology* 28(3): 292.

———. 1997. "Past Is Present: Comments on 'In the Realm of Politics: Prospects for Public Participation in African American Plantation Archaeology.'" *Historical Archaeology* 31(3): 140–45.

Colwell-Chanthaphonh, Chip, and T. J. Ferguson, eds. 2008. *Collaboration in Archaeological Practice: Engaging Descendant Communities*. Lanham, MD: AltaMira Press.

Delle, James A. 1998. *An Archaeology of Social Space: Analyzing Coffee Plantations in Jamaica's Blue Mountains*. New York: Plenum Press.

Derry, Linda, and Maureen Malloy, eds. 2003. *Archaeologists and Local Communities: Partners in Exploring the Past*. Washington, DC: Society for American Archaeology.

Flint, J. 1324. *Map of the Falls of the Ohio*. Cincinnati, OH: E.G. Gridley.

Franklin, Maria. 1997. "'Power to the People': Sociopolitics and the Archaeology of Black Americans." *Historical Archaeology* 31(3): 36–50.

Guttormsen, Torgrim, and Lotte Hedeager. 2015. "Introduction: Interactions of Archaeology and the Public." *World Archaeology* 47(2): 189–93.

Hudson, J. Blaine. 2002. *Fugitive Slaves and the Underground Railroad in the Kentucky Borderland*. Jefferson, NC: McFarland and Company, Inc.

Ingold, Tim. 1993. "A Temporality of the Landscape." *World Archaeology* 25(2): 152–74.

La Roche, Cheryl J., and Michael L. Blakey. 1997. "Seizing Intellectual Power: The Dialogue at the New York Burial Ground." *Historical Archaeology* 31(3): 84–106.

Leone, Mark P. 1984. "Interpreting Ideology in Historical Archaeology: Using the Rules of Perspective in the William Paca Garden in Annapolis." In *Ideology, Power, and Prehistory*, ed. D. Miller and Christopher Tilley, pp. 25–35. Cambridge: Cambridge University Press.

Leone, Mark P., Parker B. Potter, and Paul A. Shackel. 1987. "Toward a Critical Archaeology." *Current Anthropology* 28(3): 283–302.

Little, Barbara J., ed. 2002. *The Public Benefits of Archaeology*. Gainesville: University Press of Florida.

Little, Barbara J., and Paul A. Shackel, eds. 2007. *Archaeology as a Tool of Civic Engagement*. Lanham, MD: Altamira Press.

———. 2014. *Archaeology, Heritage, and Civic Engagement: Working toward the Public Good*. Walnut Creek, CA: Left Coast Press.

Little, Barbara J., and Larry Zimmerman. 2010. "In the Public Interest: Creating a More Activist, Civically Engaged Archaeology." In *Voices in American Archaeology*, ed. Wendy Ashmore, Dorothy T. Lippert, and Barbara J. Mills, 131–59. Washington, DC: Society for American Archaeology.

Low, Setha M. 2000. *On the Plaza: The Politics of Public Space and Culture*. Austin: University of Texas Press.

McGuire, Randall H. 2008. *Archaeology as Political Action*. Berkeley: University of California Press.

———. 2014. "Working Class Archaeology." In *Transforming Archaeology: Activist Practices and Prospects*, ed. Sonya Atalay, Lee Rains Clauss, Randall H. McGuire, and John R. Welch, 115–32. Walnut Creek, CA: Left Coast Press.

Merriman, Nick, ed. 2004. *Public Archaeology*. London: Routledge.

Messenger, Phyllis Mauch, and Susan J. Bender, eds. 2019. *History and Approaches to Heritage Studies*. Gainesville: University Press of Florida.

Miller, Henry. 1988. "Baroque Cities in the Wilderness: Archaeology and Urban Development in the Colonial Chesapeake." *Historical Archaeology* 22(2): 57–73.

Orange, Hilary, ed. 2014. *Reanimating Industrial Spaces: Conducting Memory Work in Post-Industrial Societies* London: Routledge.

Pinsky, Valerie, and Alison Wylie, eds. 1989. *Critical Traditions in Contemporary Archaeology: Essays in the Philosophy, History, and Socio-Politics of Archaeology*. Albuquerque: University of New Mexico Press.

Pool, Christopher A., and Lisa Cliggett. 2008. "Introduction." In *Economies and the Transformation of Landscapes*, ed. Christopher A. Pool and Lisa Cliggett, 1–15. Lanham, MD: Altamira Press.

Potter, Parker B., Jr. 1994. *Public Archaeology in Annapolis*. Washington, DC: Smithsonian Press.

Potter, Parker B., Jr., and Mark P. Leone. 1987. "Archaeology in Public in Annapolis: Four Seasons, Six Sites, Seven Tours, and 32,000 Visitors." *American Archaeology* 6(1): 51–61.

Prybylski, Matthew E., and M. Jay Stottman. 2010. "Reconnecting Community: Archaeology and Activism at the Portland Wharf." In *Archaeologists as Activists: Can Archaeologists Change the World?*, ed. M. Jay Stottman, 126–40. Tuscaloosa: University of Alabama Press.

Sabloff, Jeremy A. 2008. *Archaeology Matters: Action Archaeology in the Modern World*. Walnut Creek, CA: Left Coast Press.

Schein, Richard H. 2003. "Normative Dimensions of Landscape." In *Everyday America: Cultural Landscape Studies after J.B. Jackson*, ed. Chris Wilson and Paul Groth, 199–218. Berkeley: University of California Press.

Shackel, Paul A. 2001. "Introduction." In *Myth, Memory, and the Making of the American Landscape*, ed. Paul A. Shackel, 1–16. Gainesville: University Press of Florida.

———. 2003. "Archaeology, Memory, and Landscapes of Conflict." *Historical Archaeology* 37(3): 3–13.

———. 2004. "Working with Communities: Heritage Development and Applied Archaeology." In *Places in Mind: Public Archaeology as Applied Anthropology*, ed. Paul A. Shackel and Erve J. Chambers, 1–18. New York: Routledge.

Shanks, Michael, and Randall H. McGuire. 1996. "The Craft of Archaeology." *American Antiquity* 61(1): 75–88.

Silliman, Stephen W., and T.J. Ferguson. 2010. "Consultation and Collaboration with Descendant Communities." In *Voices in American Archaeology*, ed. Wendy Ashmore, Dorothy T. Lippert, and Barbara J. Mills, 48–72. Washington, DC: Society for American Archaeology.

Smith, Laurajane. 2006. *Uses of Heritage*. London: Routledge.

Stahlgren, Lori C., and M. Jay Stottman. 2007. "Voices from the Past: Changing the Culture of Historic House Museums with Archaeology." In *Archaeology as a Tool of Civic Engagement*, ed. Barbara J. Little and Paul A. Shackel, 131–50. Lanham, MD: Alta Mira Press.

Stottman, M. Jay, ed. 2010a. *Archaeologists as Activists: Can Archaeologists Change the World?* Tuscaloosa: University of Alabama Press.

———. 2010b. "Introduction: Archaeologists as Activists." In *Archaeologists as Activists: Can Archaeologists Change the World?*, ed. M. Jay Stottman, 1–18. Tuscaloosa: University of Alabama Press.

———. 2014. "From the Bottom Up: Transforming Communities with Public Archaeology." In *Transforming Archaeology: Activist Practices and Prospects,* ed. Sonya Atalay, Lee Rains Clauss, Randall H. McGuire, and John R. Welch, 179–96. Walnut Creek, CA: Left Coast Press.

———. 2016. "The Making and Remaking of Portland: The Archaeology of Identity and Landscape at the Portland Wharf, Louisville, Kentucky." Ph.D. dissertation. Lexington: University of Kentucky.

———. 2018. "Applied Archaeology (including Activist Archaeology)." In *Encyclopedia of Global Archaeology*, 2nd edn., ed. Claire Smith. Cham: Springer Press. https://doi.org/10.1007/978-3-319-51726-1_2984-1.

Stottman, M. Jay, and Matthew E. Prybylski. 2003. *An Archaeological Survey of the Portland Wharf Site (15Jf418), Louisville, Kentucky*. KAS Report #68. Lexington: Kentucky Archaeological Survey.

Tilly, Christopher. 1994. *A Phenomenology of Landscape*. Providence, RI: Berg Publishers.

Tolbert, Lisa C. 1999. *Constructing Townscapes: Space and Society in Antebellum Tennessee*. Chapel Hill: University of North Carolina Press.

Part II

Advancing Methods

CHAPTER 4

Toward a Critical Archaeological Museum

Monika Stobiecka

Introduction

"A museum needs to change if it wants to hold its—paradoxically—traditional social status" (Piotrowski 2011a: 153). Piotr Piotrowski, a Polish art historian and critic, gave pointed advice on the future of museums after the end of his directorship at the National Museum in Warsaw. A decade after he presented his practical experience of running a major museum in Poland and his profound theoretical insights immersed in the currents of the "New Museology" (Vergo 1989; Bennett 1995; Hooper-Greenhill 2002, 2005; Marstine 2006), museums are indeed in a state of transformation. The need for a global museum revolution was seen recently when the International Council of Museums (ICOM) introduced a proposition to redefine museums. According to ICOM:

> Museums are democratising, inclusive and polyphonic spaces for critical dialogue about the pasts and the futures. Acknowledging and addressing the conflicts and challenges of the present, they hold artefacts and specimens in trust for society, safeguard diverse memories for future generations and guarantee equal rights and equal access to heritage for all people. Museums are not for profit. They are participatory and transparent, and work in active partnership with and for diverse communities to collect, preserve, research, interpret, exhibit, and enhance understandings of the world, aiming to contribute to human dignity and social justice, global equality and planetary wellbeing. (Adams 2019)

This shift from collecting, conserving, and preserving past heritage for the sake of future generations to creating a democratic and inclusive space for future-oriented dialogue reflects a major change in museums' roles, their public duties, and current global challenges that museums want to address.

This switch in thinking about museums is particularly resonant in art institutions around the world. Major exhibitions dealing with global problems such as the Anthropocene and climate crisis, the migration crisis, decolonization, and growing nationalism have been organized in world-famous galleries and museums (Barry and Keane 2019) as well as in less prominent institutions.[1] Needless to say, the policy of many art museums is based on collecting contemporary artworks that in most cases touch upon pressing global problems. Given this, art museums are well-equipped to handle a visionary and thought-provoking narration that attracts and awakens visitors' interests and contributes to raising awareness of presented issues (Holmes 2007; Schlievert 2009).

In the case of archaeological museums, the challenges to addressing the present and future may be overwhelming or even barely possible to face. Indeed, when we imagine the archetype of an archaeological museum, we tend to think of a rather traditional institution presenting objects described with hermetic language and shown in rows of closed glass cases (Vergo 1989; Swain 2007). Criticized as the aesthetic illustrations of time (Olsen et al. 2012; Hamilakis 2013) and sanitized versions of archaeological practice (Lucas 2005: 127, 2012: 245), those types of exhibitions hardly trigger reflection on the meanings of the past or their relevance for the present. Even if the long-established image of an archaeological museum has changed and now includes different types of interactive engagement with objects and digital multimedia, the patterns of narration have still not radically transformed (Copplestone and Dunne 2017): the majority of the focus is put on sequences of artifacts and objects (the traditional model) or frames and technologies (the digital model), not the meanings and messages of both exhibits and artifacts (see Barker 2010).

The presented topics become irrelevant because of this visible "crisis of curation" (Nash and O'Malley 2012). This is especially alarming when thinking about current global problems and global struggles. Providing a meaningful, visionary and thought-provoking message is of crucial importance for our current times (Lafrenz Samuels 2018), which are increasingly marked by climatic decline, the Anthropocene, the migration crisis, the techno-regime, late capitalism and neocapitalism, and growing nationalistic tendencies all over the world. Can archaeology in museums be less about the remote and untouchable past and instead serve as an open forum for debating how the past can change the future? Can archaeological museums accept and handle the role of an inclusive, engaging, and attractive platform to share not only knowledge, but also the current tensions and problems that shape public debates? Furthermore, can they address ongoing archaeological discussions that deal with active public participation in (re)writing the past (Bollwerk, Connolly, and McDavid 2015)?

In this chapter, I seek to answer those questions by proposing a critical archaeological museum inspired by the concept of a "critical museum" as developed by the Polish art historian and critic Piotr Piotrowski (2010, 2011a). I am particularly interested in

Piotrowski's claim that a point of departure for a critical museum is its close relation to the paradigms and theories discussed in academic circles. Those paradigms and theories serve as active frames that influence the shape and leading message of the narration. As far as Piotrowski was concerned, only by (re)connecting museums and academies can museums actively engage in ongoing social discussions and debates. His concept, originally proposed in 2009, stands today as a forerunner to the new definition of museums as proposed by ICOM in 2019. From the idea of a critical museum, I will go further and elaborate on the concept and strategies for a critical archaeological museum. My call for a critical archaeological museum will be supported by an analysis of a piece of contemporary Polish art performed by Agnieszka Kalinowska. I will show that art inspired by archaeological objects and research is more effective in highlighting important global problems than archaeological museums, which often ignore the present and instead focus on petrifying the past. I suggest that addressing shared social dilemmas and problems by linking past and present is the best way to rethink the public image of archaeological museums and grasp them as future-oriented, (self)critical institutions that host inclusive and democratic dialogue.

From Traditional to Critical Museum

Piotr Piotrowski was a renowned Polish historian of art, art critic, and curator. One of his most famous yet controversial achievements was a practically oriented concept of a critical museum developed while Piotrowski was the director of the National Museum in Warsaw (2009–2010). His role as the director of this traditional institution was revolutionary. Piotrowski was the first to openly diagnose the anachronism of the National Museum in Warsaw and thus the need for a deep re-organization and conceptual renewal.

Until 2009, the National Museum in Warsaw had a very traditional profile. Founded in 1862 as the Museum of Fine Arts, the National Museum is one of the oldest art museums in Poland (Mazan 2011). Its collection consists of 830,000 works of art from Poland and abroad, dating from Antiquity, the Middle Ages, the Renaissance, the Baroque, and the nineteenth and twentieth centuries. The museum collection includes paintings, sculptures, drawings, prints, photographs, coins, and archaeological artifacts as well as utilitarian objects and design. The National Museum also holds Poland's most important foreign archaeological collection: frescoes and artifacts from the Faras Cathedral in Sudan, obtained by Poland during the UNESCO Nubian Rescue Mission after the construction of the Aswan High Dam in the 1960s.

Before Piotrowski's arrival at the museum, permanent galleries were arranged according to decades and schools typically defined within the fine arts. The organization of the permanent galleries was an effect of the long directorship of Stanisław Lorentz, who worked as the head of the National Museum for almost fifty years (1935–1982). Lorentz aimed to show the most precious objects in the Polish collection and to place them in a broader Western panorama of art. He followed the rules already established in the "Über-Museums," great art and archaeology collections like the British Museum, the Louvre, or the Vatican Museums (Swain 2007: 4). As in those museums, the displays in the National Museum were based on a culture-history exhibition model. Both artworks and artifacts were presented in a way that imposed an aesthetic valuation. This way of presenting exhibits refers to one of two types of exhibitions described by Peter Vergo in 1989 in edited volume *New Museology* (Vergo 1989). Even now, more than thirty years later, Vergo's elaboration of exhibitions dominating Western museums remains relevant.

Vergo distinguished between two types of exhibitions: aesthetic and contextual. Aesthetic exhibitions are characterized by isolated artifacts displayed in glass cases or cabinets, often without any information. The viewer gains knowledge about the object by experiencing a mental bond with it or by drawing from her or his own erudition and knowledge. The most important aspect in an encounter with an object of this kind is to judge its artistic quality. In putting together such exhibitions, additional materials such as texts, graphs, or diagrams are considered redundant and undesirable disturbances. This kind of relationship between visitor and exhibit corresponds with an aesthetic experience described and analyzed by Elisabeth Schellekens: "For when we appreciate things aesthetically, we do not look at the object for any practical function it may serve. Instead, we assess an object solely for its aesthetic character. This 'aesthetic attitude' is based on a kind of attention that is contemplative, discerning, and not directed at anything beyond the object" (2008: 21). The provenance of aesthetic displays is tied to nineteenth-century philosophy and the concept of a museum as a sanctuary and to the domination of visual perception in early museums and collections (Classen and Howes 2006). Ritualized by tradition, the aesthetic model of display (as understood by Vergo) remains a leading tendency in large museums and national galleries.

Lorentz wished to see the Warsaw Museum in a broader panorama of Western national galleries. Thus he applied the aesthetic model, which, in general, had not been changed until the arrival of Piotrowski.

A Critical Museum

Piotrowski recognized museum's anachronism and claimed that it needed a renewal adjusted to the contemporary realities. His idea of a critical museum was rooted in the currents of the New Museology (Vergo 1989; Hooper-Greenhill 2002, 2005; Belting 2003; Marstine 2006). Thus, he understood "critical" through the lenses of critical theory. By unraveling the hidden agendas and ideologies, he hoped to inaugurate an open forum in the National Museum. His approach was grounded in theoretical self-awareness and reflexivity that characterized also his academic scholarship (Piotrowski 2011b). Coming from the theoretically oriented University of Adam Mickiewicz in Poznań, Piotrowski was raised in the spirit of post-modernism, critical theory, Marxism, post-Marxism, and deconstruction. Bold and progressive, his vision could have the potential to foster a new approach in the traditional institution.

However, at that time neither the staff working at the museum nor the Polish audience were ready for Piotrowski's experiment. Already at odds with the employees of the museum, Piotrowski resigned after the Board of Trustees did not accept his strategic plan (Mazan 2011). However, he presented his idea for a critical museum in a book that also reported his activities as the director of the museum (Piotrowski 2011a, see Piotrowski 2010).

For Piotrowski, a critical museum was an institution open for contemporary intellectual discussions as well as a place for negotiating and mediating theories and important socio-political issues. Piotrowski, strongly inspired by Eilean Hooper-Greenhill (2002, 2005), suggested rejecting museum conservatism, observing that museums from the beginning of their history were engaged in epochal challenges, including social, political, cultural, and scientific struggles, while serving as mirrors that reflected those diverse discussions (Marstine 2006; Moser 2010). Piotrowski's vision of a critical museum serves as an instrument of democracy that encourages debates on new theories, raises awareness on shared global problems, reworks "negative memory" and trauma, is inclusive, and promotes diversity. Following Hans Belting, Piotrowski saw museums as an active political institution (Hooper-Greenhill 2005; Belting 2003).

Given that the National Museum in Warsaw is a provincial museum that cannot rival European museums in other capital cities, Piotrowski established three criteria for becoming a critical museum: (1) activeness of the institution in the public sphere, (2) institutional self-criticism, and (3) the switch within the "geography of interests." The long-standing tradition of Polish museology, as established by Lorentz, made Piotrowski's reform extremely difficult. The first challenge of attracting more people and creating a space for open dialogue was already revolutionary keeping in mind the museum's historical circumstances and its role as a national treasury of antiquities. Institutional self-criticism, obviously inspired by critical theory, and the switch in the "geography of interests" were intended to introduce a different geopolitical perspective to the museum. By the "geography of interests" Piotrowski understood Poland's gravitation toward the West and its ambition to be seen as the part of the "West." For a scholar, it was clearly visible that this kind of policy "provincializes" Poland. Piotrowski claimed that the geopolitical agenda of the museum should be different, less West-oriented and Polish heritage should be relocated through new interpretative lenses. Instead of fighting for the unreachable position of a Western country in arts and history,[2] Piotrowski acknowledged Poland's singularity as a part of Central Eastern Europe with its own national character and artistic spirit (Piotrowski 2011b). For some, Piotrowski's ambition to relocate Polish culture on the world map was heresy.

The three criteria that Piotrowski chose to execute his theoretical aims for a critical museum were too bold to be fully accepted by the museum's somewhat conservative staff. On an administrative level, Piotrowski intended to reduce job positions and introduce more contracts with outsourced specialists from universities and scientific institutions. Wanting to host a platform for sharing and exchanging experience and knowledge, Piotrowski drew plans to invite various collaborators from inside and outside Poland. Piotrowski dreamed of creating exhibitions that were the product of scientific expertise that would reflect contemporary discussions carried out in academia and thus help to distribute knowledge (Gaskell 2002) that had social and temporal relevance.

This mission of the museum was particularly visible during the exhibition *Ars homo erotica* (06 November 2010–09 May 2010). The display focused on the homoerotic ideal of art, bringing into the public debate the status of the homosexual community in Poland. As the critic Bogusław Deptuła emphasized: "This exhibition may shock especially the heteronormative people; for others, the homo-orientated may be disappointing; the curious ones may be left with no answers. Certainly, one display cannot change a lot, but it may fire up a discussion" (Deptuła 2010, my translation). According to Piotrowski, the museum had the potential to start a public debate of political and spatio-temporal importance. Plans and preparations for a future exhibition, "Democracies, democracies," further demonstrated the relevance of museum for contemporary society. The display was planned to take place when Poland was at the beginning of its presidency in the European Union (autumn 2011). The exhibition would be a presentation of different faces of democracy in Poland as well as outside the country, including illuminating the ongoing conflicts in the Middle East.

A critical museum thus had similar goals to critical theory. Exposing ideologies, promoting relevance, and encouraging self-reflection, it would have been an engaging institution where the main postulates of critical theory are presented to the broad audience.

Critical Archaeologies

Recent movements in the museum field have validated Piotrowski's claims concerning current museum and academic trends. His concept for a critical museum strongly correlates with a new definition of a museum proposed in 2019 by ICOM. Moreover, applying Piotrowski's ideas to the circumstances of archaeological museums offers an answer to recent calls for a new, critical approach in pulic archaeology (see Matsuda and Nakamura 2011).

The need for this kind of change in communicating archaeology was articulated in the 1980s, when Mark P. Leone, Parker B. Potter, Jr., and Paul A. Shackel applied the framework of critical theory in their research in Annapolis (1987, see Fracchia, this volume). Scholars emp hasized the potential of this theoretical body as a reflexive approach. Arguing that critical theory may help to achieve less contingent knowledge, they recapitulated how "the practice of archaeology is affected by political, economic, and social decisions" (Leone et al. 1987). Parker B. Potter continued this inquiry into a "critical archaeology" informed by the main objectives of critical theory later in the 1980s and early 1990s. His diagnosis "of [archaeologists'] complete scholarly detachment from issues deeply touching other people" (Potter 1994: 23) revealed a shortcoming. His study in Annapolis led to the conclusion that critical theory offers archaeology an opportunity for relevance (Potter 1994: 13). A similar perspective was offered by M. Jay Stottman who conceptualized the approach of activist archaeology. Like Potter, he underlined the importance of self-reflexivity: "through self-reflexivity, archaeologists began to understand the politics and agendas that often accompany their research" (Stottman 2010: 6). Instead of simplifying conclusions of studies for the public, archaeologists should be interested in producing relevant knowledge informed by self-awareness (Potter 1994).

Recently, interesting arguments casting new light on this debate were formulated by Kristian Kristiansen, who diagnoses a post-paradigmatic period in archaeology (Kristiansen 2014). Even though recent theoretical interests in archaeology form a vibrant body of different approaches (Domańska and Stobiecka 2020), according to Kristiansen, the main shaping factor of today's archaeology and its future challenges is not a theoretical proliferation, but rather archaeology's gravitation toward scientific methods.[3] Indeed, this global trend is reflected in increased interest in Big Data, the development of new quantitative modeling, and research on aDNA. These new scientific orientations demand new formats for public archaeology. As Kristiansen (2014: 25) writes, "new knowledge about the past has implications for how we present the past in museums and at public monuments." Complex studies based on natural scientific methods can cause archaeology to "simplify things in a dangerous, deterministic way" (Kristiansen 2014: 26). This "new" archaeology, according to Kristiansen, "demands a stronger public engagement by archaeologists, scientists and humanists, perhaps to a degree we are not used to. While archaeology has a long and glorious history of popularization, there is less experience of taking part in critical public debates, whether in newspapers, television or on the web" (Kristiansen 2014: 26). Kristiansen thus suggests that scholars should find new ways to critically engage with the past and the past's role in the present and future. The options for critical engagement are massive and "can take the form of national histories, European histories or gender histories, immigration histories etc. The sky is the limit" (Kristiansen 2014: 27).

Various political projects in archaeology, such as decolonization (Westmont, Introduction, this volume; Rizvi 2019; Matsuda and Nakamura 2011) also demand new channels "to provide openings for possible other forms of knowing and being" to be co-produced with the public (Rizvi 2019: 158). Archaeology needs a new, critical tool that opens up a debate on local, global, and glocal (global/local) problems that touch humanity from its beginnings. However, I argue that a critical museum project as proposed by Piotrowski is not adequate enough for the realities of archaeological museums. What is needed to encourage inclusive debates and fruitful dialogue within museums is not only a vibrant theoretical scholarship as encountered in contemporary archaeology, but also imagination.

A Critical Archaeological Museum

With respect to the previous discussion, I identify three requirements for a critical archaeological museum. First and foremost, with reference to the original concept of a critical museum as presented by Piotrowski, a critical archaeological institution can only function as such if a strong bond exists between universities and museums. Second, to answer Kristiansen's diagnosis, I believe that a critical archaeological museum should turn to big pictures and grand narratives that focus on global problems. Adopting this practice would re-orient archaeology toward the future by enabling museums to discuss the importance of past processes to present and future societies on different levels (global, local, glocal). Third, I posit that a critical archaeological museum must actively engage museum visitors in museum narratives in order to access an archaeological imagination that encourages visitors to create a subjective and personal vision of the past and to reflect on the past's different meanings and roles.

Visionary frameworks that echo current global challenges are especially missing today as museums turn to new media, not new messages (McLuhan 2003). Given that the digital turn brought to archaeological museums often ends in superficial engagement with multimedia (Kidd 2014) or in technological showcases (Kidd 2014; Copplestone and Dunne 2017; Stobiecka 2019), archaeological museums shall be especially interested in revising the narrations offered to the broader audience. The turn from "how" archaeology is presented and what kind of means are deployed to show it should be secondary to the question of "what" is actually displayed (Harrison 2019).

Thus, to effectively adapt Piotrowski's concept of a critical museum to the realities that archaeology as a discipline is currently facing, I acknowledged following main requirements for this future-oriented institution.

The first premise is derived from the belief that, in the age of a common mistrust in scientific expertise, archaeology needs to validate its social usefulness. Archaeological museums should not be institutions that reuse and recycle ideas established in the nineteenth century (Pearce 1990, 2006; Swain 2007; Moser 2010). Instead, archaeological museums should illustrate new theories and approaches that are the current subjects of intensive debates in academic circles (Gosden, Edwards, and Phillips 2006; Dudley 2010, 2012). As many museum scholars have emphasized, art museums in particular have always responded to the academies by mirroring the succession of new theories and paradigms (Hooper-Greenhill 2002; Pearce 1990, 2006; Marstine 2006; Moser 2010; Dudley 2010, 2012). This should be as well a task of archaeological institutions.

Archaeology in Europe is mostly financed by taxes from national and regional authorities (Kristiansen 2014; see Potter 1994: 13), so it needs to validate its social usefulness. Archaeologists should be especially aware of and responsible for the ways in which their discipline is presented to the wide public.

Moreover, as many archeological orientations relate to various forms of social injustice (e.g., decolonization, feminist and gender archaeologies, radical archaeologies, symmetrical archaeology), museums should host those debates with the active participation of their visitors (i.e., Massheder-Rigby, this volume). Archaeologists owe society an up-to-date image of archaeology that is no longer based on the traditional ways of presenting the past as is seen in many conservative archaeological or universal museums including the Louvre, the British Museum, and the Vatican Museums (Swain 2007). Changes should not be limited to the discipline itself, but they should affect also museums and presented narratives (Westmont, Introduction, this volume). Scientific relevance should be the priority (Potter 1994), especially when archaeologists are actively engaged in ongoing discussions on global (Solli et al. 2011; Rizvi 2019) and local problems (Stottman 2010).

The second requirement relates to the way we practice archaeology today. With the domination of neocapitalist forms of scientific work that promote short papers, we deprive the public of big pictures and grand narratives (Kintigh et al. 2014). Museums should not limit themselves to illustrating specialized research on displays; rather, they should attempt to draw big pictures by addressing topics that deal with human and non-human concerns, the realities of shared environments, and planetary problems that could be addressed in the past as well as in the present and future. Grand narratives have the potential to link the past, present and future, the local and the global, and the particular, the universal, and even the planetary. By answering big questions, archaeological museums validate their social, public, and political importance.

To successfully engage the public and present big pictures alongside the most valid theories, museums need to deploy an archaeological imagination, setting the third requirement for a critical archaeological museum. The role and meaning of imagination in archaeology was studied in detail by Michael Shanks, who stated that archaeological imagination allows one "to recreate the world behind the ruin in the land, to reanimate the people behind the sherd of antique pottery, a fragment of the past" (2012: 25). Shanks signifies that imagination fulfills "a creative impulse and faculty at the heart of archaeology, but also embedded in many cultural dispositions, discourses and institutions commonly associated with modernity. The archaeological imagination is rooted in a sensibility, a pervasive set of attitudes towards traces and remains, towards memory, time and temporality, the fabric of history" (Shanks 2012: 25).

Archaeological imagination in this context may answer the calls vocalized by Kristiansen as well as address challenges in the broader field of heritage studies (Harrison 2019). I understand the potential of archaeological imagination as a way of relating to archaeology's tradition (romantic and detective work on the meanings of the past), as a chance to creatively refer the past to the present, and as a possibility for nurturing our sensibility toward the past. Given this understanding, I argue that deploying archaeological imagination may give museums an opportunity to address more universal problems touching the contemporary public image of archaeology as embodied, in the discussed case, in museums.

An archaeological imagination as a creative impulse that stimulates our interests in ruins, past, and pastness and that encourages us to reinvent the lives of humans and non-humans in distant times should be the main impulse driving the museum narration. How can a museum pursue visitors' archaeological imaginations? I suggest that the power to (re)imagine archaeology may lay in collaborations with contemporary artists whose sensibility toward the past has recently been brought into conversation with the field of archaeology.

Art and Archaeology

A vibrant community of scholars have investigated the diverse connections between art and archaeology (Renfrew 1999, 2003, 2004; Jameson 2003; Vilches 2007, 2011; Harrison and Schofield 2010; Harrison 2011, 2013; Jones and Bonaventura 2011; Shanks 2012; Russell and Cochrane 2014; Chittock and Valdez-Tullett 2016; Sjöstrand 2017; Bailey 2017a, 2017b, 2018). Andrew Jones and Paul Bonaventura (2011: 6) indicate that both art and archaeology are "interested in the synoptic vision of the past and how it can function today." In a similar way, Ylva Sjöstrand is convinced that reading archaeological objects through art may have the potential to redefine the practice of studying the past. Colin Renfrew, who has promoted exploring contemporary art since the 1980s, writes that "our interest as archaeologists is to see how the work of contemporary artists in all its rich variety can aid in our own attempts to tackle the interpretative problems and to undertake the initiatives involved in gleaning information and understanding from the material cultures of past ages" (Renfrew 2004: 4). Similarly to Renfrew, Rodney Harrison and John Schofield propose three strategies to investigate the tensions between art and archaeology (2010; see Harrison 2011, 2013). Harrison and Schofield underline that contemporary art may be helpful for archaeologists in understanding the past, studying the relationship between humans and the environment, and proposing alternative analyses of material culture. According to their view, contemporary art offers a deeper insight into the past and, thanks to its imaginative potential, opens up new perspectives for examining sites and artifacts.

Harrison and Schofield identify three main trajectories in art and archaeology research: art as an archaeological record (where art is being read through the lens of archaeological methods and methodologies), archaeological investigation as a performance (where archaeological explorations are being studied from the perspective of archaeology-as-art), and art as an interpretation, narrative, and characterization (where archaeologists should use the perspective of art-as-archaeology).

This intersection of art and archaeology is also seen in the work of Doug Bailey (2017a, 2017b, 2018). He conceptualized a proposal of *art/archaeology*. Instead of theorizing on art and archaeology, he is focused on creating a rupture between archaeology and art. He openly declares that his investigations are influenced by the works of Gordon Matta-Clark, Lucio Fontana, and Ai Weiwei. Bailey's projects involve active interventions on artifacts and sites (like comparing archaeological digs to Lucio Fontana's *buchi* and *tagli*). He defines his projects as a form of negotiation between art and archaeology, creating works beyond explanation and interpretation. While Bailey uses the traditional methodological toolboxes of archaeology and art, his work questions and complicates previous practices. I would treat his projects as artistic interventions that set an important horizon for archaeological creativity.

I believe that this theoretical fusion could be operationalized in archaeological museums, providing them with an important toolbox for using creativity and archaeological imagination. This postulate is also vocalized by Elisabeth S. Greene and Justin Leidwanger in their discussion on Damien Hirst's *Treasures from the Wreck of the Unbelievable* (Greene and Leidwanger 2017; see Hirst, Geuna, and Corry 2017). In 2017, Hirst invented a fantastic story of Amotan, a wealthy Roman whose great collection of treasures sunk in the Indian Ocean. Fake treasures were recreated by the eccentric artist in collaboration with underwater archaeologists (Greene and Leidwanger 2017). Displayed in the Punta della Dogana and Palazzo Grassi in Venice at the same time as the Venice Biennale 2017, the exhibit displayed objects that were partly destroyed and covered with sea plants. The objects compelled audiences and invited them into a realm that blends two pop-cultural movies: *Indiana Jones* and *Titanic* (Greene and Leidwanger 2017: 1). Criticized by Greene and Leidwanger as imperial and based on exploitative approaches to heritage, the exhibition started a discussion on the lack of compelling stories within archaeology. Even though Greene and Leidwanger were critical about the artwork, they emphasized that "Professional archaeology could productively take note of the excitement generated not only by the site and its golden splendor but also by Hirst's juxtaposition of mysterious places and objects into an engaging and accessible story. This approach offers an opportunity for the public to interact with the past, a past that itself intersects with many pasts, both fantastic and real" (Greene and Leidwanger 2017: 7).

In this sense, art appears to be a Derridean *parergon*, a point of access to the reality of the past. Artists may help us see more in the archaeological remains by creating enchanting narrations that invite us to project our own visions of the past. Archaeological museums offer a perfect location for interventions that bring art into archaeological discourse. More and more, archaeological institutions such as the Museo dell'Ara Pacis in Rome or the Sir John Soane's Museum in London are welcoming artists at their exhibitions. The Museo dell'Ara Pacis enriched its archaeological display by introducing a contemporary artwork by Mimmo Paladino, the mosaic *Ara Pacis*, while the Sir John Soane's Museum in London regularly organizes temporary exhibitions of contemporary art.[4] Those interventions open up new perspectives, on how to understand the past, how to engage with it, how to imagine it.

I argue that art, even if it is addressed to general public with an interest in it, has the potential to affectively engage. One may like an artwork or reject it, may be puzzled or intrigued, nevertheless, there is always an affective reaction, as the one described by Greene and Leidwanger. Art does not leave people indifferent, and that is why I firmly believe in the potential of artistic interventions in the archaeological museum's spaces. Art can ignite emotions, reactions, reflections, and this capability should not be overlooked, especially with respect to the recent scholarly interest in art shared by many archaeologists.

Toward Critical Engagement:
Heavy Water by Agnieszka Kalinowska

Art's potential for reviving and improving narratives by invigorating archaeological imagination can reach further than offering only compelling stories. Colin Renfrew, Chris Gosden, and Elizabeth DeMarrais (2004: 1) suggest that "the practices of the contemporary artist, involving fresh approaches to the uses of materials and to the notion of display, may be instructive to the archaeologists." Projects at the border of art and archaeology allow one to ask questions about how the past materializes in archaeological objects, whether its image correlates with artistic representations, and what kind of vision of past history do contemporary artifacts and works of art offer us. I am convinced that contemporary art inspired by archaeological objects and research can even be effective in addressing important global problems. Agnieszka Kalinow-ska's project entitled *Heavy Water* (2017–2018) provides an example of how this may be done.[5]

Heavy Water consists of dozens of clay vessels decorated with the "migrant sign" (a symbol from the warning signs installed at the border between the United States and Mexico, 1987–1990). The jugs are replicas of water vessels found archaeologically in Ethiopia, Afghanistan, Persia, Iraq, and Syria. Kalinowska's idea for the exhibit was based on archaeological research that has reconstructed ancient migration routes by tracing fragments of clay vessels.[6] While referring to archeological studies, she wanted to show the current migration crisis as a repeated phenomenon characteristic of human history. It is not by coincidence that she chose water jugs from Ethiopia, Afghanistan, Persia, Iraq, and Syria: when she started her project, those were the countries with the highest migration rates to the European Union. The form of vessels was also intention-ally chosen, as the artist explained:

> Thanks to archaeology, we know that water vessels allow [us] to study the directions of migrations. People leave fragments, and those tell us about their life and the place where they came from . . . Water is charged with a physical and symbolical meaning. A vessel full of water becomes a physical burden, at the same time we need water to live. We may fight for it, risk, or even kill. Everyone wants to be close to the source of water. We do not have any choice—without water, no one can survive. Water equals humanity and dignity.[7]

Kalinowska wished to provoke a public debate on attitudes toward immigrants. She wanted to draw attention to the extremely hard living conditions immigrants expe-rience, including long journeys, hostility, and hatred migrants encounter when they leave their countries. *Heavy Water* was not Kalinowska's first project to discuss the mi-gration crisis. Since 2008, she has worked on a series of reconstructed fences from the refugee camps as well as on plant braids done using the same technique that is used in refugee camps and secure facilities.

Heavy Water was presented for the first time in 2017 in Lublin, Poland, during the urban art festival Open City. Dozens of vessels were hung from a tree. According to the artist's intention, the vessels were left there to be taken by passersby. During an interview that I conducted with the artist in October 2019, Agnieszka Kalinowska told me that her idea was to dispense the vessels and house them at Polish homes. In designing this performance, Kalinowska was referencing Polish attitudes toward Syrian immigrants, which was being widely discussed in the international media at that time (Leszczyński 2015). The Polish government refused to take in refugees from Syria while many other European countries accepted immigrants and actively engaged in resolving the migration crisis (Wintour 2017). Poland's decision not to accept migrants was warmly welcomed, especially in southeastern Poland, an area that is recognized for its conservatism, nationalism, and isolationism.[8] Given these circumstances, Kalinowska's decision to place the vessels in Lublin, a city in eastern Poland, stood as an important political statement. The artist believed that when the vessels were hung from a tree, people would be encouraged to take them home. In this sense, she wanted to make a symbolical gesture about welcoming the artifacts that represented refugees. It laid bare the ironic values of the vessels' new owners, especially with regard to their isolationism and nationalism.

The following year, *Heavy Water* was presented in the BWA Gallery in Warsaw alongside other artistic projects that discuss borders, the migration crisis, and the situation of refugees. Kalinowska was actively engaged in launching the debate on political and social exclusion, human rights, and basic needs. This time, the vessels were presented in a separate room, huddled together in one corner. This way of displaying objects evoked the feeling of fear and isolation experienced by immigrants.

During my talk with Agnieszka, she confessed that she wished to present the vessels with archaeological originals in an archaeological museum in order to strengthen the message conveyed by her artwork. This, unfortunately, has not happened. If the exhibit is brought into conversation with archaeological artifacts, Kalinowska's intervention has the potential to create a rupture and bring a direct political statement to an archaeological museum. This rupture could inaugurate a critical archaeological museum. Her replicas standing next to the original jars and amphoras would convey a strong message, opening the past to the discussions on the present and future. Indeed, Kalinowska stated that she wanted to bring together past and present, and by doing so, raise awareness and encourage reflection. Archaeological vessels are largely presented in typological rows, enclosed in glass cases, and are very often denuded of a deeper meaning (Ting 2010). Artistic intervention introduced by Kalinowska's replicas could convey an even more profound message by placing them next to the archaeological originals.

Kalinowska's artwork is, however, not an isolated case. In 2019, Chinese artist and activist Ai Weiwei presented a series of porcelain plates decorated with scenes he had documented in a refugee camp. Ai Weiwei's project, *Odyssey*, openly referred to the ancient Greek mythological travel epic, sets yet another artistic intervention that uses archaeological imagination to convey deeply relevant and important social and political messages. Unfortunately, this project did not attract scholars as did the work by Hirst. Nevertheless, this oversight shows that the connection between archaeology, art, and social injustice are yet unexplored. The artwork by Ai Weiwei is another example, that could be discussed in a context of its further potential in archaeological museums.

Discussion

The critical museum is a response to the recent calls for a revision of museums' public roles. Given that museums should be democratizing, inclusive, and polyphonic spaces that host critical dialogue about the past and the future, museums are in need of a change as vocalized by Piotrowski in 2010. In the opening quotation of this chapter, Piotrowski states that change will be the only way for museums to hold their traditional social status. I argue here that this unspecified tradition relates not to a museum's role as a treasury that collects and protects heritage nor to its function as a sanctuary. "Tradition" here reveals the deep history of museums and their connection to the Greek provenance, when a museum (*museion*) stood as a space for academic dialogue. Museums should prioritize dialogues that provide relevant insight into scholarly inquiries today. There is, however, danger behind the idea of (re)connecting museums and academies[9] within the framework of a critical archaeological museum. The risk lays in the way knowledge, theories, and new perspectives are presented. Museums can easily take an imperial or patriarchal attitude if they do not acknowledge the role and impact of visitors in producing new perspectives and views. To avoid this kind of "power-knowledge" position, museums should be especially aware of visitors' interests within the field of archaeology.

My observations of Polish archaeology enthusiast groups on Facebook demonstrated how divergent the interests of the public are from the narrations of archaeological museums. When Polish archaeological institutions present very traditional views on the past framed in the culture-history paradigm, the wider public instead discusses press releases on human and non-human relations, health and sickness in the past, past diets, the shape of the environment, or social relationships; in other words, the public is interested in subjects that relate to contemporary life and universal questions. Thus, I firmly believe that museums should be especially concerned with how to connect visitors' interests with current theories on those matters. This approach is a means of creating a space for dialogue where visitors are understood not as passersby, but as active users who participate in the decision-making process on the presented narratives. Nowadays, museums are equipped with a variety of tools that can help them assess the actual interests of the public in archaeology. Paradoxically, search engines, Google Trends, and observations on Facebook, Instagram, YouTube, and Twitter may be more efficient ways to collect data on the profile of a museum's users than face-to-face surveys.

Nevertheless, the question of access to the past through artifacts remains. As I have argued throughout this chapter, the (re)connection of museums to academies and a

response to universal questions is impossible to achieve without a bridge. I have suggested that art can serve as this special bridge to enter the past, to evoke associations
and discover connections, and to ground one's personal vision of the distant epochs;
at the same time, when chosen wisely, art can assist in helping visitors see a different
world in archaeological remains. Artworks that are derived from the archaeological
imagination allow us to debate universally important problems such as the migration
crisis, as exemplified here by Kalinowska's work, as well as other issues such as neocapitalism, growing nationalism, the Anthropocene, and ecological disasters. With the
artists' help, archaeological museum curators can build a platform to bridge past and
present and to critically discuss what can we learn from bygone times.

Conclusion

Throughout this chapter I presented an idea of a future-oriented archaeological museum that prioritizes critical dialogue. The three requirements for a critical archaeological museum that I recognized include: strengthening the bonds between universities
(sites of new knowledge production) and museums (sites of presenting and engaging
new knowledge); addressing big pictures and grand narratives focused on universal
problems; and utilizing archaeological imagination. The biggest challenge in executing
this vision is to actively engage the audience by triggering their archaeological imagination. I proposed that a possible impulse may be given by contemporary art that refers
to archaeology. I recapitulated how art can be a point of access to the reality of the past
and illustrated this claim with the example of *Heavy Water* by Agnieszka Kalinowska.
While discussing this artwork, I suggested that art can also offer archaeological museums relevance, being a major point of departure for critical archaeology.

The intentional entanglement of imagination and reality (of the academic discourse
and/or shared values) should be the way forward for a future-oriented critical archaeological museum. Compiling new theories with big picture and timeless questions,
and archaeological imagination offers a way to reaffirm the status of archaeology as the
discipline of universally important problems. Archaeology is not about the past, and
museums should not be either. Archaeology is the study of the past to understand the
present and future. Mirroring this idea should be the main task of critical archaeological museums to come.

Acknowledgments

Here I would like to thank Camille Westmont for important comments on this chapter and language correction, Agnieszka Kalinowska for sharing with me her work and
thoughts, Ewa Domańska and Maria Poprzęcka for recommending Hirst's artwork to
me, and finally the participants of session 174, "Archaeological Heritage and Museum

Management: Future Chances, Future Risks" at the 2019 European Association of Archaeologists Conference, Bern, Switzerland, where I presented the idea of a critical archaeological museum for the first time. I would like to thank Sara Perry and Cornelius Holtorf for providing thought-provoking feedback during the conference.

Monika Stobiecka, PhD is an art historian and archaeologist, and an assistant professor at the Faculty of Liberal Arts, University of Warsaw. A fellow of the Lanckoroński from Brzeź Foundation (2016), the Kościuszko Foundation (2018), the Foundation for Polish Science (2019). She collaborated with several Polish museums, i.e. the Museum of Modern Art and the National Gallery Zachęta in Warsaw and the Museum of Architecture in Wrocław. She is interested in critical museum and heritage studies, archaeological theory and methodology.

Notes

1. Here I refer to the current popularity of the Anthropocene and ecological discussions as presented in many art exhibitions in Poland, to mention few of them: *Human-Free Earth* at the U-jazdowski Castle Center for Contemporary Art in Warsaw (see https://u-jazdowski.pl/en/programme/exhibitions/bezludzka-ziemia) or the *Penumbral Age: Art in the Time of Planetary Change* at the Museum of Modern Art in Warsaw (https://artmuseum.pl/en/wystawy/wiek-polcienia).
2. Poland, a former USSR satellite country, is located in Central Eastern Europe, a region that differs from Western Europe in terms of economy, culture, and politics.
3. This issue was intensively discussed during the 2019 European Archaeologists Association Conference in Bern, Switzerland. Concerns on how aDNA would shape future narratives in archaeological museums were brought to light during the session *Populism, Identity Politics and the Archaeology of Europe*.
4. See, for example, Sir John Soane's Museum London. 2017. "Marc Quinn: Drawn from Life." *Sir John Soane's Museum London*. Retrieved 5 March 2022 from https://www.soane.org/whats-on/exhibitions/marc-quinn-drawn-life.
5. *Agnieszka Kalinowska — Ciężka woda* [Heavy Water], 3 October 2017, https://2017.opencity.pl/artysci/agnieszka-kalinowska/index.html.
6. While interviewing the artist, I asked for particular books she referred to. She did not provide me with exact titles.
7. *Agnieszka Kalinowska. Ciężka woda* [Heavy Water], 27 January 2018. Retrieved 1 July 2020 from https://news.niezlasztuka.net/event/agnieszka-kalinowska-ciezka-woda/, (my translation).
8. Recently targeted also at the Polish LGBTQ+ community.
9. Here, I am referring mostly to European museums. Contrary to American museums that are not housed at universities.

References

Adams, Geraldine Kendall. 2019. "ICOM Unveils New Museum Definition." 31 July. Retrieved 20 February 2020 from https://www.museumsassociation.org/museums-journal/news/3107 2019-icom-reveals-updated-museum-definition.

Bailey, Doug. 2017a. "Art/Archaeology: What Value Artistic-Archaeological Collaboration?" *Journal of Contemporary Archaeology* 4(2): 246–56.

———. 2017b. "Disarticulate—Repurpose—Disrupt: Art/Archaeology." *Cambridge Archaeological Journal* 27(4): 691–701.

———. 2018. *Breaking the Surface: An Art/Archaeology of Prehistoric Architecture*. Oxford: Oxford University Press.

Barker, Alex W. 2010. "Exhibiting Archaeology: Archaeology and Museums." *Annual Review of Anthropology* 39: 293–308.

Barry, Kaya, and Jodi Keane. 2019. *Creative Measures of the Anthropocene. Art, Mobility, and Participatory Geographies*. Singapore: Springer and Palgrave Macmillan.

Belting, Hans. 2003. *Art History after Modernism*, trans. Caroline Saltzwedel, Mitch Cohen, Kenneth Northcott. Chicago: The University of Chicago Press.

Bennett, Tony. 1995. *The Birth of the Museum: History, Theory, Politics*. London: Routledge

Bollwerk, Elisabeth, Robert Connolly, and Carol McDavid. 2015. "Co-Creation and Public Archaeology." *Advances in Archaeological Practice* 3(3): 178–87.

Chittock, Helen, and Joana Valdez-Tullett. 2016. "Archaeology with Art: A Short Introduction to This Book." In *Archaeology with Art*, ed. Hellen Chittock and Joana Valdez-Tullett, V–VIII. Oxford: Archaeopress.

Classen, Constance, and David Howes. 2006. "The Museum as Sensescape: Western Sensibilities and Indigenous Artifacts." In *Sensible Objects: Colonialism, Museums and Material Culture*, ed. Elisabeth Edwards, Chris Gosden, and Ruth B. Phillips, 199–222. Oxford: Berg.

Copplestone, Tara, and Daniel Dunne. 2017. "Digital Media, Creativity, Narrative Structure and Heritage." *Internet Archaeology* 44. https://doi.org/10.11141/ia.44.2.

Deptuła, Bogusław. 2010. "Catching Up." *BiWeekly.pl*, Issue 6, July. Retrieved 20 February 2020 from https://www.biweekly.pl/article/1335-catching-up.html.

Domańska, Ewa, and Monika Stobiecka. 2020. "Archaeological Theory: Paradigm Shift." In *Encyclopedia of Global Archaeology*, ed. Claire Smith, 1–7. Cham: Springer Nature Switzerland AG. https://doi.org/10.1007/978-3-319-51726-1_1557-2.

Dudley, Sandra H. 2010. "Museum Materialities: Objects, Sense and Feeling." In *Museum Materialities: Objects, Engagements, Interpretations*, ed. Sandra H. Dudley, 1–18. London: Routledge.

———, ed. 2012. *Museum Objects: Experiencing the Properties of Things*. London: Routledge.

Gaskell Ivan. 2002. "Magnanimity and Paranoia in the Big Bad Art World." In *Two Art Histories*, ed. Charles Haxthausen, 14–24. Williamstown, MA: Clark Art Institute and Yale University Press.

Gosden, Chris, Elisabeth Edwards, and Ruth B. Phillips, eds. 2006. *Sensible Objects: Colonialism, Museums and Material Culture*. Oxford: Berg.

Greene, Elisabeth S., and Justin Leidwanger. 2017. "Damien Hirst's Tale of Shipwreck and Salvaged Treasure." *American Journal of Archaeology* 122(1): 2–11.

Hamilakis, Yannis. 2013. *Archaeology and the Senses: Human Experience, Memory, and Affect*. New York: Cambridge University Press.

Harrison, Rodney. 2011. "Surface Assemblages: Towards an Archaeology in and of the Present." *Archaeological Dialogues* 18(2): 141–61.

———. 2013. "Scratching the Surface: Reassembling an Archaeology in and of the Present." In *Reclaiming Archaeology beyond the Tropes of Modernity*, ed. Alfredo González-Ruibal, 44–55. London: Routledge.

———. 2019. "On Heritage Ontologies: Rethinking the Material Worlds of Heritage." *Anthropological Quarterly* 91 (4): 1365–84.

Harrison, Rodney, and John Schofield. 2010. *After Modernity. Archaeological Approaches to the Contemporary Past*. Oxford: Oxford University Press.

Hirst, Damien, Elena Geuna, and Amie Corry, eds. 2017. *Damien Hirst: Treasures from the Wreck of the Unbelievable*. Venezia: Pinault Collection.

Holmes, Tiffany. 2007. "Eco-Visualization: Promoting Environmental Stewardship in the Museum." *Journal of Museum Education* 32(3): 273–83.

Hooper-Greenhill, Eilean. 2002. *Museums and the Shaping of Knowledge*. London: Taylor and Francis.

———. 2005. *Museum and the Interpretation of Visual Culture*. New York: Routledge.

Jameson, John H. 2003. "Art and Imagery as Tools for Public Interpretation and Education in Archaeology." In *Ancient Muses: Archaeology and the Art*, ed. John H. Jameson, John E. Ehrenhard, and Christine A. Finn, 57–65. Tuscaloosa: The University of Alabama Press.

Jones, Andrew, and Paul Bonaventura. 2011. "Shaping the Past: Sculpture and Archaeology." In *Sculpture and Archaeology*, ed. Paul Bonaventura and Andrew Jones, 1–17. Surrey-Burlington: Routledge.

Kidd, Jenny. 2014. *Museums in the New Mediascape: Transmedia, Participation, Ethics*. Surrey-Burlington: Routledge.

Kintigh, Keith W., Jeffrey H. Altschul, Mary C. Beaudry, Robert D. Drennan, Ann P. Kinzig, Timothy A. Kohler, W. Fredrick Limp, Herbert D. G. Maschner, William K. Michener, Timothy R. Pauketat, Peter Peregrine, Jeremy A. Sabloff, Tony J. Wilkinson, Henry T. Wright, and Melinda A. Zeder. 2014. "Grand Challenges for Archaeology." *Proceedings of the National Academy of Sciences* 21 111(3): 879–80. https://doi.org/10.1073/pnas.1324000111.

Kristiansen, Kristian. 2014. "Towards a New Paradigm? The Third Science Revolution and Its Possible Consequences in Archaeology." *Current Swedish Archaeology* 22: 11–34.

Lafrenz Samuels, K. 2018. *Mobilizing Heritage: Anthropological Practice and Transnational Prospects*. Gainesville: University of Florida Press.

Leone, Mark P., Parker B. Potter, Jr., and Paul A. Shackel. 1987. "Toward a Critical Archaeology." *Current Anthropology* 28(3): 283–302.

Leszczyński, Adam. 2015. "Poles Don't Want Immigrants: They Don't Understand Them, Don't Like Them." *The Guardian*, 2 July. Retrieved 20 February 2020 from https://www.theguardian.com/world/2015/jul/02/poles-dont-want-immigrants-they-dont-understand-them-dont-like-them.

Lucas, Gavin. 2005. *The Archaeology of Time*. London: Routledge.

———. 2012. *Understanding the Archaeological Record*. New York: Cambridge University Press.

Matsuda, Akira, and Katsuyuki Nakamura. 2011. "Introduction: New Perspectives in Global Public Archaeology." In *New Perspectives in Global Public Archaeology*, ed. Katsuyuki Okamura and Akira Matsuda, 1–18. New York: Springer.

Marstine, Janet, ed. 2006. *New Museum: Theory and Practice*. Malden, MA: Blackwell Publishing.

Mazan, Kazimierz. 2011. "National Museums in Poland." In *Building National Museums in Europe 1750–2010: Conference Proceedings from EuNaMus, European National Museums: Identity Politics, the Uses of the Past and the European Citizen, Bologna 28–30 April 2011*, ed. Peter Aronsson and Gabriella Elgenius, 667–87. Linköping: Linköping University Electronic Press.

McLuhan, Marshall. 2003. *Understanding Media: The Extensions of Man*. London: Gingko Press.

Moser, Stephanie. 2010. "The Devil Is in the Detail: Museum Displays and the Creation of Knowledge." *Museum Anthropology* 33(1): 22–33.

Nash, Stephen E., and Nancy O'Malley. 2012. "The Changing Mission of Museums." In *Archaeology in Society: Its Relevance in the Modern World*, ed. Marcy Rockman and Joe Flatman, 97–110. New York: Springer.

Olsen, Bjørnar, Michael Shanks, Timothy Webmoor, and Christopher Witmore. 2012. *Archaeology: The Discipline of Things*. Berkeley: University of California Press.

Pearce, Susan M. 1990. *Archaeological Curatorship*. London: Leicester University Press.

———. 2006. *Interpreting Objects and Collections*. New York: Routledge.

Piotrowski, Piotr. 2010. "An Art Historian between the University and the Museum: Towards the Idea of the Critical Museum." *Índex Barcelona: MACBA* 0: 12–15.

———. 2011a. *Muzeum krytyczne*. Poznań: Rebis.

———. 2011b. *In the Shadow of Yalta: Art and the Avant-Garde in Eastern Europe, 1945–1989*, trans. Anna Brzyski. London: Reaktion Books.

Potter, Parker B. 1994. *Public Archaeology in Annapolis: A Critical Approach to History in Maryland's Ancient City*. Washington DC: Smithsonian Institution Press.

Renfrew, Colin. 1999. "It May Be Art but Is It Archaeology? Science as Art and Art as Science." In *Mark Dion: Archaeology*, ed. Mark Dion, 12–23. London: Black Dog Publishing.

———. 2003. *Figuring It Out: What Are We? Where Do We Come From? The Parallel Visions of Artists and Archaeologists*. London: Thames and Hudson.

———. 2004. "Art for Archaeology." In *Substance, Memory, Display: Archaeology and Art*, ed. Colin Renfrew, Chris Gosden, and Elisabeth DeMarrais, 7–34. Cambridge: McDonald Institute for Archaeological Research.

Renfrew, Colin, Chris Gosden, and Elizabeth DeMarrais. 2004. "Introduction: Art as Archaeology and Archaeology as Art." In *Substance, Memory, Display: Archaeology and Art*, ed. Colin Renfrew, Chris Gosden, and Elizabeth DeMarrais, 1–6. Cambridge: McDonald Institute for Archaeological Research.

Rizvi, Uzma Z. 2019. "Archaeological Encounters: The Role of the Speculative in Decolonial Archaeology." *Journal of Contemporary Archaeology* 6(1): 154–67.

Russell, Ian A., and Andrew Cochrane, eds. 2014. *Art and Archaeology*. New York: Routledge.

Schellekens, Elisabeth. 2008. *Aesthetics and Morality*. London: Continuum Books.

Schlievert, Chelsea. 2009. "Take This Moment: Sexual Violence Awareness and the Art Museum as a Vehicle for Social Change." *Journal of Cultural Research in Art Education* 27: 63–76.

Shanks, Michael. 2012. *The Archaeological Imagination*. Walnut Creek, CA: Left Coast Press.

Sjöstrand, Ylva. 2017. "The Concept of Art as Archaeologically Applicable." *Cambridge Archaeological Journal* 27(2): 371–88.

Solli, Brit, Mats Burström, Ewa Domańska, Matthew Edgeworth, Alfredo González-Ruibal, Cornelius Holtorf, Gavin Lucas, Terje Oestigaard, Laurajane Smith, and Christopher Witmore. 2011. "Some Reflections on Heritage and Archaeology in the Anthropocene." *Norwegian Archaeological Review* 44(1): 40–88.

Stobiecka, Monika. 2019. "Digital Escapism: How Objects Become Deprived of Matter." *Journal of Contemporary Archaeology* 5(2): 194–212.

Stottman, M. Jay. 2010. "Introduction: Archaeologists as Activists." In *Archaeologists as Activists: Can Archaeologists Change the World?*, ed. M. Jay Stottman, 1–16. Tuscaloosa: University of Alabama Press.

Swain, Hedley. 2007. *An Introduction to Museum Archaeology*. Cambridge: Cambridge University Press.

Ting, Wing Yan Vivian. 2010. "Dancing Pot and Pregnant Jar? On Ceramics, Metaphors and Creative Labels." In *Museum Materialities: Objects, Engagements, Interpretations*, ed. Sandra H. Dudley, 189–203. Oxon: Routledge.

Vergo, Peter, ed. 1989. *The New Museology*. London: Reaktion Books.

Vilches, Flora. 2007. "The Art of Archaeology: Mark Dion and His Dig Projects." *Journal of Social Archaeology* 7(2): 199–223.

———. 2011. "Mirrored Practices: Robert Smithson and Archaeological Fieldwork." In *Sculpture and Archaeology*, ed. Paul Bonaventura and Andrew Jones, 97–112. Surrey-Burlington: Routledge.

Wintour, Patrick, 2017. "EU Takes Action against Eastern States for Refusing to Take Refugees." *The Guardian*, 13 June. Retrieved 20 February 2020 from https://www.theguardian.com/world/2017/jun/13/eu-takes-action-against-eastern-states-for-refusing-to-take-refugees.

CHAPTER 5

"You Can't Replant Old Trees"
The Combined Approach of Memory and Public Archaeology to Reinvestigate Court Housing in Liverpool, UK

Kerry Massheder-Rigby

Introduction

Have we, as UK-based historical archaeologists, failed to recognize the full value of oral history as a form of public archaeology? Written sources often dominate as more legitimate, with memory obliterated by the written word (Kasabova 2008) and the heavily scientific approach of archaeology skeptical of oral sources (Mason 2000). However, David Lowenthal (2015) quoting L. P. Hartley argues that "the past is a foreign country"; what better way to find out about the past than to converse directly with the individuals and communities who experienced it? Oral history has the potential to act in the absence of other sources, providing information that cannot be found elsewhere. Although the discipline of archaeology has a lengthy tradition of using oral testimony, particularly the testimony of Indigenous Peoples, it has yet to be applied fully and in a meaningful way within UK archaeology. Jay Stottman (2010) questioned what value archaeology has for the general public. From a critical theory perspective, a combined approach of archaeology and oral history has the potential to challenge existing understandings of the past, placing the public as a key partner in the archaeological process.

Scholars of critical theory in historical archaeology (Kellner 1989; Leone, Potter, and Shackel 1987; Leone 2020; McGuire 2014; Orser 1996; Pragnell 2020) questioned the commercialization of history and how class structures exclude people from the archaeological process. Archaeologists have sought to overcome this exclusion in several ways. For example, Richard Handler and Eric Gable (1997) conducted an ethnographic study of the "living museum" at Colonial Williamsburg, highlighting the conflict and negotiation of public history that takes places between various audiences, including historians, front of house staff, and visitors. Camille Westmont (chap. 6, this volume) established how archaeology can be used as a tool for social justice through researching the lived experiences of nineteenth-century convicts. By using critically based public narratives to build empathy for the historic convicts, Westmont demonstrates how racial disparities were built into the convict leasing system and how racial inequality continues in the US prison system today. Randall H. McGuire (2008) called on historical archaeologists to identify mechanisms of capitalism and establish programs of public archaeology that could enable working-class communities to create their own histories. Oppressed by slum labels and assumptions about working-class housing by external observers, the participation of the historic working class in the archaeology of housing challenges the potential for the misinterpretation of archaeological features. James Symonds (2011) criticized historical archaeological approaches that interpreted the archaeology of people who lived in poverty through the lens of the twenty-first century. Taking a critical approach to the archaeology of working-class housing by including the residents in the archaeological process via oral history can break down the barriers to their inclusion in archaeology.

Recent research has shown the potential for combining archaeology and oral history in the UK context. The oral history project, *Our Humble Abodes*, was conducted by the author and Dr. Elizabeth Stewart in 2013–14 on behalf of the National Museums Liverpool. The project interviewed, for the first time, former residents of courtyard-style, "court," housing in Liverpool and collected their testimonies for the Museum of Liverpool repository. The nineteenth-century descriptions of court housing dominate the historic literature, characterizing this form of housing as unsanitary, overcrowded, dilapidated, and slum-like. This research, via the oral history testimony, introduced an alternative, twentieth-century account based on firsthand experiences. The memories shared by the oral history narrators demonstrate the ways oral testimony from the former community can challenge the official, historic record, which typically reflects a biased mainstream narrative. These personal experiences and accounts cannot be found in the archaeological record and demonstrate the unique nature of oral history in an archaeological context.

This chapter focuses on how the combined approach can challenge our understanding of working-class housing by including the opinions and memories of those with lived experience as a form of public archaeology. The former residents, via oral history, provide insight that may otherwise go unrecorded. It provides a case study of court housing in Liverpool, UK, using oral history memories as a means to engage the public with the archaeological process, providing an alternative perspective of this vanished and misunderstood housing type.

Oral History and the Combined Approach

Oral history is both a research methodology for data collection (the process of interviewing) and an object (the audio of the interview with the testimony of the narrator plus other documentation created as a result of the interview, such as a transcript). Oral history relies on firsthand testimony about the past elicited by an interviewer from a narrator and recorded as an audio or audio-visual file. Oral history is situated as a discipline within memory studies alongside collective and individual memory, identity, folklore, myth, oral traditions, post memory, autobiography, and nostalgia. The founders of oral history (Evans 1956; Portelli 1981; Samuel 1994; Thompson 2000) saw it as a radical approach able to challenge the dominant historical narrative by exploring the histories of marginalized communities and those previously excluded or misrepresented in the historical record. Oral history is used as a tool to record emotional responses, personal experiences, and expert knowledge. It is an opportunity to engage directly with living memory and, as a form of public archaeology, it can engage the public in interpreting material culture and breaks down barriers to inclusion in archaeology for those with a lived experience of the site.

The use of memory and oral history in archaeology has gained momentum in recent years. Memory has become a theme at major conferences such as the 2008 World Archaeological Congress in Dublin, which held several sessions on memory and oral traditions and the 2017 Society for Historical Archaeology conference held sessions on memory and materiality, and historic memory. Chapters on oral history have been included in recent historical archaeology-themed handbooks and journals (Orser 2017; Orser et al. 2020; Jones and Russell 2012). They continue the work of fellow advocates of the combined approach (Adams 1984; Moshenska 2007; Purser 1992).

The integration of oral history testimony with site-based archaeological evidence is referred to as the combined approach (Massheder-Rigby 2020). This combined approach recognizes and values the expert knowledge that exists in the community. In addition, oral history is a participatory and engaging way for non-archaeologists—the public—to take part in the process of archaeology as collaborators rather than contributors. It is also a way for archaeologists, typically from a particular background and level of education, to better understand the historic environment they did not personally experience and participate in a knowledge exchange with the public as equals rather than as experts.

Evidence suggests that together archaeology and oral history can better inform our understanding of the past (Bennett and Fowler 2017). Pooling our strengths as archaeologists, historians, and geographers, we can provide an account of the people of the modern past that is as accurate as evidence will allow (Mayne 2011). Both disciplines are compatible without diminishing the significance of either (Lyons et al. 2010), but we need a more theoretically informed approach to memory-work within archaeology (Moshenska 2006). The memories shared within oral history interviews could be used to interpret material culture, identify objects, and make sense of object collections. The testimony can transmit knowledge that is of continuing importance to a community, inform the public about historic events, identify and interpret sites of human occupation, inform about past social life and culture, and challenge long-held assumptions. Archaeology and oral history offer two complementary ways of considering human history (McKechnie 2015) and their use together has the potential to offer a fuller picture by each filling gaps in the information not available to the other. Oral history and archaeology are both placed-based and fieldwork disciplines and the value of oral history for historical archaeology lies in its ability to provide personal memories, feelings, and reflections about archaeological features from living memory.

Archaeology and Oral History Memory of Working-Class Housing

In the UK, working-class housing has typically been approached from the perspective of the discipline of history with a concentrated focus in the 1970s (Chapman 1971; Gauldie 1974; Sutcliffe 1972; Tarn 1971) and a revival in interest in the 1990s (Daunton 1990; S. M. Gaskell 1990; Rodger 1995). The subject then received attention from an archaeological perspective (Dewhurst 1989; Crosby, Garwood, and Corder-Birch 2008; Newman and Newman 2008) although the research focused on geographical areas, archaeological sites or housing types, rather than the subject of working-class housing more generally.

Household archaeology is a diverse and eclectic field of study to which researchers bring multiple perspectives, with scholars researching household archaeology in the ancient Near East (Parker and Foster 2012), several cultures of the Ancient Americas (Douglass and Gonlin 2012; Joyce and Gillespie 2000), ancient Israel (Yasur-Landau, Ebeling, and Mazow 2011), and Chinese immigrant communities in America (Williams and Voss 2008), for example. The term "household archaeology" was coined by Richard R. Wilk and William L. Rathje (1982) and includes domestic spatial patterning, social archaeology, and the study of household behaviors. Studying households is significant because it is within the context of the household that cultural consciousness, social choices and status are performed (Barile and Brandon 2004; Beaudry 2004; King 2006; Prossor et al. 2004). Households are the primary arena in which space is experienced and life is lived (Lefebvre 1971). Mary Beaudry (2015) argues that archaeologists should attempt to integrate social history approaches, with a focus on ordinary people, and anthropological approaches looking at development cycles within domestic groups and households more generally. Archaeologists should strive to excavate household sites in such a way that they can make persuasive links between the life histories of sites and site formation processes and identify episodes of household stasis, upheaval, transformation (Beaudry 1995). Although urban neighborhoods have received increased attention from historical archaeologists (Mayne and Lawrence 1999; Mayne and Murray 2001; Yamin 2002), the combined perspective of archaeology and oral history offers new ways to investigate these vanished inner-city housing forms, particularly in the UK context.

Historical archaeologists have conducted ethnographies of place (Connelly 2011; Mayne 2011; Mayne and Lawrence 1999; Mayne and Murray 2001; Rimmer 2011) that demonstrate the potential for documentary, oral, and archaeological evidence to work together. There are examples of archaeologists and historians working together to investigate vanished inner-city neighborhoods and reinvestigate the slum stereotypes (Connelly 2011; Mayne and Lawrence 1999; Mayne and Murray 2001; Murray and Mayne 2001; Solari 2001; Yamin 2002). Alan Mayne and Tim Murray (2001) introduced methods that underpinned new research agendas, aiming to address distortions embedded in the historical record that confuse the imagined realities of slums with the actualities of working-class neighborhoods. This methodology was further developed by York Archaeological Trust at the Hungate excavations in York (Connelly 2018; Mayne 2011; Rimmer 2011).

Although oral history and the public's involvement are equal in significance, it is the oral history testimony that has the most potential to increase our understanding of the working-class housing experience. It cannot be assumed from the archaeology that residents used the space in the way they were originally intended and so while archaeology, including desk-based research, can provide physical remains and historic documents as evidence, oral history has the unique ability to illuminate the physical archaeological remains by providing lived experience from community-based experts. Nancy Janovicek (2013) argues unequal power relations cannot be addressed if researchers consider themselves to be the only experts, giving a voice to marginalized people. Oral history narrators are community-based experts and can participate in archaeology as collaborators, rather than simply as contributors. The public can, and should be encouraged to, work with archaeologists to set the research agenda, representing their community while interpreting physical archaeological structures and objects. The combined approach can enable the public to be involved in archaeology in a meaningful way, contributing firsthand knowledge of the physical landscape and the people who inhabited it. Oral history provides the opportunity to capture accounts of the working-class housing experience that may otherwise go unrecorded. Traditionally, the historic working class, marginalized communities, and those inhabiting housing labeled slums have been underrepresented in the historical record. Oral history can potentially address this underrepresentation by recording memories, opinions, interpretations, thoughts, and life histories. Indigenous Peoples have pioneered storytelling, oral history, and the verbal sharing of memory to preserve the heritage of their community. Indigenous archaeologists have demonstrated the value of Indigenous People participating in the archaeological process as equal partners and have shared the often tumultuous relationship between archaeology and Indigenous culture (McMillan and Yellowhorn 2004; Yellowhorn 2000; Watkins 2000). Their methods illustrate that the practice of public archaeology, community involvement and community-led archaeology and memory work does not necessarily mean amateur, unprofessional or inaccurate. So, although the combined approach is not new, it has been widely practiced within the archaeological approaches to Indigenous Peoples, it has yet to be fully practiced within UK archaeology.

Within historical archaeology, working-class housing has received increased attention more recently, a symposium "Archaeologies of Workers' Housing" organized by

Harold Mytum, Charlotte Newman, and Suzanne Lilley was held at the 2017 Society for Historical Archaeology conference in Fort Worth, Texas, and a session "Housing the Industrious Workforce" was held at the Theoretical Archaeology Group conference in 2015 in Bradford, UK (Lilley 2015). These sessions both encouraged alternative perspectives of working-class housing. There are examples of UK-based archaeological studies with a focus on housing that have included oral history (Belford 2003; Casella 2012; Casella and Croucher 2010; Dwyer 2014; Moshenska 2006, 2007, 2010) however the combined approach has been slow to develop in the UK despite these examples of the profession heading in the right direction. These previous UK-based studies provided the foundations for a methodological approach of both archaeology and oral history to study working-class housing. Their observations and evaluation have worked to develop the combined approach however gaps remain in the research such as a framework of the combined approach that goes beyond a single site, a critical look at what survives in the different sources of evidence and what the potential for the combined approach is. Developing an approach that treats archaeology and oral history as equals rather than one as a supplementary source should be a priority.

In the UK there are only a handful of twentieth-century accounts from those with a lived experience of working-class housing (London 1903; O'Mara 1933; R. Roberts 1971). Potentially oral history, as part of the combined approach, can help address this gap.

Public Archaeology and Sites of Memory

In collaborating with the public, oral history can help the survivors of repressive military dictatorships, such as those in Latin America, oppose and reclaim the official narrative (Hiner 2018; Huyssen 2011; Zarankin and Salerno 2008). The collective memory of past violence can be used as a vehicle for assuming and attributing responsibility (Leccardi 2016; Sodaro 2018). The Museo De La Memoria Y Los Derechos Humanos (Museum of Memory and Human Rights) in Santiago, Chile, and the Espacio Memoria Y Derechos Humanos Ex ESMA (Space for Memory and Human Rights, formally ESMA) in Buenos Aires, Argentina, are two examples of this. Sites of memory, such as the Seodaemun Prison in South Korea (Lee 2019) or the former Khmer Rouge prison in Cambodia (Sirik 2015) have the ability to help the public come to terms with the violence of the past, specifically the detainment, torture, and murder of political prisoners. Sites of memory provide an arena for the sharing of oral histories by allowing them to play a prominent role in the memorialization of past events.

Memory, both historical and deep time tribal memory, within the field of the archaeology of Indigenous Peoples has made huge contributions to and further developed the combined approach. The rights of Indigenous Peoples and communities to engage in archaeological work and collaborate with heritage research is included within some legislation. In the United States, the Native American Graves Protection and Repatriation Act (National Park Service 1990), which requires federally funded institutions to make human remains and associated materials available for return to their associated tribes, accepts oral history as evidence for the identification of human remains as Native American. The United Nations Declaration on the Rights of Indigenous Peoples, adopted by the UN General Assembly in 2007, recognized the right of Indigenous Peoples to have control over their heritage. Some localized legislation has also recognized the rights Indigenous Peoples have to their heritage, such as the Ontario Heritage Act R.S.O. 1990, which regulates archaeology and grants licenses to archaeologists to investigate heritage. Additionally, several archaeology organizations have codes of conduct that set out the responsibilities archaeologists have to Indigenous Peoples. For example, the Australian Archaeological Association (2022) has a code of ethics for members that requires them to acknowledge the special importance of the cultural heritage of Indigenous communities and the Canadian Archaeological Association (2022a; 2022b) has principles for ethical conduct pertaining to First Nations Peoples.

Memory work allows Indigenous Peoples to assume the rights to their own history (Beck and Somerville 2005; Gould et al. 2020; Lyons et al. 2010; Watkins 2000), to participate within archaeological research (Basso 1996; Herrmann et al. 2017), and to add narrative to the archaeological data (Bennett and Fowler 2017; Mason 2000; McKechnie 2015). Archaeologists who examine sites related to Indigenous Peoples recognize that memories and community knowledge are embedded in geographical locations within the historic landscape, that "wisdom sits in places" (Basso 1996). Iain McKechnie (2015) proposes that a skepticism of oral history has resulted in the continued privileging of colonial history accounts over Indigenous accounts. It is possible to apply methodologies developed during archaeological projects of Indigenous Peoples by using the combined approach at non-Indigenous sites; however, McKechnie (2015) observes that even Indigenous oral history has yet to be integrated or evaluated effectively alongside conventional archaeological chronologies.

Even in places like the UK where there is no Indigenous community, several funders and organizations require public engagement and participation within archaeology. Oral history is one way to encourage the community to participate in archaeology (Marshall 2002; Tully 2007). With public money being spent on archaeology and heritage, there is a duty to include and engage the public in the archaeological process. The National Lottery Heritage Fund (formally Heritage Lottery Fund), a UK-based public funding body, supports projects that help local people explore, enjoy and protect their heritage while Historic England (formally English Heritage, the national agency for the protection of built heritage in England), within their report *Conservation Principles, Policies and Guidance* (English Heritage 2008), state that everyone should be able to participate in sustaining the historic environment and should have the opportunity to contribute his or her knowledge of the value of places. Additionally, the European Association of Archaeologists (2009) has a collection of codes and principles that guide members to take active steps to inform the public about their archaeological work. As these organizations indicate, it is considered best practice to facilitate the engagement of non-archaeologists in heritage, and archaeology and oral history is one way this can be achieved in a meaningful way. As the combined approach recognizes that expert knowledge exists in the community, it has the potential to challenge the dominant historical narrative, offer alternative narratives, and can include the public in archaeological work by engaging them with their heritage.

However, despite the increased popularity and use of oral history, there are concerns over the reliability of memory and its ability to contribute to historical narratives. There are studies that investigate the relationship between data sets, particularly archaeology and documentary evidence (Little 1992; Moreland 2001, 2006; Purser 1992), and the abilities of each, however, oral history uniquely relies on the process of recalling memories that may be influenced by the passing of time (Connerton 2008; Larsen 2011; Portelli 1981). Mark Riley and David Harvey (2005) acknowledge the ongoing issues oral history has in being recognized as a credible set of data. The often partial, subjective, ambiguous, tensioned, and contradictory nature of oral history accounts means archaeologists need to be careful in using them; however, if, as a profession, we can move beyond the opinion that there is a single, truthful historical narrative, then we can begin to use these alternative accounts to challenge what we think we know. For example, Denis Byrne (2003) called for archaeologists in Australia to challenge the white-settler practice of ignoring the presence of Aboriginal Peoples in the historical landscape. A verification of memories approach was used for oral testimony in the 1950s in African archaeology (Schmidt 1990); however, this approach still places archaeology as the dominant and accurate source with oral accounts needing to be verified. The example of Inuit Elders at Arivat illustrates one way these concerns can be addressed (Lyons et al. 2010). The Inuit Elders used their own form of fact-checking of testimonies by debating whose word was the best authority and, therefore, whose memory was most accurate. Sian Jones (2012) found that a community in Scotland privileged some sources of memory over others, such as locals' over newcomers', as those with greater social authority. An integrated approach where memory is valued as equal to archaeology is essential for the combined approach to work in practice. Gabriel Moshenska (2006) suggests archaeologists need to pay close attention to developments in the field of memory work, particularly elements that relate to material culture, place, and memorials.

History of UK Court Housing

Inadequate and substandard housing long pre-dated the Industrial Revolution (Ashworth 1951; S. M. Gaskell 1990), but it increased in that era of rapid urbanization and widespread overcrowding. Casual workers were inclined to base themselves close to places of potential employment, urban centers and ports, which coincided with where the oldest buildings and housing were located. To meet the rising demand for low-cost accommodation, houses were constructed in the rear yards and streets surrounding the existing houses and multi-roomed properties were developed to provide for multi-occupancies. It was impossible for those without a steady income, or a disposable income, to spend on their home or living environment. There was no clearly defined housing policy between 1850 and 1880. All legislation on housing up to 1875 fell within public health legislation and law rather than being a priority in its own right (Flinn 1965; Rodger 1995). These low-cost, high-density forms of working-class housing rapidly declined into what became known as slum housing.

By the late nineteenth century, housing acts used slum housing as a point of reference to debate and agree upon a program of demolition and replacement (Burnett 1978; Pooley and Irish 1994; Rodger 1995; Tarn 1971). S. M. Gaskell (1990) suggests, further supported by S. Hayton (1998), that much of the evidence surrounding nineteenth century-slum housing are likely tinged with xenophobia as a result of these areas being inhabited by migrants, particularly Irish and Jewish people. There was frequent turnover of inhabitants as a result of unstable employment, so these communities were in a permanent state of fluidity. Later statistical studies (C. Booth 1889; Rowntree 1901) demonstrated the variations in the people who lived in slum areas. Their skills, race, religion, and wages all varied.

With novelists, social investigators, journalists, and the housing reform movement bringing public attention to slum housing (W. Booth 1890; Engels 1845; Mayhew 1851; Rowntree 1901), those in authority needed to explain their continued existence. Authorities blamed the existence of slums on the inhabitants and their lack of moral qualities. Gaskell (1990) suggests that the presentation of slum life to the public gave it an exotic and mysterious character, otherworldly, to outsiders. A slum was both a physical, geographically designated space, an abyss, and a primitive, dangerous space inhabited by those with few morals. This is suggestive of class fear and fear of the unknown. Suggesting slum dwellers were less than the deserving poor and that the physical attributes of a slum were a result of the failings of its inhabitants allowed those in authority to explain away the ongoing existence of these problem areas. By the twentieth century, the slum was a high-profile threat to a country proposing a land fit for heroes.

In 1933, local authorities were requested by the central government to prepare five-year plans to demolish slums. By 1967, 900,000 "slum" houses in Britain had been demolished with approximately 2.5 million people rehomed (Rees 2001). The prejudices of parliamentary commissioners, legislators, officers, and journalists determined the questions they asked and the approaches they took during their investigations. Popular attitudes toward the working-class suggested that the working-class caused their own poverty, often through drunkenness, idleness and crime, and that their lifestyle choices were to blame (C. Booth 1889; P. Gaskell 1883; H. Roberts 1855; Rowntree 1901). The public voiced concerns that government assistance would encourage a lack of motivation in the poor, and they would be unwilling to help themselves. However, investigative journalism and poverty surveys challenged this widely held belief. The need for public expenditure on public health and housing resulted in alternative explanations prevailing (Wohl 1977). However, with limited firsthand accounts from the working-class themselves (London 1903; O'Mara 1933; R. Roberts 1971), assumptions and myths about these communities have continued into the present day.

Our Humble Abodes: Court Housing in Liverpool

Liverpool courtyard housing, or court housing, was the regional form of low-quality, high-density housing and was home to half of the working class in the city during the nineteenth century. Court housing was a form of back-to-back housing behind the frontage houses, or shops, of the main street. The typically rectangular courtyard was entered through a narrow passageway from the main street. The houses inside the court faced one another across a shared courtyard that housed shared facilities such as a toilet, standpipe, and ashbin. They varied in size from two houses to twenty and were two or three stories high often with a cellar and a garret (attic). The houses were back-to-back with the next court and so did not have a rear exit or yard. The major shortcomings of back-to-back and court housing was the lack of ventilation due to built-up proximity, a rear wall in common, the temptation to build as many houses as possible onto a small piece of land to maximize profits. This resulted in shared spaces, such as streets and passageways, being small so that as much land as possible could be dedicated to housing. These houses were mostly constructed by speculative builders, small-scale and motivated by profit, these builders became known as Jerry Builders (Ashton 1954) who constructed inexpensive, temporary, inferior housing with a lack of durability and comfort.

As with other large urban towns and cities, Liverpool suffered a crisis of housing, health, and overcrowding and, consequently, attracted the attention of medical observers, public health reformers, middle-class social commentators, and town planners. By the 1840s, unsanitary housing in England was gaining public attention encouraged by reformers through pamphlets and investigative journalism. In Liverpool, officials, health professionals, and commentators were identifying the abundance of court and cellar dwellings in the city as hazardous to health. Nineteenth-century investigations into housing and health found that conditions in court dwellings could spread of disease. At the local level, Medical Officers of Health were key figures in the development of housing policy and in identifying areas of low quality, slum-like, housing (Pooley 1985; Pooley and Irish 1994). Medical observers concluded that poor housing, specifically airless and dirty living conditions, resulted in a high mortality rate. Court housing and cellar dwellings were identified in public health pamphlets as types of housing that provided an airless and dirty existence. They recognized that these property types lacked proper sanitation and drainage, lacked a water supply, lacked adequate ventilation, were poorly constructed of cheap materials, and the yards and streets surrounding these properties were not cleaned. In 1863, Dr. William Stewart Trench, Liverpool's second Medical Officer of Health, commented in his *Report of the Medical Officer for*

Health that disease was a result of "the number of poor . . . collected in certain squalid localities; filth and penury pent up in airless dwellings, frequent changes of residence, . . . crowding together of many families in single houses, . . . the preponderance of narrow ill-ventilated courts and alleys, [and] the construction and position of middens and cesspools" (Trench 1863: 7).

Based on these observations, an enthusiastic and thorough program of slum clearance occurred in Liverpool during the early to mid-twentieth century. The slum clearances began in the late nineteenth century with the 1875 Artisans Dwelling Act, which enabled local authorities to demolish slum housing. This was followed by the 1890 Housing of the Working-Classes Act, which gave local authorities the power to close unsanitary dwellings, and the 1930 Slum Clearance Act, which encouraged the demolition of court housing. New tenements and, later, estates of newly constructed housing in suburbs were created to house the displaced. The Liverpool Corporation, a municipal corporation that later became Liverpool City Council, built housing as a means of remediating the unsanitary housing that was responsible for health issues in the city. However, providing new homes for the displaced also became a means of controlling and improving their morals and behavior, as residents were required to follow Corporation rules and a certain level of conduct was expected. Typically, those displaced from the worst housing were unable to afford the Liverpool Corporation rents and found alternative accommodations. This resulted in overcrowding issues elsewhere. Sir Lancelot Keay, Director of Housing, was reluctant to allow former court residents to reside in the newly constructed dwellings. He suggested a stop gap alternative, called special preparatory tenements, to teach tenants to live in decent housing before moving into permanent accommodation.

Court housing was once prevalent throughout Liverpool; however, a widespread clearance program in the twentieth century left only three court houses extant. An oral history project, *Our Humble Abodes,* conducted in 2013–2014, provided the unique opportunity to challenge the mainstream narrative of court housing in Liverpool by introducing a previously under-acknowledged source: the memories of former residents. The oral histories contributed to our understanding of this form of working-class housing, within living memory and yet under-explored.

Oral Histories of Liverpool Court Housing

Court housing has faded from social memory and has now taken on a mythical, Dickens-like existence in the Liverpool consciousness. The generally held impression of the court housing experience is not necessarily incorrect or untrue, but it is limiting. Carrying out oral history interviews with former residents has led to the emergence of alternative narratives of court housing.

Most of what we know about court housing comes from nineteenth-century accounts, reports and legislation in response to poor-quality housing and outbreaks of disease, as described above. Little is known about the housing experience for twentieth-century court residents.

The *Our Humble Abodes* was delivered by the Archaeology Department of the Museum of Liverpool (Massheder-Rigby 2018; Stewart 2019). The project was intended to engage the public with the history of working-class housing in Liverpool through the recording of oral histories and the sharing of memories. The project aimed to record oral histories of court housing potentially providing an unofficial view of life in a Liverpool court house.

The project was featured in local media in order to help locate potential narrators. Ten narrators were interviewed, eight of whom had been former residents of court houses and two who had lived in close proximity to court housing, although one of the eight residents was keen to point out that while he lived in a court house, he did not live in a court as only two of the houses of the court remained. Four of the narrators lived in the same court providing a unique insight. The narrators were given the option of where the interview would take place, some chose the comfort of their own home, and some opted to visit the Museum of Liverpool. Siblings and family members were welcome to be present for the interview and take part in the interview. Although this makes for confusing transcribing at times, it gave the narrators the opportunity to make the decision of who was present during the sharing of their, potentially traumatic, memories. The interviews took a conversational approach around a set of themes related to housing, all involved looking at historic maps of the area the narrators lived in, and several included discussing photographs the narrators had brought along. All narrators signed a consent form to allow their full names, memories, and the audio recordings to be used in a variety of ways, including in National Museums Liverpool venues, academic outputs, broadcasting, and educational activities. The author has chosen to use the narrator's initials in this chapter to afford them a level of anonymity.

Introduction to the Narrators

KS lived in a court house in Mann Street, L8. KS and JT are cousins, and JT lived with their mutual grandmother on Beaufort Street, which abutted the Mann Street court with through access. Their grandparents also lived in the Mann Street court. They were interviewed together as KS invited JT to accompany him as he thought that as she was older, she would most likely have memories to add to his account. MM and MH are cousins (their mothers were half-sisters) and both lived in houses in the same Mann Street court as KS. MM contacted the project after seeing his old neighbors, KS and JT, talking about court housing to the Liverpool Echo newspaper in December 2013. MM advised he would bring his cousin MH along as she lived in the court at the same time. MH moved in with her grandmother, who lived in the next street, at the age of eighteen months following an illness attributed by the family to damp conditions in the court house. She recalled spending most of her time in the court house despite

Figure 5.1. Mann Street court, Liverpool, 1953. Photograph by MM. Courtesy of National Museums Liverpool, Museum of Liverpool collection, used with permission.

residing elsewhere. AS was the eldest child in a family of eight children. RL was an only child until his cousin moved in with the family. His family moved into the court house, one of only two still standing, and joined an existing tenant, an elderly lady. BR lived with his seven siblings in a court house on Saltney Street, L3. He left the court with his family in 1954, although it had been condemned in 1900, and moved to tenements on Vauxhall Road, L3. AM and AR are brother and sister among four siblings. AM contacted the project team following the BBC Radio Merseyside appeal and asked if he could bring along his older sister AR who lives in South Africa but was currently on holiday in the UK.

For some, the interviews were an opportunity to take a stroll down memory lane and reminisce about their childhoods. Several narrators expressed a sense of gratitude toward their former community for lessons learned, or shared feelings about life, not necessarily being better than today, but certainly a way of life that is now lost to them and to modern society. One narrator shared feelings of bitterness toward a hard childhood where court life forced her to grow up quickly and take on the responsibility of caring for her siblings and household resulting in memories being formed that echoed the existing, negative, historical view of life in courts.

Description of Court Housing

From the memories of those with lived experience from the twentieth century, a Liverpool court house can be described as three stories, some with cellars, each identical as the next house with the front elevation facing the front of your neighbor's house

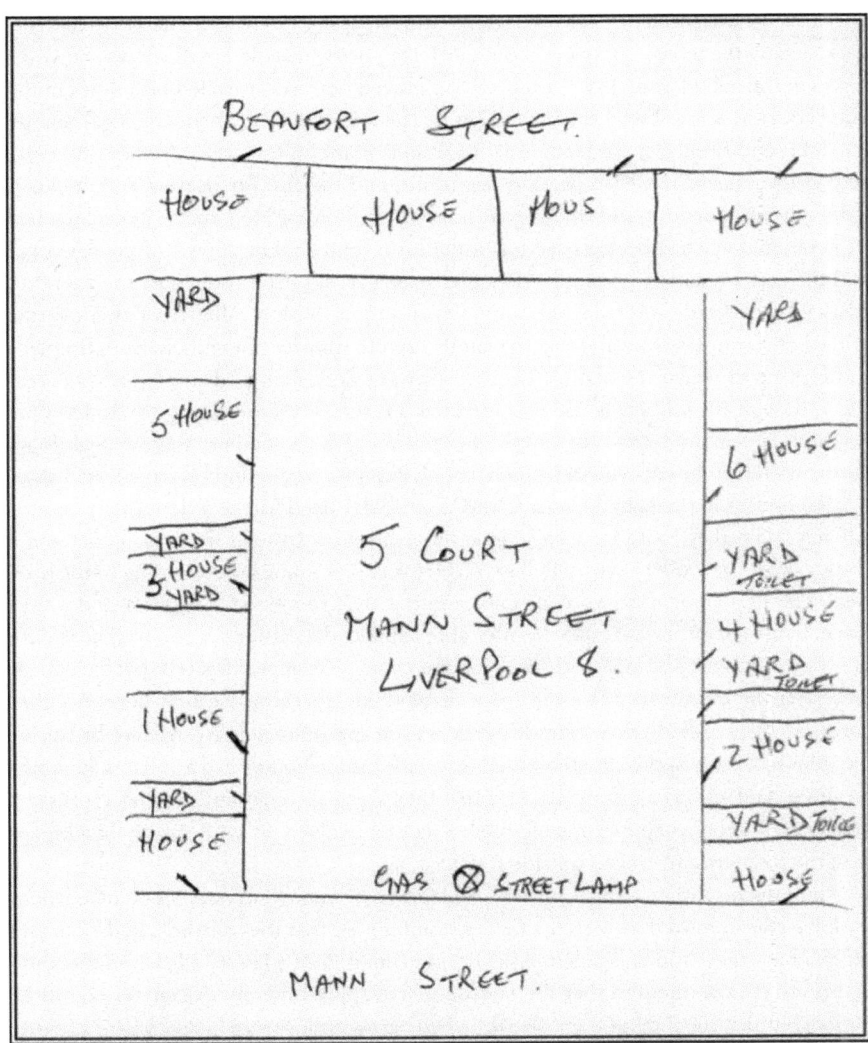

Figure 5.2. Plan of the Mann Street court, Liverpool, by KS. Courtesy of National Museums Liverpool, Museum of Liverpool collection, used with permission.

with the front houses classed as being part of the court. Houses that had cellars rarely used them as they were either flooded or full of rubbish. Some had a single ground floor living room and some had two downstairs rooms, one for living and one used as a kitchen. Each room had one window, sash style, at the front of the house, no windows to the rear, and one narrator, RL, recalled the glass being replaced with opaque industrial glass following a number of Blitz blasts, which he described as distorting the view. There were no standard fixtures and fittings, and typically no internal sink or cupboards. The houses did not have electricity until at least 1956. KS recalled the residents approaching the power company about electricity being installed in the court, however it was not installed until 1957, after KS had moved out. MM recalled his house, in the same court as KS, as being the first to get it. The houses had a gas cooker, a gas mantle for light, and fireplaces for traditional coal fires. Some of the houses did not have gas and so used paraffin oil lamps, one per room, and the fire for heating and cooking, although each narrator said the gas was not switched on for long due to being attached to a coin meter. The fire was used for both heating and cooking. Some of the narrators said the court houses were cold, particularly the garret (attic) room and one narrator, AR, said their house was cold and damp. One narrator, MM, recalled frost on the inside of the bedroom windows and that the family used to transfer hot embers from fireplace to fireplace to warm the rooms. The houses were described as damp by other narrators although BR said his house was warm as a result of the fire being lit all day. One narrator, AM, commented the houses were "drab." RL remembers the internal doors having metal latches instead of handles, much like you would find on an external gate.

The houses in the court where KS, MM, and MH lived had two downstairs rooms, a living room that could be accessed via the front door straight from the court and a "little parlor" or scullery with a Belfast-style sink and draining board leading to the back yard. The first floor had two bedrooms and the attic room had a window and a fireplace. Some narrators were able to offer approximate dimensions of rooms. Those with one room downstairs, AM and AR, said the room was approximately twelve square meters at the most with the same space divided into three on the first floor. Another narrator, RL, recalled two rooms downstairs each approximately twelve feet by twelve feet plus a hallway approximately three feet wide. Some houses had a cellar, which was not used, and all had a garret. RL said that they were all very similar in his locality— high ceilings, rooms approximately twelve feet by twelve feet with the kitchen bigger than the living room, and an outside toilet.

All of the narrators, except RL who was fortunate enough to have his own bedroom until his cousin moved in with the family, commented that they shared a bedroom and often a bed, they "top and tailed it," as KS explained. MM's family all shared the same bedroom. AS commented that the bedroom was approximately five meters by three meters but that she did not mind sharing a bed because they were lucky to have a house. This was either because there was only one room upstairs or because there was only enough room for one bed in the upstairs rooms. AM and AR said that two of their siblings slept in the garret when overcrowding became an issue. Others, for example BR, said they did not use the garret, preferring to send female members of the family to sleep with relatives in the nearby landings, another form of working-class housing. AR commented that they were lucky to only have four children in the family as some had ten. BR said he regularly ate his dinner sitting on the stairs as the room was not large enough to fit the family table. BR commented he did not spend much time in the house as there was little room. He also mentioned that court residents were more prone to having accidents due to the houses being so small.

Toilets were situated in external brick blocks at the top end of the court. The toilet block may have been split into several units with a shared wooden platform with a hole through for each unit. Narrators recalled they could look through the hole and see the channel of excreta from the other units. Some families were fortunate enough to have their own toilet, such as KS, AR, and AM, however most shared with neighbors in the court. BR recalled two toilet units being used by eight households whereas AR recalls one toilet unit being used by seven or eight households.

Wider Neighborhood and Community

In the court itself were other shared facilities including a water pump, or tap, and an ashbin. The outside tap was often the only source of water, although one narrator had a cold water tap inside their court house. Another recalled the water at the outside tap only being available for parts of the day and mentioned occasions where she was scolded by adults for wasting water or reminded that water from the pump was not intended for resident use but was for the cart horses. Laundry was carried out using a bowl or several bowls. Residents bathed using boiled water in the sink with a bar of soap to their wash hands and face and used a tin bath once a week for a full bath, or they visited the local public baths. KS recalls using his grandparents washing facilities at their home, which was not a court house. Narrators recalled that limited access to hot water led to neighborliness and that their neighbors would pass along used washing water to be reused. It was mentioned that despite the limited nature of washing facilities the court and houses were scrubbed so clean by residents you could eat off the surface. AS was keen to point out that there was no internal hot water and no bath. This was her favorite thing about moving from a court house into a landings style property. Flooring was flag tile paving, sometimes with linoleum covering or oilcloth, sometimes with no covering particularly in the upstairs rooms, which had wooden floorboards. Some houses had wallpaper, some were wallpapered with newspaper and flour paste, and some were bare horsehair and plaster, occasionally whitewash/lime painted along with the furniture. The woodwork was painted with a dark green/brown tar paint described by KS as being smelly.

It is possible from the testimonies to identify a less built-up residential neighborhood than described in the historical written records as the Blitz and slum clearance program helped to remove back houses and create gaps where center houses once stood. AR said the court was just wide enough for a Shire horse to enter. Narrators described the court itself as paved with flagstones, although AR and AM's landlord had concreted over the paving flags, this memory a result of a young AR slipping on the concrete and hurting herself. Shared facilities in the court include features previously discussed: toilets, water pump and ashcan. There was also one gas lamp for light, although NS recalled the court on her street was "dark" but could not say exactly why this was. In some courts, center houses were demolished to create space to improve the living conditions for residents or to build alternative residences such as landings.

BR said the space created by removing center houses in his court was used for washing and drying laundry or for placing mangles. RL said he lived in a court house but not in a court as all the back houses had been demolished. Others thought their area was more built up when the landings or gardens were built, such as Caryl Gardens. Narrators recalled they did not play in their own court as it was small; AR recalled the ladies of the court sitting in the court to play bingo. Many played in the ruins of the sites of bombings. Some games, such as football, were popular.

Narrators could describe the wider neighborhood that, due to being in the city center, was made up of warehouses and shops. Testimonies were able to provide details on services available and offered to court residents such as that of a "knocker upper," a gentleman who would act as an alarm clock and knock on your bedroom window to wake you. A local bakehouse was a useful service on a Sunday, advised AR, as one could take a pot of prepared meat and vegetables to the bakehouse for it to be cooked so the family could have a hot meal. For residents in North Liverpool Great Homer Street was a location of a large market where individual stalls could compete for custom. RL said it was a fantastic shopping center, better than our modern supermarkets. AR recalls Great Homer Street for another reason—the courts in the area were filthy. There were public baths available and shops where you could buy lime for whitewashing walls. The butchers and bakers were also shops that a number of narrators could recall. The community spirit of the court was recalled by many of the narrators. KS described his court as being "like a clan" and AR recalled, "The people were lovely. We were all together, it's not like now, you know. You don't even know your next-door neighbors now or anything. People were nice, people were interested in people . . . everyone knew everyone's name . . . I loved the people."

The demolition of court housing and the relocation of residents appears in the memories of former residents. When asked about how the family felt about the courts being condemned and families being relocated KS replied, "Pleased! I think my mum was pleased, yeah . . . lovely house with a bathroom and garden—wow!" When asked about her feelings about the courts being demolished, AR commented, "They put people out in Kirkby . . . out in the sticks. There was no shops . . . there was no comradeship between old neighbors. And you were stuck. People went out of their mind. It was absolutely a disaster and all people wanted was to come back to the city where it was bustling and vibrant and your neighbors was neighbors, and everyone knew one another . . . so my mam wouldn't go there." RL quoted something his grandmother frequently said when discussing the relocation of court residents, "you can't replant old trees."

Supplementary Evidence of Court Housing

Long before the oral history interview, RL had been researching and making sense of his own life history by engaging in recalling, processing, and recording his memories in a creative written form. These writings particularly focus on his childhood using the form of poetry and a diary style memoir, which falls into the categories of nostalgia, reminiscence, and family history research. RL's creative writing, approximately 10,000 words of poetry and autobiography, can also help to construct a description of court housing. Creative writing is designed to suit a purpose, for example, words used in RL's poems may have been chosen to fit within the context and style of the poem rather than as a reflection of the truth. The intention of creative writing is to tell a story not to provide a clinical account. RL choose to write his story because "My purpose is to recall what things were like for ordinary people like me who grew up in Liverpool during the early part of the twentieth century" (RL 2014: 1). Unlike the oral history interview RL had time to consider the words he used and the memories he shared and had time to shape and amend the writing to enable it to be in a readable format. There is the potential this written testimony influenced the memories shared during the oral history interview. By already revisiting these memories, it shaped and focused them and affected what was recalled during the oral history interview. RL focused on these memories because they had already been shared as his version of the past. However, it is possible the written memoir serves as a more focused transcript for the oral history interview, a written version to factcheck against. Through the memoir a more detailed and a clearer description of court housing can be constructed.

RL commented that he had lived in one of the worst and poorest slum districts in Liverpool in one of the two remaining court houses on Prince Edwin Street as the back houses of the court had already been demolished. From his written memoir it is possible to construct a description of court housing that complements the account provided during the oral history interview. The house was three stories high with a cellar that the family did not use due to it being flooded. The ground floor was two to three feet higher than street level and was accessed by several steps from the street. On this floor were two "basic"-sized rooms, a parlor and a kitchen, a "long lobby" and stairs to the first floor. The first floor had bedrooms and a landing with a spiral staircase to a garret room that the family did not use. Each bedroom had its own fireplace. The floor covering downstairs was lino with wooden boards upstairs and on the stairs. Each room had large windows with shutters although the family used blinds instead. There was a coal fire used for cooking and heating as it was kept on a low heat constantly and was raised according to need. The family used oil lamps and candles for light. RL said he was programmed to look after his belongings and not wish for new, which made him value what he had "there were always others worse off than us" (RL 2014: 13). There was a brick toilet unit with two separate doors leading to two toilets—a wooden bench seat with a hole in the center and a channel below. The toilets had previously been used by all houses in the court but was now only used by them. RL described this as "lucky." They used cold water daily to wash their hands and faces and boiled water over the fire to fill the galvanized tin bath once a week.

The family moved into the house and rented only part of it initially. The main occupant was an elderly lady who died when RL was two. RL lived in the house with his parents, sister and cousin. He wrote "so much light in the street unlike inside our house, it was so dark and dreary in there" (RL 2014: 7). The court was concrete and quite large due to the absence of the back houses. RL described this as a "holler" with rubble where the courts had been. He and friends used the space to play football. He wrote that the street was not very clean but that the women would keep the front of their house clean by scrubbing the pavement and steps in front of their houses. "I wasn't aware of any danger or of the condition of the street which must have been in a bad way with dirt and rubbish lying around because we were in one of the worst slum areas" (RL 2014: 7). It must be noted that this statement sounds suspiciously like it has been influenced by the mainstream narrative of court housing as a slum. RL recalled a small park nearby with swings and a childhood game of "wishful thinking" where they would gather outside of sweet shop, Crane's, and play a choice game of who would have each type of sweet, despite not having the means to purchase anything. Maggie Saxons was the local chandlers where the family would buy paraffin oil and candles. It also provided used comic books. RL commented on the neighborhood, "We were living in a community where everyone seemed to play a part. There always seemed to be someone with knowledge or ability to cater for most problems that came our way and the help came without asking" (RL 2014: 14).

It is possible to use the photographs KS and MM provided to construct a factual description of court housing. The court is an open style with a gas lamp at the street opening, is brick built with stone mantles, and is at least two stories high. The court is paved with flagstones with a gulley down the center, an ashbin on the rear wall of the court, and the rear of the court abuts a building with windows. The ground floors of the houses are whitewashed and the window frames on the houses are painted both black and white. There appears to be private access for each house to a side or rear yard, possibly home to a toilet block. The court appears to be clean and clear of rubbish. The photographs were taken of a street party to celebrate the coronation and depict a large table running down the center of the court with a tablecloth, flags and bunting. KS provided a sketch of the Mann Street court during his oral history interview. The sketch closely resembles the photograph but is intriguing as, although not to scale, KS gave prominence to the court yard, which is drawn much larger than the houses. Perhaps experiencing produced memories focused on the space where he spent the most time. The oral history testimonies also provided memories of other relevant themes, not within my housing experience criteria but important as themes that the combined approach can better interpret such as poverty and attitudes.

These memories and opinions give a richer understanding of what life was like in a court house and in court housing plus the community they were a part of as children. It is in these memories we can begin to find evidence of attachment to place, place identity and grief, community spirit, a lively and thriving community, relative poverty, survival, comradery, and nostalgia. This oral history evidence introduces an alternative, early to mid-twentieth century view of court housing.

Oral History and the Potential to Challenge
Existing Historical Narratives

Liverpool court housing provides a unique opportunity with which to investigate the value that memories contribute to and challenge the accepted historical view of this type of housing due to an absence of physical archaeological investigation. During the nineteenth century, cellars were commonly rented out as a separate dwelling, providing a self-contained dwelling space for a family. In the twentieth century, when cellar dwellings were abolished, the residents of courts had the liberty not to use the space as the oral history testimony suggested. The Blitz changed the Liverpool landscape and was responsible for the demolition of court houses on Saltney Street, home to BR. Once the spaces between the extant houses was cleared, the residents made use of the space for laundry, but this is likely to have improved ventilation in the courts also. The oral history testimony suggested the houses and outdoor spaces were used differently over time, seemingly in a more humane way than their nineteenth-century counterparts.

Narrators contributed a range of perspectives. For example, one narrator was the lone, negative voice and spoke out against court housing, citing reasons why this form of housing was responsible for her tough childhood and questioned why anyone would be nostalgic for that way of life. Two things that are unique about this narrator is that she was the head of the household while her parents were unavailable, "We say 'God, do you remember the courts?' We've come a long way since the courts." AR was the only narrator who commented she did not feel like she had a childhood because when her mother was hospitalized, for reasons AR attributed to the poor conditions of the court house, she was responsible for taking care of the younger children in the family. Curiously, her brother AM could not recall any "bad times" during his childhood. AR assumed the role of mother to the younger siblings, and it is this responsibility that makes her narration less like a memory formed during childhood and more like a review of her life through the lens of an adult. She is also the only narrator no longer living in Merseyside, living abroad in a hot climate in a large house with a swimming pool. It is this extreme juxtaposition of housing and lifestyles that make her contribution unique.

A particularly successful aspect of the oral history project was the photographs of the Mann Street court shared by KS and MM. The photographs were taken during a street party to celebrate the coronation of Queen Elizabeth in June 1953. They depict the children seated at a long table that runs down the center of the court, with adults standing behind the children and the court houses surrounding. The photographs are taken from both ends of the court and so show the court open to the street and the ash-bin. These, plus the sketch of the court, provide a unique insight into the housing experience as they are rare examples of photographs taken by residents of court housing rather than by health inspectors with an agenda to document the courts in preparation for their clearance. These written accounts and photographs sharply contrast with our own understanding of a home making it very easy to fall into the trap of remembering and memorializing the mid-nineteenth century to mid-twentieth century working-class housing experience as a Monty Python "Four Yorkshiremen" style parody.[1] Many of the second-hand memories, or oral tradition, fall into what could be categorized as dark nostalgia, in the sense that, much like dark tourism (White and Frew 2013; Cai et al. 2021) and dark heritage (McAtackney 2014), there is a public curiosity for landscapes of suffering. "Dark tourism" is a term coined in 1996 by John J. Lennon and Malcolm Foley (1996) to describe the practice of visiting places associated with death and suffering such as battlefields, prisons, and places of natural disasters. The term "dark heritage" followed and is broader in that it includes a focus on understanding the cultural practice of why people engage with landscapes of trauma (Thomas 2019). It worth noting that the term "dark" can be problematic due to its association with racism and perhaps a more appropriate term to use is "thanotourism" (Seaton 1996), although this is much narrower in scope, or alternatively traumatic heritage, taboo heritage, or difficult pasts. Those who did not experience life in a court can often be the most vocal when discussing what it was like and here the official historical narrative is accepted, shared, and perpetuated. Those who were not part of the community of courts appear to view this form of housing and way of life with nostalgia, but a rather dark nostalgia, a nostalgia for a difficult past they did not themselves experience. For example, "It's a wonder half of those courts didn't fall down before they were cleared. Different world that was. You had to have proper Scouse nouse to get through those times" (Goldenface 2007; Yo Liverpool). Pablo42 continues the theme in the online forum, "Amazing that people lived like that. You wonder what gave them the strength to go on" (2009, Yo Liverpool). With the decline of Liverpool as a result of a lack of public funding in the 1980s, it is worth considering this destructive end to a once prevalent housing type may have left its mark on the memory of Liverpool residents. The courts are described by AR as "worse than slums" and that people in the courts "lived like rats." However, narrators shared conflicting memories and opinions that suggested their housing experience was on the whole a positive one. AR described the court as "close-knit" where everyone knew each other's name and shared mixed feelings of relief and sadness over that way of life being lost forever. "They were lovely days, you know. I wouldn't change them for the world. I wouldn't change anything. We can appreciate what we've got and it's a way of life that's gone forever, you know? There's nothing to cry about, not really."

The significance of public inclusion becomes evident with the examples from within the oral histories that provide instances of the housing experience that cannot be found in the archaeological record or documentary sources. Memories that display traits of an attachment to place or grief for a lost home, for example,

> I have this little dream now and again . . . our house is still standing there, and I'm walking over rubble, you know, up the court, and I go in the house . . . there's an armchair there, and the old steel fireplace, it's got the oven and the range and everything, and I'm standing looking round and I see a

little flicker in the ash like that, and I goes over and the pokers there so I just give it a little nudge and the next thing the fire lights up! So I just sit down there and look at the fire and then puff—it just disappears! It's like, you know, you were happy there so that dream is like, you get that little flicker of light and when you touch it, it all becomes lovely and warm again, so you're . . . . home. (MM)

MM left his court house to serve in the military and returned to rubble as the courts had been demolished. His dream, above, displays an attachment to his former home and displacement grief, a longing for home. RL seemed to summarize the attachment to place well.

It's just my opinion, like, but . . . it's about people not places. And the more people, everybody was packed in, and you learnt something from everybody, so all those people you could virtually say that it was a mass of opinions and skills, helping you to judge things. That was the good part of living in a packed area where people found it hard to live. And they found out how to get on with one another, put all the things that they worry about went out the window, the first thing they wanted to do was survive so that meant getting on with one another.

It must be noted that these memories were formed as young children rather than literally from birth. The concept of memories being formed through the eyes of childhood is intriguing. That any aspects of the house were remembered, particularly in such detail, is impressive given the more exciting, carefree experiences children tend to have. Many of the memories shared by the narrators contrast with the documentary opinions from the previous century. "The sight of these children as they huddled together in this smokey, miserable house, was distressing. What will be the remembrance of home be to them in future years?" (Shimmin 1864: 14). Shimmin (1864) found it hard to imagine what could improve the dreary life that children of courts were doomed to live whereas some of the narrators noted how, as children, they were always outside playing. BR shared, "As children, you know we had a great childhood . . . .'cuz we were all the same. We had no expectations 'cuz we got what we could afford." AR felt similarly, "How can you say they are lovely memories?! It's 'cuz you were happy and it's hard to be happy." An opinion in sharp contrast to the nineteenth-century accounts from non-residents of court housing.

This example of the combined approach has shown the potential for oral history to reinvestigate and challenge the official historical record. The potential for oral history to aid the development of an archaeological approach to the excavation of court housing is exciting. The oral histories are valuable because they provide an alternative view of court housing that both confirm and challenge the existing historical record. For example, Colin G. Pooley and Sandra Irish (1994) comment that Liverpool was facing an acute housing shortage in the 1920s citing the 1925 Medical Officer Health Report that estimated a shortfall of 18,000 houses and noted that overcrowding continued to be severe. However, only two interviews revealed signs of overcrowding. One family, then of three, moved into a property that had a single older lady already residing in it. AR recalled people fearful when the inspector called and that parents would hide children in neighboring properties so not to draw attention to the number of children residing in the house. So, overcrowding existed, but in many forms and with different experiences.

Although some of the testimonies showed hints of nostalgia and reminiscence it does not necessarily mean these memories are false or unreliable. However, one should question and determine how much of an effect popular culture has had on the narrators and the lens through which they recalled the housing experience. Liverpool is a particularly nostalgic place, from Facebook sites, to walking tours and Beatlemania. Heritage and culture in Liverpool are geared toward the nostalgia of being Scouse and being proud of the city and its accomplishments. Facebook groups are a clear example of how past communities and geographical neighborhoods can reconnect to reminisce about times and people gone by, and Liverpool has several prominent groups. The *Liverpool Echo* newspaper has a regular column for times gone by, and there is an active Liverpool History Society. It must be acknowledged, however, that memories supporting popular culture, or each other, or that are quaint, are not necessarily untrue. Despite the wider public displaying a nostalgia for times of slum housing in the city, the narrators provide accounts that are remarkably average, rich in detail of the housing experience, but with no overwhelming nostalgia or condemnation of court housing as slums.

Conclusion

The combined approach of archaeology and oral history provides physical evidence and firsthand accounts with which to investigate the housing experience beyond the official historical narrative about working-class housing. It allows the investigation, revision and challenge of the mainstream narrative. Although all sources of evidence, and disciplinary approaches, have their challenges, they are all incomplete in some way, together they can contribute to our understanding of an area, a housing form, and the housing experience of the residents. The public, as experts through oral history, can potentially make valuable contributions to the interpretation of a site and the surrounding landscape and so sites of any period would work as an arena for memory recall. Any place-based project could apply the combined approach since place serves as a nexus for both oral history and archaeology. Indeed, it is the places where people spent their time and established place-based bonds that perhaps work best. Currently, within UK archaeology, oral history is rarely applied and tends to only be included on funded projects, those with the objective to engage the public rather than on commercial archaeological projects (for example, Casella and Croucher 2010; Moshenska 2007), and then they tend not to follow a framework.

The primary advantage of looking at the housing experience using the combined approach is that it can inform us about how a place was experienced, provide firsthand testimony to interpret the archaeology, and enable former residents to reclaim the narrative. In Liverpool, despite a lack of excavated remains and limited extant remains, the oral history reveals this once prevalent housing type provides information to design an archaeology brief, should the opportunity to conduct a building recording or excavation occur, and the testimony is preserved for future use.

Elements of the housing experience appear in documents, archaeology, and oral history but only the community aspects, the lived experience and place-based narratives appear in oral history. Combined, they can provide a full picture of the housing experience, yet it is the oral history that can humanize the archaeological remains. A study by Wendy E. Beck and Margaret Somerville (2005) provides a framework to assess the combined approach proposing "conversations" between the disciplines that involve co-opting, intersecting, parallel, complementary, and contradictory conversations where both sources are considered to have equal importance. The possibilities of the combined approach go beyond the housing experience to slum studies, place attachment, memory studies, and developing an anthropological approach to studying the recent past in the UK. The combined approach as practiced elsewhere, particularly in the archaeology of Indigenous Peoples, could be more widely applied in the UK. There is huge potential to develop a model to apply to UK archaeology to facilitate the inclusion of oral history.

While archaeology in the UK usually follows a standardized methodological approach, this is not the case with oral history, even though best practice guidance is available from the Oral History Society (2017). The rise in popularity of oral history collected by community-led heritage projects suggests a more formal framework for the collection, processing, curation, and storage of oral history could be beneficial. A more formalized and standardized framework could result in oral history interviews that are of similar quality, are recorded and processed in the same manner, and are stored and accessible in the same way. A universal framework could be used by archaeologists on site in the same way the Museum of London Archaeology (1990) manual is used. The concept of a site is also useful for enabling archaeology and oral history to interact (Beck and Somerville 2005). Moshenska's (2007) pioneering site-based approach to oral history as community archaeology in the UK provides the foundation to develop a framework for UK archaeologists to use to include oral history in their work. Ideally, the oral history element of an archaeology project would be developed during the project design phase rather than as an afterthought (Morton, Walker, and Gardner 2008) to ensure the public can shape the research agenda and methodologies.

Oral history, like archaeology, is finite and, furthermore, is only available for a limited time. Both archaeology and the practice of oral history recover evidence that will eventually be lost by recording it. The primary reason for conducting oral history within UK archaeology should be to uncover evidence, memories, and prevent them from being lost. However, the meaningful inclusion of the public in archaeology as contributors of equal significance to the professional archaeologists should be considered essential.

Acknowledgments

I owe a depth of gratitude to Dr. Elizabeth Stewart for her collaboration on the *Our Humble Abodes* project and my employer at the time National Museums Liverpool (Museum of Liverpool) for their generous support of the project. Thanks especially go to the narrators and their families for kindly sharing their memories with such warmth and humor.

Kerry Massheder-Rigby is an Honorary Research Fellow at the University of Liverpool (Archaeology, Classics and Egyptology) and a Policy Advisor for the Department for Education. Her research has focussed on the inclusion of the community as collaborators in the archaeological process in the form of oral history. She has over fifteen years experience in commercial and community archaeology, oral history, and audience engagement in culture. Kerry is the Treasurer of the Society for Post-Medieval Archaeology.

Notes

1. A series of comedy sketches called 'the good old days' that parody nostalgic conversations amongst friends. In the sketches, four Yorkshiremen, played by Monty Python writers/actors, share memories of their impoverished childhoods, with each story becoming increasingly exaggerated and eventually improbable.

References

Adams, William Hampton. 1984. "Ethnoarchaeology as a Merging of Historical Archaeology and Oral History." *North American Archaeologist* 4(4): 293–305.

Ashton, Thomas Southcliffe. 1954. "The Treatment of Capitalism by Historians." In *Capitalism and the Historians*, ed. F. A. Hayek, 32–52. London: Routledge & Kegan Paul.

Ashworth, William. 1951. "British Industrial Villages in the Nineteenth Century." *Economic History Review* 3: 378–87.

Australian Archaeological Association. 2022. Code of Ethics. Retrieved 3 April 2022 from http://australianarchaeology.com/governance/code-of-ethics/.

Barile, Kerri, and Jamie Brandon. 2004. "Introduction." In *Household Chores and Household Choices: Theorizing the Domestic Sphere in Historical Archaeology*, ed. K. Barile and J. Brandon, 1–14. Tuscaloosa: University of Alabama Press.

Basso, Keith. 1996. *Wisdom Sits in Places: Landscape and Language among the Western Apache*. Albuquerque: University of New Mexico Press.

Beaudry, Mary C. 1995. "Scratching the Surface: Seven Seasons Digging at the Spencer-Pierce-Little Farm, Newbury, Massachusetts." *Northeast Historical Archaeology* 24: 19–50.

———. 2004. "Doing the Housework: New Approaches to the Archaeology of Households." In *Household Chores and Household Choices: Theorizing the Domestic Sphere in Historical Archaeology*, ed. K. S. Barile and J. C. Brandon, 254–62. Tuscaloosa: The University of Alabama Press.

————. 2015. "Households beyond the House: On the Archaeology and Materiality of Historical Households." In *Beyond the Walls: New Perspectives on the Archaeology of Historical Households*, K. R. Fogle J. A. Nyman, and M. C. Beaudry, 1–22. Gainesville: University Press of Florida.

Beck, Wendy, and Margaret Somerville. 2005. "Conversations between Disciplines: Historical Archaeology and Oral History at Yarrawarra." *World Archaeology* 37(3): 468–83.

Belford, Paul. 2003. "Forging Ahead in Coalbrookdale: Historical Archaeology at the Upper Forge." *Industrial Archaeology Review* 25(1): 59–62.

Bennett, Kurt, and Madeline Fowler. 2017. "'In My Memory, It Says Rarawa!': Abandoned Vessel Material Salvage and Reuse at Rangitoto Island, Aotearoa/New Zealand." *International Journal of Historical Archaeology* 21(1): 27–48.

Booth, Charles. 1889. *Life and Labour of the People*. London.

Booth, William. 1890. *In Darkest England and the Way Out*. Oxford: Diggory Press. Reprinted in 2006.

Burnett, John. 1978. *A Social History of Housing 1815–1970*. London: Methuen.

Byrne, Denis. 2003. "The Ethos of Return: Erasure and Reinstatement of Aboriginal Visibility in the Australian Landscape." *Historical Archaeology* 37(1): 73–86.

Cai, Yanting, Gang Li, Chang Liu, and Long Wen. 2021. "Post-pandemic Dark Tourism in Former Epicentres." *Tourism Economics* (August): 1–18.

Canadian Archaeological Association. 2022a. Principles of Ethical Conduct. Retrieved 7 April 2022 from https://canadianarchaeology.com/caa/about/ethics/principles-ethical-conduct.

————. 2022b. CAA Objectives. Retrieved 7 April 2022 from https://canadianarchaeology.com/caa/about/objectives.

Casella, Eleanor C. 2012. "'That's Just a Family Thing, You Know': Memory, Community Kinship, and Social Belonging in the Hagg Cottages of Cheshire, North-West England." *International Journal of Historical Archaeology* 16(2): 284–99.

Casella, Eleanor C., and Sarah Croucher. 2010. *The Alderley Sandhills Project: An Archaeology of Community Life in (Post-)Industrial England*. Manchester: Manchester University Press.

Chapman, Stanley David. 1971. "Introduction." In *The History of Working Class Housing: A Symposium*, ed. S. D. Chapman, 9–12. London: David and Charles Newton Abbot.

Connelly, Peter A. 2011. "Flush with the Past: An Insight into Late Nineteenth-Century Hungate and Its Role in Providing a Better Understanding of Urban Development." *International Journal of Historical Archaeology* 15(4): 607–16.

————. 2018. "When Hungate was taken down" Solid and Ephemeral: The Dichotomy at the Heart of the Archaeology of Clearance in 1930s York." Society for Historical Archaeology, New Orleans, 4 January 2018. New Orleans, LA: Society for Historical Archaeology.

Connerton, Paul. 2008. "Seven Types of Forgetting." *Memory Studies* 1(1): 59–71.

Crosby, Tony, Adam Garwood, and Adrian Corder-Birch. 2008. "Workers Housing in Essex." *Industrial Archaeology Review* 30(2): 101–25.

Daunton, Martin J. 1990. "Introduction." In *Housing the Working-Class, 1850–1914: A Comparative Perspective*, ed. M. J. Daunton, 1–31. Leicester: Leicester University Press.

Dewhurst, Lucy. 1989. "Housing the Workforce: A Case Study of West Yorkshire, 1750–1900." *Industrial Archaeology Review* 11(2): 117–35.

Douglass, John, and Nancy Gonlin, eds. 2012. *Ancient Households of the Americas: Conceptualizing What Households Do*. Boulder: University Press of Colorado.

Dwyer, Emma. 2014. "Historical and Contemporary Archaeologies of Social Housing: Changing Experiences of the Modern and New, 1870–Present." Ph.D. dissertation. Leicester: University of Leicester.

Engels, Friedrich. 1845. *The Condition of the Working Class in England*. London: Penguin. Reprinted in 2009.

English Heritage. 2008. *Conservation Principles, Policies and Guidance for the Sustainable Management of the Historic Environment*. London: English Heritage.

European Association of Archaeologists. 2009. EAA Codes and Principles. Retrieved 7 April 2022 from https://www.e-a-a.org/EAA/About/EAA_Codes/EAA/Navigation_About/EAA_Codes .aspx.

Evans, Ewart. 1956. *Ask the Fellows Who Cut the Hay*. London: Faber and Faber.

Flinn, Michael W. 1965. "Introduction." In *Report of the Sanitary Condition of the Labouring Population of Great Britain*, ed. E. Chadwick, 1–73. Edinburgh: Edinburgh University Press.

Gaskell, Peter. 1833. *The Manufacturing Population of England, Its Moral, Social and Physical Conditions*. London: Baldwin and Cradock.

Gaskell, S. Martin. 1990. *Slums*. Leicester: Leicester University Press.

Gauldie, Enid. 1974. *Cruel Habitations: A History of Working-Class Housing 1780–1918*. London: George Allen and Unwin Ltd.

Goldenface. 2007. Yo Liverpool. Retrieved 5 April 2022 from https://www.yoliverpool.com/fo rum/showthread.php?4273-Pre-Slum-Clearances-Housing-Images.

Gould, D. Rae., Holly Herbster, Heather Law Pezzarossi, and Stephen. A. Mrozowski. 2020. *Historical Archaeology and Indigenous Collaboration: Discovering Histories that Have Futures*. Gainesville: University Press of Florida.

Handler, Richard, and Eric Gable. 1997. *The New History in an Old Museum: Creating the Past at Colonial Williamsburg*. Durham, NC: Duke University Press.

Hayton, Sandra. 1998. The Archetypal Irish Cellar Dweller." *Manchester Region History Review* 12: 66–77.

Herrmann, Edward W., Rebecca A. Nathan, Matthew J. Rowe, and Timothy P. McCleary. 2017. "*Bacheeishdiio* (Place Where Men Pack Meat)." *American Antiquity* 82(1): 151–67.

Hiner, Hillary. 2018. "Putting the Archive in Movement." In *Beyond Women's Words: Feminisms and the Practices of Oral History in the Twenty-First Century*, ed. Katrina Srigley, Stacey Zembrzycki, and Franca Iacovetta, 204–16. London: Routledge.

Huyssen, Andreas. 2011. "International Human Rights and the Politics of Memory: Limits and Challenges." *Criticism* 53(4): 607–24.

Janovicek, Nancy. 2013. "'If You'd Told Me You Wanted to Talk about the '60's, I Wouldn't Have Called You Back': Reflections of Collective Memory and the Practice of Oral History." In *Oral History off the Record: Towards an Ethnography of Practice*, ed. Anna Sheftel and Stacey Zembrzycki, 185–99. New York: Palgrave Macmillan.

Jones, Sian. 2012. "'Thrown like Chaff in the Wind': Excavation, Memory and the Negotiation of Loss in the Scottish Highlands." *International Journal of Historical Archaeology* 16(2): 346–66.

Jones, Sian, and Lynette Russell. 2012. "Archaeology, Memory and Oral Tradition: An Introduction." *International Journal of Historical Archaeology* 16(2): 267–83.

Joyce, Rosemary A., and Susan D. Gillespie, eds. 2000. *Beyond Kinships: Social and Material Reproduction in House Societies*. Philadelphia: University of Pennsylvania Press.

Kasabova, Anita. 2008. "Memory, Memorials and Commemoration." *History and Theory* 47(3): 331–50.

Kellner, Douglas. 1989. *Critical Theory, Marxism, and Modernity*. Baltimore, MD: Johns Hopkins University Press.

King, Julia. 2006. "Household Archaeology, Identities, and Biographies." In *The Cambridge Companion to Historical Archaeology*, ed. Dan Hicks and Mary Beaudry. Cambridge: Cambridge University Press, 293–314.

Larsen, S. Erik. 2011. "Memory Constructions and Their Limits." *Orbis Litterarum* 66(6): 448–67.

Leccardi, Carmen. 2016. "Memory, Time and Responsibility." In *Routledge International Handbook of Memory Studies*, ed. A. L. Tota and T. Hagan, 109–20. London: Routledge.

Lee, HyunKyung. 2019. *"Difficult Heritage" in Nation Building*. Cham: Palgrave Macmillan.

Lefebvre, Henri. 1971. *Everyday Life in the Modern World*. London: Athlone Press. Reprinted in 2000.

Lennon, John J., and Malcolm Foley. 1996. "JFK and Dark Tourism: A Fascination with Assassination." *International Journal of Heritage Studies* 2(4): 198–211.

Leone, Mark P. 2020. "Critical Theory." In *The Routledge Handbook of Global Historical Archaeology*, ed. C. E. Orser, Jr., A. Zarankin, P. Funari, S. Lawrence, and J. Symonds, 289–95. London: Routledge.

Leone, Mark P., Parker B. Potter, Jr., and Paul A. Shackel. 1987. "Towards a Critical Archaeology." *Current Anthropology* 28(3): 283–302.

Lilley, Suzanne. 2015. "Housing the Industrious Workforce." Theoretical Archaeology Group Conference, Bradford, UK, 14–16 December. Retrieved 11 April 2022 from https://www.antiquity.ac.uk/sites/default/files/downloads/tag/TAG_2015_abstracts.pdf.

Little, Barbara J., ed. 1992. *Text-Aided Archaeology*. Boca Raton, FL: CRC Press.

London, Jack. 1903. *The People of the Abyss*. London: Hesperus Press Limited. Reprinted in 2013.

Lowenthal, David. 2015. *The Past Is a Foreign Country-Revisited*. Cambridge: Cambridge University Press.

L, R. 2014. Untitled memoir and collection of poems. Unpublished.

Lyons, Natasha, Peter Dawson, Matthew Walls, Donald Uluadluak, Louis Angalik, Mark Kalluak, Philip Kigusiutuak, Luke Kiniski, Joe Karetak, and Luke Suluk. 2010. "Person, Place, Memory, Thing: How Inuit Elders Are Informing Archaeological Practice in the Canadian North." *Canadian Journal of Archaeology* 34(1): 1–31.

Marshall, Yvonne. 2002. "What Is Community Archaeology?" *World Archaeology* 34(2): 211–19.

Massheder-Rigby, Kerry. 2019. "The Housing Experience of the Working Classes 1790–1970: The Potential of the Combined Approach of Archaeology, the Historical Record and Oral History." Ph.D. dissertation. Liverpool: University of Liverpool.

———. 2020. "Oral History." In *The Routledge Handbook of Global Historical Archaeology*, ed. Charles E. Orser, Jr., Andres Zarankin, Pendro Funari, Susan Lawrence, and James Symonds, 478–95. London: Routledge.

Mason, Ronald. 2000. "Archaeology and Native North American Traditions." *American Antiquity* 65(2): 239–66.

Mayhew, Henry. 1851. *London Labour and the London Poor*. Hertfordshire: Wordsworth Classics of World Literature. Reprinted in 2008.

Mayne, Alan. 2011. "Beyond Metrics: Reappraising York's Hungate 'Slum.'" *International Journal of Historical Archaeology* 15(4): 553–62.

Mayne, Alan, and Susan Lawrence. 1999. "Ethnographies of Place: A New Urban Research Agenda." *Urban History* 26(3): 325–48.

Mayne, Alan, and Tim Murray, eds. 2001. *The Archaeology of Urban Landscapes: Explorations in Slumland*. Cambridge: Cambridge University Press.

McAtackney, Laura. 2014. *An Archaeology of the Troubles: The Heritage of Long Kesh/Maze Prison*. Oxford: Oxford University Press.

McGuire, Randall. H. 2008. *Archaeology as Political Action*. Berkeley: University of California Press.

———. 2014. "Capitalism in Archaeological Theory." In *Encyclopedia of Global Archaeology*, ed. Claire Smith, 1131–40. New York: Springer.

McKechnie, Iain. 2015. "Indigenous Oral History and Settlement Archaeology in Barkley Sound, Western Vancouver Island." *BC Studies* 187: 193–228.

McMillan, Alan, and Eldon Yellowhorn. 2004. *First Peoples in Canada*. Vancouver: Douglas & McIntyre.

Moreland, John. 2001. *Archaeology and Text*. Bristol: Bristol Classical Press.

———. 2006. "Archaeology and Texts: Subservience or Enlightenment." *Annual Review of Anthropology* 35: 135–51.

Morton, Diana, David Walker, and Laura Gardner. 2008. *M74 Public Archaeology Programme Evaluation Report*. Unpublished report. *please note, the oral historian on the project was David Walker.

Moshenska, Gabriel. 2006. "Scales of Memory in the Archaeology of the Second World War." *Institute of Archaeology, UCL*, 17: 58–68.

———. 2007. "Oral History in Historical Archaeology: Excavating Sites of Memory." *Oral History* 35(1): 91–97.

————. 2010. "Gas Masks: Material Culture, Memory, and the Senses." *The Journal of the Royal Anthropological Institute* 16(3): 609–28.

Murray, Tim, and Alan Mayne. 2001. "Imaginary Landscapes: Reading Melbourne's 'Little Lon.'" In *The Archaeology of Urban Landscapes: Explorations in Slumland*, ed. Alan Mayne and Tim Murray, 1–7. Cambridge: Cambridge University Press.

Museum of London Archaeology. 1990. *Archaeological Site Manual*, 3rd edn. London: Museum of London.

Mytum, Harold, Charlotte Newman, and Suzanne Lilley. 2017. "Archaeologies of Workers' Housing." Society for Historical Archaeology Conference, Fort Worth, Texas, 4–8 January. Retrieved 11 April 2022 from https://sha.org/wp-content/uploads/2015/05/2017-Conference-on-Historical-and-Underwater-Archaeology-Abstract-Book.pdf.

National Park Service. 1990. National Native American Graves Protection and Repatriation Act. Retrieved 7 April 2022 from https://home.nps.gov/subjects/archeology/napgra.htm.

Newman, Caron, and Richard Newman. 2008. "Housing the Workforce in Nineteenth Century East Lancashire." *Post-Medieval Archaeology* 42(1): 181–200.

O'Mara, Pat. 1933. *The Autobiography of a Liverpool Irish Slummy*. Liverpool: The Bluecoat Press. Reprinted in 2009.

Orser, Charles E., Jr., 1996. *A Historical Archaeology of the Modern World*. New York: Plenum Press.

————. 2017. *Historical Archaeology*, 3rd edn. London: Routledge.

Orser, Charles E., Jr., Andres Zarankin, Pedro Funari, Susan Lawrence, and James Symonds, eds. 2020. *The Routledge Handbook of Global Historical Archaeology*. London: Routledge.

Pablo42. 2009. Yo Liverpool. Retrieved 5 April 2022 from https://www.yoliverpool.com/forum/showthread.php?4273-Pre-Slum-Clearances-Housing-Images/page2.

Parker, Bradley J., and Catherine P. Foster, eds. 2012. *New Perspectives on Household Archaeology*. State College: Pennsylvania State University Press.

Pooley, Colin G. 1985. "Housing for the Poorest Poor: Slum Clearance and Rehousing in Liverpool, 1890–1918." *Journal of Historical Geography* 11(1): 70–88.

Pooley, Colin G., and Sandra Irish. 1994. "Housing and Health in Liverpool, 1870–1940." *Transactions of the Historic Society of Lancashire and Cheshire* 143: 193–219.

Portelli, Alessandro. 1981. "The Peculiarities of Oral History." *History Workshop Journal* 12(1): 96–107.

Pragnell, Jonathan. 2020. "Capitalism and Globalisation." In *The Routledge Handbook of Global Historical Archaeology*, ed. Charles E. Orser, Jr., Andres Zarankin, Pendro Funari, Susan Lawrence, and James Symonds, 117–32. London: Routledge.

Prossor, Lauren, Susan Lawrence, Alasdair Brooks, and Jane Lennon. 2012. "Household Archaeology, Lifecycles and Status in a Nineteenth-Century Australian Coastal Community." *International Journal of Historical Archaeology* 16: 809–27.

Purser, Margaret. 1992. "Oral History and Historical Archaeology." In *Text-Aided Archaeology*, ed Barbara J. Little, 165–71. Boca Raton, FL: CRC Press.

Rees, Rosemary. 2001. *Poverty and Public Health 1815–1948*. Portsmouth, NH: Heinemann Educational Publishers.

Riley, Mark, and David Harvey. 2005. "Landscape Archaeology, Heritage and the Community in Devon: An Oral History Approach." *International Journal of Heritage Studies* 11(4): 269–88.

Rimmer, Jayne. 2011. "People and Their Buildings in the Working-Class Neighbourhood of Hungate, York." *International Journal of Historical Archaeology* 15(4): 617–28.

Roberts, Henry. 1855. *The Physical Condition of the Labouring Classes, Resulting from the State of Their Dwellings, and the Beneficial Effects of Sanitary Improvements Recently Adopted in England*. Knowsley Pamphlet Collection, University of Liverpool.

Roberts, Robert. 1971. *The Classic Slum: Salford Life in the First Quarter of the Century*. London: Penguin. Reprinted in 1990.

Rodger, Richard. 1995. *Housing in Urban Britain 1780–1914*. Cambridge: Cambridge University Press.

Rowntree, Benjamin Seebohm. 1901. *Poverty: A Study of Town Life*. Bristol: The Policy Press. Reprinted in 2000.

Samuel, Raphael. 1994. *Theatres of Memory: Past and Present in Contemporary Culture*. New York: Verso Books. Reprinted in 2012.

Schmidt, Peter R. 1990. "Oral Traditions, Archaeology and History: A Short Reflective History in Africa." In *A History of African Archaeology*, ed. P. Robertshaw, 252–70. Oxford: James Currey.

Seaton, Anthony V. 1996. "Guided by the Dark: From Thanatopsis to Thanatourism." *International Journal of Heritage Studies* 2(4): 234–44.

Shimmin, Hugh. 1864. *The Courts and Alleys of Liverpool*. The Porcupine.

Sirik, Savina. 2015. "Everyday Experiences of Genocide Survivors in Landscapes of Violence in Cambodia." MA thesis. Kent, OH: Kent State University.

Sodaro, Amy. 2018. *Exhibiting Atrocity: Memorial Museums and the Politics of Past Violence*. New Brunswick, NJ: Rutgers University Press.

Solari, Elaine-Maryse. 2001. "The Making of an Archaeological Site and the Unmaking of a Community in West Oakland, California." In *The Archaeology of Urban Landscapes: Explorations in Slumland*, ed. Alan Mayne and Tim Murray, 22–38. Cambridge: Cambridge University Press.

Stewart, Elizabeth J. 2019. *Courts and Alleys: A History of Liverpool Courtyard Housing*. Liverpool: University of Liverpool Press.

Stottman, M. Jay, ed. 2010. *Archaeologists as Activists*. Tuscaloosa: University of Alabama Press.

Sutcliffe, Anthony. 1972. "Working Class Housing in Nineteenth-Century Britain: A Review of Recent Research." *Society for the Study of Labour History* 24: 40–47.

Symonds, James. 2011. "The Poverty Trap: or, Why Poverty Is Not about the Individual." *International Journal of Historical Archaeology* 15(4): 563–71.

Tarn, John N. 1971. *Working-Class Housing in Nineteenth Century Britain*. London: Lund Humphries Publishers Limited.

Thomas, Susie, Vesa-Pekka Herva, Oula Seitsonen, and Eerika Koivisto. 2019. "Dark Heritage." In *Encyclopedia of Global Archaeology*, ed. Claire Smith, 1-11. Cham: Living Edition, Springer.

Thompson, Paul. 2000. *The Voice of the Past*, 3rd edn. Oxford: Oxford University Press.

Trench, William S. 1863. *Annual Report of the Medical Officer of Health for Liverpool*. Liverpool.

Tully, Gemma. 2007. "Community Archaeology: General Methods and Standards of Practice." *Public Archaeology* 6(3): 155–87.

Watkins, Joe. 2000. *Indigenous Archaeology: American Indian Values and Scientific Practice*. Walnut Creek, CA: Altamira.

White, Leanne, and Elspeth Frew, eds. 2013. *Dark Tourism and Place Identity*. Melbourne: Routledge.

Wilke, Richard R., and William L. Rathje. 1982. "Household Archaeology." *American Behavioural Scientist* 25: 617–39.

Williams, Bryn, and Barbara L. Voss. 2008. "The Archaeology of Chinese Immigrant American Communities." *Historical Archaeology* 42(3): 1–4.

Wohl, Anthony S. 1977. *The Eternal Slum: Housing and Social Policy in Victorian London*. London: Edward Arnold.

Yamin, Rebecca, ed. 2002. *Tales of Five Points: Working-Class Life in Nineteenth Century New York*, vol. 7. West Chester, PA: John Milner Associates.

Yasur-Landau, Assaf, Jennie R. Ebeling, and Laura B. Mazow, eds. 2011. *Household Archaeology in Ancient Israel and Beyond*. Leiden: Brill.

Yellowhorn, Eldon. 2000. "The Evolving Relationship between Archaeologists and First Nations." *Canadian Journal of Archaeology* 24(2): 162–64.

Zarankin, Andres, and Melisa A. Salerno. 2008. "'Looking South': Historical Archaeology in South America." *Historical Archaeology* 42(4): 38–58.

CHAPTER 6

Archaeological Narratives as Critical Public Archaeology

Illuminating the Realities of Past and Present Forced Prison Labor through Story

V. Camille Westmont

Introduction

Slavery did not end in the United States with the Emancipation Proclamation. In Tennessee, it carried on deep in the hollows and hills for decades after emancipation under the label "convict leasing." Indeed, immediately following the Civil War, states across the US South implemented convict leasing schemes at their state prisons. Convicts were leased by the state to private businesses for cash; in return, the businesses could use the convicts as unpaid labor for the length of the convicts' prison sentences. In Tennessee, this practice continued into the 1890s, a full thirty years after the end of the war; in some states, such as Alabama, convict leasing persisted into the 1920s (Shapiro 1998). Convict leasing was also the first US manifestation of a racialized incarceration system. White voters' fears around social change after the war were assuaged through the targeted oppression of recently freed African Americans. Racially specific legislation and opportunistic enforcement of the law caused African Americans to be imprisoned at unprecedented rates (Blackmon 2008). Although the private convict leasing system was abandoned, the legislation that enabled it is still in force, and thousands of imprisoned persons today are still forced to work without pay for the duration of their sentences in prisons across the United States.

The largest private convict stockade in Tennessee was the Lone Rock Stockade, located outside Tracy City, Tennessee. Today, archaeologists from the University of the South are using archaeological and archival research to understand the lived experiences of the thousands of individuals who were forced to live in the stockade and work in nearby coal mines and coke ovens over the nearly twenty-five years that the stockade was in use. Although this archaeology project examines the material and architectural remains of nineteenth-century convict leasing, the public engagement aspects of the project adopt a critical theory perspective by tracing the roots of racialized incarceration, its origins in slavery and unpaid labor, and its continued presence in the United States today. This work aims to underscore how structural racism became embedded in US incarceration and demonstrate that these issues continue to plague the system. By highlighting the origins of this practice, the work aims to demystify and denaturalize our current treatment of incarcerated individuals.

Critical theory, with its focus on critiquing culture to highlight otherwise unnoticed power structures, has the ability to play a leading role in exposing the origins of prison labor as a replacement for slavery (Geuss 1981). In defining the stockade site as a form of negative cultural heritage (Westmont 2021), I am drawing on the stockade's history as a site of racially motivated and unjust incarceration to address issues of social, economic, and racial inequality in the US prison system today; however, bringing those injustices to the surface can also serve as a source of pain for descendant communities. Using critical approaches, I mobilize this heritage to direct public attention toward social justice initiatives with the ultimate goal of promoting social justice action (e.g., Johnston and Marwood 2017). In this way, cultural heritage can be "an instrument of cultural power" that fulfills the moral imperative archaeologists and other heritage researchers have for the well-being of modern communities (Harvey 2001: 327; e.g., Kiddey 2017; Smith, Shackel, and Campbell 2011).

This project piloted the use of archaeological narrative to achieve social justice goals. Narrative and storytelling have become accepted parts of archaeological interpretation over the last two decades (Praetzellis 2014) and have played an instrumental role in advancing other critical archaeological projects (see Spector 1993). Situating archaeological knowledge as "stories" de-intellectualizes the endeavor, thereby evoking emotional rather than intellectual responses (Praetzellis 1998, 2014). In cases where the history in question is negative or otherwise painful for some communities, the addition of storytelling helps to humanize the endeavor by encouraging the audience to recognize the shared humanity of the characters; while painful, such an approach is necessary for accounting for the realities of history and helps to set the tone for ongoing and future conversations in a way that encourages empathy with victims rather than blame. In this project, narrative and storytelling are central to the public archaeology project's overarching goal of advocating a permanent end to forced prison labor. In this way, archaeological narrative is utilized as a method for achieving emancipation from culturally naturalized conceptions of imprisonment and punishment by examining the origins of the system.

The work of the Lone Rock Stockade Project falls within a long and growing tradition of social justice-oriented archaeology. While the movement initially sought to increase representation in the past by promoting archaeological projects that focused on marginalized groups, particularly African Americans, Indigenous peoples, and women, the scope of social justice-oriented work has expanded dramatically in the last twenty years and adopted new methods for carrying out this type of work. The work done by the Lone Rock Stockade Project specifically uses narrative as its means of achieving social change. This chapter begins with a discussion of archaeology's role in culture change and the role archaeological interpretations and narratives play in realizing those goals. It then moves into a more detailed discussion of historical convict leasing in Tennessee and the work of the Lone Rock Stockade Project. Finally, the chapter examines how the Lone Rock Stockade Project's framing of its findings for a public audience could be used to promote culture change through the use of a critical perspective on historic and modern racialized incarceration.

Theory

The application of critical theory to public archaeology has gained traction within the field over the past forty years. Starting with the Archaeology in Annapolis project directed by Mark Leone at the University of Maryland in the mid-1980s (Leone, Potter, and Shackel 1987), archaeology projects that take up goals of reflexivity, in particular, have proliferated (see Hodder 2003). To a lesser extent, projects have also adopted goals that explicitly pursue liberating or revelatory ends (see Atalay et al. 2016; Stottman 2010). Today, critical theory has been thoroughly integrated into archaeological practice, particularly historical archaeology and projects that engaged with descendant communities. Critical theory has proven particularly useful for projects that seek social justice ends (Alì 2017). However, in the context of public archaeology that engages critical theory, the means by which critical theory is introduced to public audiences has not been explored in depth. This work focuses on archaeological narratives, or accounts of the past derived at least in part by archaeological data, as a means for communicating critical theory-based perspectives of archaeological sites.

Narratives are a constant aspect of modern life. Narratives are frequently used to both communicate facts and influence opinions. Although narratives at their most basic level simply recount a sequence of events in the past along a plot line with one or more characters (Labov and Waletzky 1967; Toolan 2012; Pluciennik 1999), narratives are not straightforward or unbiased accounts. Narratives are "vehicles of ideology," even though the ideology that guides the narrative is not always obvious to the listeners (Polletta and Gardner 2015: 536). Narratives appeal to listeners because they draw on a concept of storytelling—an activity available to and understood by most people. In the process of creating a narrative, the author dictates which details to emphasize, the tone, repetitions, and even fictive details to weave into the story (Hight 2005). The structure of a narrative is more accessible because the narrative's point or moral is communicated through the sequence of events (whether good or bad) rather than relying on logic to communicate the point (Polletta 2006). That makes narrative a particularly useful tool for activists interested in inspiring social change.

Although activism often relies upon explanation and arguments, storytelling and the development of directed narratives can provide additional appeal for public audiences and be more persuasive than other forms of communication (Viterna 2013; Jones 2013; Slater and Rouner 2002). In the activist context, the most successful stories are those that can connect to the audiences' personal ideology or elicit emotional connections (Polletta and Gardner 2015; Haltom and McCann 2004; Van Dyke and Bernbeck 2015). Recent scholarship has identified that individuals who "identify emotionally with the story's protagonist" and who feel empathy for the characters are more likely to oppose characters that stymie the protagonist from reaching their goal (Polletta and Redman 2020: 3). In other words, narratives define the "good" and "bad" characters in a story for the audience, thereby inculcating the audience into the storyteller's point of view from the outset. Audiences' preconceived perceptions of both the story (e.g., Is it plausible? Is it important?) and the narrator (e.g., Does the delivery seem authentic? Is the narrator the right person to tell this story?) also affect their response to the story (Bruner 1991). Therefore, while narratives and storytelling can be a powerful tool for conveying intention, it also needs to be done with thought and attention in order to be effective.

Narrative has a long tradition within archaeology; indeed, archaeological narratives and storytelling that explored "imaginary, but by no means unimaginable" scenarios experienced a surge in popularity beginning in the 1970s and 1980s (Mouer and Edwards-Ingram 1998 quoted in Gibb 2000: 1; Praetzellis 2014). Janet Spector's (1993) *What This Awl Means*, Ian Hodder's (1989) "Writing Archaeology" article, and Adrian Praetzellis's Archaeologist as Storyteller session at the 1997 Society for Historical Archaeology conference, among others, have served as a foundation for this type of archaeological interpretation and, potentially, a form of archaeological analysis in itself (Gibb 2000; see Little 2000). The power inherent in this type of narrative is apparent as the method continues to develop in theoretical and methodological complexity (see Joyce 2008; Van Dyke and Bernbeck 2015). Narratives in archaeology are not just valued for their ability to engage, entertain, and inform, but for their functional ability to address misconceptions about archaeology and archaeologists (Thomas 2015), its ability to mediate conflicting perspectives in order to unmask power dynamics (Little and Shackel 2014), and their ability to "highlight subtleties of social relations overlooked in more conventional analyses" (Gibb 2000: 5).

Narratives are already being used within archaeological practice to promote social justice initiatives. Martin Gallivan and Danielle Moretti-Langholtz (2007) examine the ways that working in consultation with the Pamunkey tribe of Virginia on archaeological research at Werowocomoco ensured civic engagement and that Indigenous values were represented in the academic research agenda. The project had the additional benefit of highlighting the persistence of Indigenous groups in the state. In that instance, Indigenous narratives of the site's history were instrumental in achieving greater societal recognition for the Pamunkey's presence and their right to play a leading role in interpreting the site and its history. This helped to break down colonized perspectives on native groups and re-assert autonomy and agency for the Pamunkey. In other instances, the narratives that arise from archaeological objects themselves provide a form of social justice through enfranchisement and ownership of the past. Gabby Omoni Hartemann's (2022) work with the Afrodiasporic and Indigenous communities in eastern Guiana illustrate the ways that narratives can be used to heal wounds caused by structural racism and colonialism. In their work, Hartemann draws on Indigenous practices related to storytelling to break down the barriers between "public" and "expert" in order to begin the process of healing. Because archaeology is managed as part of the French bureaucratic structure in Guiana, Afrodiasporic and Indigenous peoples are most often excluded from participating in archaeological research, which serves to continue the trauma of colonization on these marginalized groups (Clay 2021). Using storytelling, a traditional way of knowing, the La Caroline archaeological project is using narrative to help address long-standing colonial traumas and re-invest communities in their own histories. Sonya Atalay suggests that archaeologists can draw on Indigenous traditions of storytelling to promote dissemination of historical knowledge in ways that "entwine archaeological data with present-day communities and present-day problems" (2020: 10–11).

Projects like La Caroline and the Indigenous collaboration at Werowocomoco demonstrate the power that narratives can have in challenging power structures by telling alternative stories about different places, times, and peoples. In the Lone Rock Stockade Project, we used narratives not just to tell an alternative story, but to demonstrate the brutality of the convict lease system and to show that the worst part of convict leasing—coerced, unpaid labor—is still a part of incarceration today. In this way, we used narratives about real prisoners and real historical events to highlight the obscured, racist roots of prison labor and advocate for ending the practice altogether by building empathy for historical and, by extension, modern prisoners. In the spirit of critical theory, we are using archaeological interpretations to highlight the obscured historical roots of institutionalized inequalities such as forced prison labor in order to provide people with the knowledge they need to liberate themselves from such situations. In order to understand how the archaeology of an 1870s private prison connects to modern controversies like the Angola Prison Farm and Parchman Prison, we used narratives that embed people in place and emphasize the shared experience of historic and modern prisoners.

Slavery and Convict Labor: Historical Roots and Modern Legacies

Slavery is a social and economic circumstance that has existed since the beginning of recorded history (Bales and Robbins 2001:18). In the American context, slavery has existed on the continent since 1526, with slavery for life being established in 1640 and chattel slavery, or slavery that can be passed from parent to child, being established in 1662 (Foner 1975). Although exact definitions of slavery are often opaque (see Allain

2009, Allain and Hickey 2012), the prevailing definition of slavery relies on three key aspects: "the use of violence, and the ability to control, for economic exploitation" (Allain and Bales 2012: 3; Bales 2005); of these, the concept of physical control over another person is the primary consideration.

Chattel slavery was outlawed in the United States with the ratification of the Thirteenth Amendment to the US Constitution on 6 December 1865. Although Abraham Lincoln had issued the Emancipation Proclamation as a wartime act nearly three years prior, the executive order only freed enslaved people in the states under active rebellion, thereby providing no relief for those individuals enslaved in Kentucky, Maryland, Delaware, and Missouri. Although the Thirteenth Amendment outlawed slavery as it had been practiced in the country for nearly two hundred years, the Thirteenth Amendment also provided the means for a new form of legalized slavery: forced labor. The text of the amendment reads, "Neither slavery nor involuntary servitude, *except as a punishment for crime* whereof the party shall have been duly convicted, shall exist within the United States, or any place subject to their jurisdiction" (Amendment Thirteen, United States, emphasis mine). The specific exception included in that text—"except as punishment for a crime"—enabled a new system of term enslavement to arise across the country. This system, in which prisoners were sold by states to private concerns where they would be forced to work under threat of violence, was known as convict leasing.

Developed in the early nineteenth century, the concept of forcing prisoners to work was originally rooted in a desire for prisoners to develop Christian morality and repentance as well as the standard desire to inflict punishment. Inspired by Quaker ideas, prison reformers hoped that keeping prisoners in isolation where they would be forced to read from the Bible would cause the prisoners to experience a spiritual conversion. High rates of illiteracy paired with total isolation, however, contributed to despair rather than piety (Moulder 1976). Although the direct approach to improving prisoners' moral character had failed, reformers continued to hope that instituting a regular work schedule under direction of a supervisor might encourage industriousness and reform in a different way. In the Northeastern United States where industrialization had already taken root, the idea of a prisoner work system was paired with industrial production. Prisoners were forced to work in small shops inside the prisons producing goods such as shoes that could be sold, thereby providing income for the prison. Following this model, state prisons across the nation, including the Tennessee state penitentiary in Nashville opened in 1831, built on-site prison labor workshops and partnered with outside contractors to operate the workshops (Moulder 1976). However, the penitentiary was constructed to hold only two hundred inmates, a limit that was rapidly surpassed in the years leading up to the Civil War and completely disregarded after the war. Enormous state debt prevented the expansion of the prison after the war as social conditions imposed harsher and longer prison sentences. To deal with this disaster, the state legislature opted in 1866 to lease the penitentiary to furniture manufacturers but required the lessees to keep the prisoners on the penitentiary grounds. When this arrangement disintegrated the following year, the practice was temporarily abandoned. Arthur Colyar, president of the Tennessee Coal and Railroad (TCR) company in Tracy City, Tennessee, renewed interest in the practice when he convinced state legislators to authorize a convict leasing "branch" prison at his mines in Tracy City and Battle Creek in February 1871 (Crowe 1956). Impressed by Colyar's success, in November 1871 the Governor and State Assembly authorized a five-year lease of the state penitentiary to Thomas O'Connor and Robert Looney. O'Connor became deeply involved with Colyar and TCR and would eventually take control of the company from Colyar (Moulder 1976).

Postbellum convict leasing took two forms. In states such as Tennessee, businesses leased the entire state penitentiary and all of the prisoners inside. In states such as Alabama, companies paid fees to the state on a per-convict basis. In both cases, convicts worked for the duration of their sentences. In Tennessee, the lessees would make annual payments to the state for the duration of the lease, which lasted from five to six years. Larger prison populations could garner larger lease payments, which created an incentive for states to imprison more people. Leasing convicts to private businesses where convict labor was in direct competition with private labor became increasingly unpopular during the late nineteenth and early twentieth centuries; by the 1920s, convict leases to private businesses had largely been replaced by chain gangs in which convicts worked on public construction projects such as roads or completed other physical tasks such as rock breaking. Convicts were forced to do this work through physical violence such as whippings or psychological violence such as solitary confinement that was threatened as punishment for noncompliance.

The convict lease system quickly became infamous for its brutality. State leases explicitly removed lessees' liability for injury or death of prisoners, effectively removing any incentives for lessees to invest in working or living conditions for prisoners. With a captive yet expendable labor force, companies quickly reverted to brutal and efficient management practices. Individuals incarcerated for minor crimes such as petit theft and vagrancy soon found life and limb at serious risk. The problem became so pronounced that the phrase "one dies, get another" became a defining feature of the Southern convict lease system (Mancini 1996: 1).

Although leasing state penitentiaries to private companies has largely disappeared, forced prison labor persists in the United States. Shortly after the turn of the century, the first federal effort was made to curtail the impact of prison labor on the free labor market. In 1905, President Theodore Roosevelt issued Executive Order No. 325A, which prohibited the use of prisoner labor for the fulfillment of federal contracts. However, despite this and other state-level prohibitions on forced prison labor, the text of the Thirteenth Amendment ensures that "slavery and servitude" will continue to be legally allowed in American prisons until a constitutional amendment closing that loophole is made. A series of other federal laws aimed at regulating prisoner-produced goods was passed in the late 1920s and 1930s. However, these restrictions were greatly reduced in 1973 when the Nixon administration effectively reversed the

1905 executive order and again in 1979 with the establishment of the Prison Industry Enhancement Certification Program (PIECP) through an act of Congress (Sloan 2010; Federal Register 1973). Although the PIECP has instituted standards, not all prisons are part of PIECP, and six states continue to force prisoners to work without pay as part of their sentence (Sawyer 2017). At an international level, the ethics of prison labor continue to be a contentious issue. The International Labour Organization (ILO) currently considers forced labor under threat of menace to be a form a "modern slavery" (ILO 2019); however, the ILO specifically exempts "any work or service exacted from any person as a consequence of a conviction in a court of law, provided . . . that the said person is not placed at the disposal of private individuals, companies, or associations" (Forced Labour Conviction 1930 [No. 29]: Article 2.2[c]). The fact that the enslavement of US citizens is legal according to the US Constitution and continues to be the law of the land is a little-known legacy of the Civil War and American slavery. This legacy continues to touch individuals and families, particularly African American and Latino individuals and families, across the nation in devastating ways.

Historical Background of the Lone Rock Stockade

Although convict leasing existed prior to the Civil War, it took on a new scale and aggressiveness in the postbellum South. This occurred for two primary reasons economic and social stability. The businesses that leased convicts from the state were responsible for the inmates' upkeep, including food, housing, and medical care. This significantly reduced the financial burden on state budgets while simultaneously providing a new revenue stream. The importance of this financial aspect of convict leasing for state budgets cannot be overstated. Tennessee, Texas, Alabama, Mississippi, Georgia, South Carolina, Arkansas, Florida, and Louisiana—nine of the eleven Confederate states—all implemented convict leases in the years following emancipation. One prominent plantation owner in Nashville, Confederate General Benjamin Cheatham, stated in 1878 that "This State is making more money by its convicts than any sister State in the Union" (*Daily American*, 21 March 1878). In effect, convict leasing enabled former Confederate states to mobilize free labor in the service of state economies by holding the monopoly on legalized slavery in the postwar period. However, the effect on state budgets was not the only economic consideration created by convict leasing. Following the war, the South experienced a dramatic labor crisis. The Southern agricultural economy had been built upon the availability of enslaved labor, and the South's limited prewar industrial economy had likewise begun relying on unpaid labor (Blackmon 2008). Now expected to pay wages to their formerly enslaved employees, many businessmen found their previous business models untenable. The availability of convict labor, however, returned the availability of a cheap, below-market-rate labor supply. While convict leasing played a prominent role in the state's postbellum finances, convict leasing also served an important social function.

Emancipation of America's enslaved population brought massive social changes. White anxieties about the role of African Americans in society hit a fever pitch, especially as a crime wave spurred by "demoralized social and economic circumstances" hit the country immediately following the war (Rosenbaum 1940: 722). With little to no formal training, little to no personal wealth, and a general ignorance of the law, recently freed peoples were already at a massive disadvantage in entering free society. White society used their influence, particularly in politics, to advocate for a "law and order" political movement. This led to harsher sentences for minor crimes and new legislation targeted at controlling the freedoms of African Americans. As prison populations grew under these new laws, the prospect of convict leasing as a means of alleviated overcrowded prisons grew. Convict leasing, then, once again provided white Southerners with a means of total physical and economic control over Black people and Black labor in the South. These social and economic roots formed the foundation of a practice that still today continues to exert these forms of control over Black people in the United States.

This chapter examines the use of narratives within public archaeology at the site of the Lone Rock Stockade, a circa 1883 prison used to house prisoners leased from the state of Tennessee and forced to work in TCR's coal mines and coke ovens near Tracy City, Tennessee. Convict labor was used consistently by TCR from 1871 until 1896 when the practice ended in Tennessee. After experiencing success with the first set of one hundred prisoners leased to the company in 1871, TCR purpose-built a new convict stockade next to the Lone Rock Mine in 1883 to coincide with an expansion of the company's industrial activities. The stockade was built to hold up to two hundred prisoners, although the actual occupancy hovered between 300 and 650 for much of the 1880s and 1890s. Due to the concerted efforts of Black Codes and racial discrimination in the enforcement of the law, African Americans represented between 70 and 90 percent of those incarcerated at the Lone Rock Stockade. Conditions inside the stockade were horrible: as much as 10 percent of the stockade's occupants died annually from diseases like tuberculosis, typhoid fever, and organ and bowel failure. A high number of prisoners successfully escaped while dozens of others were shot and killed in botched escape attempts. Prison inspectors reports regularly cited inhumane and illegal conditions inside the stockade, including excessive whippings, a lack of vegetables, unsanitary living conditions, and rampant physical and sexual violence. Despite these and other complaints, TCR managed to maintain their control over the state's convict population for nearly twenty-five years. Despite TCR playing a major role in the building of Tennessee's and the South's industrial economy after the Civil War, its use of convict labor in both Tennessee and Alabama is frequently overlooked or downplayed. In addition to archaeological investigations aimed to shed light on prisoners' living conditions inside the stockade, an extensive public archaeology program was developed to highlight the legacy of convict leasing and expose the realities of the forgotten system—and its continued legacies in the modern day (Westmont 2021).

Critical Public Narratives of the Stockade

The Lone Rock Stockade Project has benefited immensely from the availability of state convict records. Because all of the prisoners at the stockade were convicted and sentenced in state courts and processed by the Main Penitentiary in Nashville, the prisoners' identities are well documented. These records vary in their amount of detail, but all records include names, crimes, county, sentence, date sentenced, and information on the prisoners' period of incarceration, such as if they tried to escape, if they were pardoned, if they completed their sentence, or if they died while imprisoned. Other records provide even more information, such as physical descriptions that include scars and tattoos, employment, education, marital status, place of birth, and religious affiliation. These documents are in the process of being transcribed by volunteers and eventually we hope to make the transcriptions available through an online database. In the meantime, however, the records have become a prime source for archaeological narratives that aim to emphasize the politics of incarceration and the human toll of a form of slavery that is still legal today.

Drawing on convict records, newspaper accounts, and archaeological data, the Lone Rock Stockade Project uses critically based public narratives to build empathy for the historic prisoners before revealing the fact that unpaid forced labor continues to legally happen in prisons across the United States today. By demonstrating the roots of the practice in slavery and the control of African American bodies and demonstrating the continuity of the practice from rural 1871 Tennessee to modern prisons in 2022, members of the public are forced to reckon with the implications of the system not only for prisoners and their families but also for the free laborers who are deprived of jobs at private corporations and the state bureaucrats who financially benefit from unpaid labor.

Using patterns in the records and newspaper reports, we were able to glean stories about the circumstances of prisoners at the Lone Rock Stockade. The archaeology project then turned these stories into grounded experiences. Rather than just tell a story, we were able to identify the place on the landscape where that part of the story occurred, then move to the next place on the landscape where the story continued. Using a little imagination, visitors were able to "see" the story taking place as it had happened at the site 150 years ago. In this way, archaeology offered a means of reviving and reliving the brutality of the convict lease system and forced labor. Public tours of the site focused on showing visitors how the extant industrial structures on the site contributed to a larger landscape defined by industrial efficiency, control, and social hierarchy (see Westmont 2021). During these tours, three prison narratives were told. While the prisoners themselves and the events described in the narratives are real, the archaeologists' placement of these events on the landscape and the reference to specific artifacts represents a form of archaeological interpretation that falls under James Gibb's "imaginary but by no means unimaginable" form of archaeological narration (2000: 1).

Narrative #1: RJ

RJ's story illustrates the human cost of convict leasing. RJ's story begins at the former gates of the stockade.

> RJ Campbell was sixteen years old when he was caught shoplifting in Memphis. The boy had recently run away from his family in rural Mississippi after a disagreement with his father and thought he'd try his luck in the big city just across the border. Although RJ was white, his family lacked the political connections in Tennessee necessary to secure a pardon from the governor. RJ arrived at the stockade in late 1887 to serve his one-year prison term. However, things quickly took a turn for the worse.
>
> Like all prisoners, RJ's first interaction with the stockade's physician occurred at the gates of the stockade. However, the stockade physician was not just there to check on RJ's and the other prisoners' overall health: the physician was primarily there to make a determination about how much labor he and the other prisoners could be expected to do in a day given his physical stature, much in the same way an enslaved person was evaluated. This evaluation would determine RJ's daily quota, or the amount of coal he would be expected to mine every day. If RJ reached his quota, he could relax in the evenings; if he failed to reach his quota, he would be forced to lay on the ground as he was whipped with a 2.5-pound, leather and wood ox whip. The next day, RJ would be expected to complete his daily quota plus produce the coal he lacked the day before. RJ had to do this Monday through Saturday, or six days per week, from 5 a.m. to 4 p.m., for the duration of his sentence. For this work, RJ was paid nothing.
>
> Although RJ had never done work like this before, he settled into the pattern of stockade life for the first few months of his sentence; however, his luck would change. RJ's second meeting with the prison physician was not as straightforward as the first. In February 1888, RJ was stooping to load coal into his mine cart when a block of slate fell from the ceiling and struck his back. Unable to walk, RJ's work partner called for help and, with the assistance of a few other convicts, RJ was carried out of the mine on a litter to the stockade hospital.

At this point in the narrative, the tour group would move to the location of the stockade hospital. The hospital was one of two structures investigated archaeologically during the summer of 2020. Visitors were shown artifacts related to the hospital, including patent medicine bottle finishes and a shirt collar stud that likely belonged to the physician. Walking through the former footprint of the hospital, it was once again reiterated that the place where the visitors stood was the location where RJ was carried more than a 130 years earlier. RJ's story continued:

RJ was given two weeks of "rest" to recuperate from his injury, although he was often forced to help whitewash buildings during his rest period. At the end of his two-week hospital stay, RJ was forced to return to work in the mines. Although he was young, RJ's injured back hadn't fully healed. As RJ crawled on his knees through the mines, unable to bend his back to stoop through the low-ceiling passages, he knew what awaited him at the end of the day: the prison guard's whip. With his injury, RJ knew he wouldn't be able to meet his daily quota. RJ pleaded with his parents to send him money so he could pay other convicts to mine his quota for him; although his mother secretly sent him some money, it wasn't enough. Less than two weeks after returning to the mines, RJ was in yet another mine accident. This time, a block of slate fell from the ceiling and smashed RJ's arm against an iron mine track. Unable to save RJ's mangled arm, the physician was forced to amputate RJ's arm above the elbow.

RJ eventually sued Tennessee Coal and Iron for $20,000 for the loss of his arm, arguing that the injury was caused by TCR's failure to properly maintain their mine and that RJ's employment prospects were seriously hindered by his injury. TCR fought the lawsuit. Eventually, TCR settled with RJ's guardian for just $1,000. That would be the equivalent of about $30,000 today for the loss of his arm.

RJ's story was intended to highlight the brutality of the convict lease system, particularly the low value placed on human life and well-being through the system's design. Convict leasing's ability to inflict and re-inflict trauma on convicts in a consistent manner is highlighted through RJ's repeated physical traumas. The visceral details of the story—whippings, crawling, amputation—further underscore the human cost of convict labor. While this first narrative helped to humanize the trauma of an otherwise anonymous system, the second narrative sought to illustrate the unreasonable and unfair aspects of the system.

Narrative #2: Eliza Owens and Richard Schooler

One refrain encountered during public events at the stockade was the idea that because the individuals in the stockade had committed a crime, they deserved their punishment. To counteract this concept, the narrative of Eliza Owens and Richard Schooler was added to the public tours. The only historical information available about Eliza and Richard comes from their convict records and the US Census. However, this is enough to outline the basics of a narrative that are later brought to life through their connections to the landscape.

> Richard Schooler and Eliza Owens were in love. Richard, the son of slaves from Alabama, had been born in Virginia in 1857. As a young man, he moved to Roane County, Tennessee, where he worked as a blacksmith.

There he met Eliza, the daughter of a white farming family from Eastern Tennessee. In 1878, the pair were both twenty-one. Their relationship, however, provoked the ire of their fellow citizens, and in the early 1880s, they were convicted of miscegenation and sentenced to four years in the state penitentiary. Shortly after sentencing, the pair arrived at the Lone Rock Stockade in Tracy City, Tennessee, where they would be forced to work without pay for the duration of their prison sentences. While Eliza was one of just five women in the prison responsible for doing the laundry of more than four hundred people every week, Richard was forced to work in TCR's Lone Rock Mine for eleven hours per day, six days per week. Richard and Eliza are just two of the tens of thousands of convicted criminals who were swept up by Tennessee's convict lease system.

As the tours proceeded through the different areas of the stockade, Richard and Eliza's story is situated on the landscape. The racially segregated prisoner barracks and wash houses were identified, emphasizing the differences in Richard's and Eliza's experiences at the stockade. At the stockade gates, guests were told about Richard's transfer to the Battle Creek mine to help put down a strike. Visitors were asked to imagine watching one of their loved ones be marched down the hill to the train not knowing if they would ever see them again. Throughout this narrative, visitors were repeatedly reminded that Richard and Eliza were forced into their situation for daring to love the person they loved. Emphasizing that the majority of prisoners trapped in the convict lease system were often convicted of crimes such as miscegenation, petty theft, or receiving stolen goods helped to drive home the idea that the punishment did not equal the crime and that convict leasing was not about punishment but rather about cheap labor.

Richard and Eliza's story and RJ's story aimed to situated the horrors of convict leasing on the physical landscape of the stockade in order to solidify the argument that convict leasing was a terrible practice and a stain on the history of the United States. However, as mentioned previously, forced prison labor continues to happen at prisons across the United States today. In order to connect the history of convict leasing to the modern practice of forced prison labor, a third narrative was relayed to the tour guests.

Narrative #3: Jason

Toward the end of the tour, a final story was told. The story was prefaced by the fact that although the story did not take place at the Lone Rock Stockade, it was relevant for understanding the Lone Rock Stockade. The precise context of the story was not revealed until the end of the story.

Jason's experiences were not unlike Eliza's, Richard's, or RJ's, although Jason was located at a different prison. Jason had been convicted of second-degree murder and was sentenced to life in prison. When Jason arrived at the prison, he was evaluated by the prison's physician who determined Jason was physically fit enough to work. Jason was assigned to do manual field labor at a farm that supplied vegetables for the prison. For this work, Jason was paid 2 cents per hour. Although the prison's doctor said Jason was well enough to work, Jason's eyesight was rapidly deteriorating, making it impossible to complete the manual labor that was expected of him. Although Jason continued to complain about his eyesight, the prison doctor did nothing to address his concerns. Eventually, another physician visiting the prison diagnosed Jason with severe cataracts in both eyes and determined he was fully blind in one eye and nearly blind in the other. Even after he was determined to be almost completely blind, Jason was sent back into the farm fields, where he was expected to perform just like the rest of the other prison workers. Unable to judge distances or identify objects, Jason regularly injured himself as he tried to keep up with the pace of work in the fields. He complained constantly that he was in pain. The prison doctor told Jason that without treatment he would soon be entirely blind, but the prison lacked the funds to get him treatment. Jason eventually sued the prison warden and the doctors for not getting him treatment.

Jason is, at this moment, a prisoner in Angola, the Louisiana State Penitentiary, and his legal battle against the state occurred in 2016. Forced prison labor continues to occur every day in the United States and has not changed significantly since the time of the Lone Rock Stockade. If slavery and forced labor were wrong in 1896 when the Lone Rock Stockade was abandoned, it is still wrong today. Jason is just the latest victim in the long history of convict labor that began in the deep recesses of the postwar South. However, we can end this for good.

Jason's story was used to bring the historically distanced horrors of convict leasing into the modern day. The intentional withholding of certain details of Jason's story was used to draw parallels between nineteenth-century convict leasing and current twenty-first-century forced prison labor practices. Jason's story is one of dozens of instances of prisoner abuses and neglect at Angola Prison in recent years, highlighting the fact that forced labor in prisons continues to be ethically problematic and a violation of individuals' civil rights (Covert 2018; Benns 2015).

The stories intended to highlight not only the atrocities embedded in the convict lease system, but the fact that forced, essentially unpaid, prison labor continues to happen today. Although all three narratives refer to real people and real events, the archaeological narrator used storytelling as a means to highlight specific parts of the stories and invoked repetition as a way to emphasize the central message: forced convict labor, while legal, is a morally reprehensible practice. By approaching the public interpretation of the archaeological site from a critical perspective, the interactions with the public were able to take a form that not only entertained but advocated for a rejection of modern legalized enslavement by situating it in its historical context.

Discussion

The Lone Rock Stockade Public Archaeology Tours were intended to instruct visitors about the history of the site and educate them about the human legacy of convict leasing through a series of narratives that conveyed "improbable but not impossible" prisoner experiences in both the past and the present. All of the narratives presented on the public tours are based on real people and real situations; only the details of the stories have been inferred in order to bring the stories and their characters to life. This work adopted an explicitly critical perspective that sought to highlight the origins of convict leasing as a substitute for slavery and the racial disparities that were built into the convict leasing system. Drawing on narrative scholarship, the narratives were designed to elicit feelings of empathy for the protagonists (the convict laborers) while simultaneously encouraging visitors to think critically about the structures that victimized the protagonists, primarily the convict lease system and the Thirteenth Amendment (see Polletta and Redman 2020).

History and narratives of the past are neither apolitical nor harmless; in archaeology, the question then becomes not if archaeological narratives are political, but whose politics will be represented (Colwell-Chanthaphonh 2012; Southgate 2001). While the politics of the narratives are intentional and explicit in this instance, the potential harm caused by such portrayals is not as apparent. The deployment of potentially emotion-laden stories within the context of forced labor risks re-opening old wounds and re-victimizing those who have been directly or indirectly affected by the legacies of slavery, racial prejudice, or the US judicial system (Hartemann 2022). To put it another way, post-colonial and decolonizing archaeologies that seek a truthful accounting of historical wrong-doings can also harm communities (Haviser 2015). However, denying the historical experiences of Black and other marginalized populations within US history risks perpetuating the systemic forms of violence that have oppressed them. In this project, narratives were used not to needlessly re-open old wounds, but to advocate for modern-day change in the US system of incarceration. While the narratives are intended to be emotional, the structure and content of the narratives seek to channel those emotions toward civic action that will prevent future incarcerees from being exposed to further harm.

At the same time that narratives represent a clear break from claims of scientific or intellectual objectivity, the validity of the argument is not lost in the careful blurring between what we know and what we speculate (Praetzellis 2014: 5136; see Kristiansen 2011). Narratives are not just a rhetorical device; they provide archaeologists with a means of eliciting a different response to archaeological information—a response based in emotions rather than rationality. Given the topic under consideration, an emotional response that builds empathy for the past and present victims of legalized forced labor is preferable to one that requires a simple digestion of facts. As a critical archaeology project that aims to address an ongoing social issue, the narratives presented here generate an urgency to act that typical archaeological interpretations might not.

Conclusion

Narrative stories help to contextualize the stockade by emphasizing the human costs of the convict lease system. Archaeological interpretations often focus on the tangible things left behind—objects, buildings, and human-modified landscapes. In this instance, focusing on the material legacies of the convict lease system and the Lone Rock Stockade would have been a disservice not just to the individuals who were enslaved at this location historically, but to the thousands of individuals who continue to be forced to work under threat of violence every day across the United States. Narratives are a powerful way to invoke empathy and measure the human impact of history. When employed at archaeological sites, narratives can transcend the time gap between past and present and highlight the shared humanity among humans of all time periods. This is a major potential avenue for archaeological interpretations that adopt a critical perspective. Narratives can help illuminate the historical roots of socially naturalized phenomena in the present, thereby making narratives an apt vehicle for a critical public archaeology.

Acknowledgments

This work was made possible through a grant from the Tennessee Civil War National Heritage Area and the University of the South's Southern Studies Program. I am indebted to the Grundy County Historical Society, George Shinn, Daniel Wescoat, Sarah Sherwood, John Grammer, Woody Register, and the Sewanee VISTA Program. This manuscript was improved through the generous efforts of Jay Stottman.

V. Camille Westmont is the Andrew Mellon Foundation Postdoctoral Fellow in Historical Archaeology at the University of the South in Sewanee, Tennessee. She received her PhD in anthropology from the University of Maryland. Her work focuses on labor archaeology, industrial cultural heritage, landscape analyses, and public engagement. She currently serves as the co-chair of the Public Archaeology Community in the European Association of Archaeologists.

References

Alì, Nunzio. 2017. "Critical Theory, Relations of Domination, and a Certain Idea of Social Justice." *Cadernos de Ética e Filosophia Política* 30: 75–90.

Allain, Jean. 2009. "The Definition of Slavery in International Law." *Howard Law Journal* 52(2): 239–76.

Allain, Jean, and Kevin Bales. 2012. "Slavery and Its Definition." *Global Dialogue* 14(2): 6–14.

Allain, Jean, and Robin Hickey. 2012. "Property and the Definition of Slavery." *The International and Comparative Law Quarterly* 61(4): 915–38.

Atalay, Sonya. 2020. "Indigenous Science for a World in Crisis." *Public Archaeology*. https://doi.org/10.1080/14655187.2020.1781492.

Atalay, Sonya, Lee Rains Clauss, Randall H. McGuire, and John R. Welch, eds. 2016. *Transforming Archaeology: Activist Practices and Prospects*. London: Routledge.

Bales, Kevin. 2005. *Understanding Global Slavery: A Reader*. Berkeley: University of California Press.

Bales, Kevin, and Peter T. Robbins. 2001. "'No One Shall Be Held in Slavery or Servitude': A Critical Analysis of International Slavery Agreements and Concepts of Slavery." *Human Rights Review* 2: 18–45.

Benns, Whitney. 2015. "American Slavery, Reinvented." *The Atlantic*, 21 September.

Blackmon, Douglas. 2008. *Slavery by Another Name: The Re-Enslavement of Black Americans from the Civil War to World War II*. New York: Doubleday.

Bruner, Jerome. 1991. "The Narrative Construction of Reality." *Critical Inquiry* 18: 1–21.

Clay, Elizabeth C. 2022. "'Mo té la': Community-Engaged Plantation Archaeology in Guyane." *International Journal of Historical Archaeology* 26(1): 211-41.

Colwell-Chanthaphonh, Chip. 2012. "Archaeology and Indigenous Collaboration." In *Archaeology Theory Today*, ed. Ian Hodder, 267–91. Cambridge: Policy Press.

Covert, Bryce. 2018. "Louisiana Prisoners Demand an End of 'Modern-Day Slavery.'" *The Appeal*, 8 June.

Crowe, Jesse. 1956. "The Origin and Development of Tennessee's Prison Problem, 1831–1871." *Tennessee Historical Quarterly* 15(2): 111–35

Federal Register. 1973. *Executive Order 11755 of Dec. 29, 1973 (Relating to prison labor), United States*. Retrieved 20 November 2020 from www.archives.gov/federal-register/codification/executive-order/11755.html.

Foner, Philip S. 1975. *History of Black Americans: From Africa to the Emergence of the Cotton Kingdom*. Santa Barbara, CA: Praeger.

Forced Labour Convention. 1930 (No. 29), International Labour Organization.

Gallivan, Martin D., and Danielle Moretti-Langholtz. 2007. "Civic Engagement at Werowocomoco: Reasserting Native Narratives from a Powhatan Place of Power." In *Archaeology as a Tool of Civic Engagement*, ed. Barbara J. Little and Paul A. Shackel, 47–66. Lanham, MD: AltaMira Press.

Geuss, Raymond. 1981. *The Idea of a Critical Theory: Habermas and the Frankfurt School*. Cambridge: Cambridge University Press.

Gibb, James G. 2000. "Imaginary, but by No Means Unimaginable: Storytelling, Science, and Historical Archaeology." *Historical Archaeology* 34(2): 1–6.

Haltom, William, and Michael McCann, (2004). *Distorting the Law: Politics, Media, and the Litigation Crisis*. Chicago: University of Chicago Press.

Hartemann, Gabby Omoni. 2022. "Unearthing Our Colonial Wounds: Griotic Archaeology and Community-Engagement in Eastern Guiana." *International Journal of Historical Archaeology* 26: 79–117. https://doi.org/10.1007/s10761-021-00596-6.

Harvey, David C. 2001. "Heritage Pasts and Heritage Presents: Temporality, Meaning and the Scope of Heritage Studies." *International Journal of Heritage Studies* 7(4): 319–38.

Haviser, Jay B. 2015. "Truth and Reconciliation: Transforming Public Archaeology with African Descendant Voices in the Dutch Caribbean." *Journal of African Diaspora Archaeology and Heritage* 4(3): 243–59.

Hight, Jeremy. 2003. "Narrative Archaeology: Reading the Landscape." *Streetnotes* Summer. Retrieved 5 June 2022 from www.web.mit.edu/comm-forum/legacy/mit4/papers/hight.pdfs.

Hodder, Ian. 1989. "Writing Archaeology: Site Reports in Context." *Antiquity* 63(239): 268–74.

———. 2003. "Archaeological Reflexivity and the 'Local' Voice." *Anthropological Quarterly* 76(1): 55–69.

International Labour Organization (ILO). 2019. "Eliminating Forced Labour: Handbook for Parliamentarians No. 30." Geneva: Inter-Parliamentary Union.

Johnston, Robert, and Kimberley Marwood. 2017. "Action Heritage: Research, Communities, Social Justice." *International Journal of Heritage Studies* 23(9): 816–31.

Jones, Michael D. 2013. "Cultural Characters and Climate Change: How Heroes Shape Our Perception of Climate Science." *Social Science Quarterly* 95: 1–39.

Joyce, Rosemary. 2008. *The Languages of Archaeology: Dialog, Narrative, and Writing*. Oxford: Blackwell Publishers.

Kiddey, Rachael. 2017. "From the Ground Up: Cultural Heritage Practices as Tools for Empowerment in the Homeless Heritage Project." *International Journal of Heritage Studies* 24(7): 694–708.

Kristiansen, Kristian. 2011. "Theory Does Not Die, It Changes Direction." In *The Death of Archaeological Theory?*, ed. J. Bintliff and M. Pearce, 72–79. Oxford: Oxbow Books.

Labov, William, and Joshua Waletzky. 1967. "Narrative Analysis: Oral Versions of Personal Experience." In *Essays on the Verbal and Visual Arts*, ed. J. Helm, 12–44. Seattle: University of Washington Press.

Leone, Mark P., Parker B. Potter, Jr., and Paul A. Shackel. 1987. "Toward a Critical Archaeology." *Current Anthropology* 28(3): 283–92.

Little, Barbara J. 2000. "Compelling Images through Storytelling: Comment on 'Imaginary, but by No Means Unimaginable: Storytelling, Science, and Historical Archaeology.'" *Historical Archaeology* 34(2): 10–13.

Little, Barbara J., and Paul A. Shackel. 2014. *Archaeology, Heritage, and Civic Engagement: Working towards the Public Good*. Walnut Creek, CA: Left Coast Press.

Mancini, M. 1996. *One Dies, Get Another: Convict Leasing in the American South, 1866–1928*. Columbia: University of South Carolina Press.

Moulder, Rebecca Hunt. 1976. "Convicts as Capital: Thomas O'Conner and the Leases of the Tennessee Penitentiary System, 1871–1883." *East Tennessee Historical Society's Publications* 48: 40–70.

Pluciennik, M. 1999. "Archaeological Narratives and Other Ways of Telling." *Current Anthropology* 40(5): 653–78.

Polletta, Francesca. 2006. *It Was Like a Fever: Storytelling in Protest and Politics*. Chicago: University Chicago Press.

Polletta, Francesca, and Beth Gharrity Gardner. 2015. "Narrative and Social Movements." In *The Oxford Handbook of Social Movements*, ed. Donatella Della Porta and Mario Diani, 534–48. Oxford: Oxford University Press.

Polletta, Francesca, and Nathan Redman. 2020. "When Do Stories Change Our Minds?: Narrative Persuasion about Social Problems." *Sociology Compass* 14(4): e12778.

Praetzellis, Adrian. 1998. "Introduction: Why Every Archaeology Should Tell Stories Once in a While." *Historical Archaeology* 32(1): 1–3.

—————. 2014. "Narrative and Storytelling for Archaeological Education." In *Encyclopedia of Global Archaeology*, ed. Claire Smith, 5135–38. New York: Springer-Verlag.

Rosenbaum, Betty B. 1940. "Relationship between War and Crime in the United States." *Journal of Criminal Law and Criminology* 30(5): 722–40.

Sawyer, Wendy. 2017. "How Much Do Incarcerated People Earn in Each State?" Prison Policy Initiative. Retrieved 20 November 2020 from www.prisonpolicy.org/blog/2017/04/10/wages/.

Shapiro, Karin. 1998. *A New South Rebellion: The Battle Against Convict Labor in the Tennessee Coalfields, 1871–1896*. Chapel Hill: University of North Carolina Press.

Slater, Michael D., and Donna Rouner. 2002. "Entertainment-Education and Elaboration Likelihood: Understanding the Processing of Narrative Persuasion." *Communication Theory* 12: 173–91.

Sloan, Bob. 2010. "The Prison Industries Employment Certification Program: Why Everyone Should Be Concerned." *Prison Legal News*, 15 March, 1.

Smith, Laurajane, Paul Shackel, and Gary Campbell. 2011. "Introduction: Class Still Matters." In *Heritage, Labour and the Working Classes*, ed. Laurajane Smith, Paul Shackel, and Gary Campbell, 1–16. Abingdon: Routledge.

Southgate, Beverly. 2001. *History: What and Why? Ancient, Modern, and Postmodern Perspectives*, 2nd edn. London: Routledge.

Spector, Janet D. 1993. *What this Awl Means: Feminist Archaeology at a Wahpeton Dakota Village*. St. Paul: Minnesota Historical Society Press.

Stottman, M. Jay, ed. 2010. *Archaeologists as Activists: Can Archaeologists Change the World?* Tuscaloosa: University of Alabama Press.

Thomas, Jonathan T. 2015. "The Archaeologist as Writer." In *Subjects and Narratives in Archaeology*, ed. Ruth M. Van Dyke and Reinhard Bernbeck, 169–88. Boulder: University Press of Colorado.

Toolan, Michael. 2012. *Narrative: A Critical Linguistic Introduction*. London: Routledge.

Van Dyke, Ruth M., and Reinhard Bernbeck. 2015. *Subjects and Narrative in Archaeology*. Boulder: University Press of Colorado.

Viterna, Jocelyn. 2013. *Women in War: The Micro-Processes of Mobilization in El Salvador*. New York: Oxford University Press.

Westmont, V. Camille. 2022. "Dark Heritage in the New South: Remembering Convict Leasing in Southern Middle Tennessee through Community Archaeology." *International Journal of Historical Archaeology* 21(1): 1–21.

CHAPTER 7

Expanding Critical Archaeology in the Digital Age

Building User Interfaces and Sharing the Assemblages of Archaeology in Annapolis across the Globe

Adam Fracchia

Introduction

The Archaeology in Annapolis (AiA) collections represent more than forty years of scholarly research on the development of the modern world centered on the city of Annapolis, the capital of Maryland and former capital of the United States. Grounded in critical archaeology, the archaeological research program, established and run by Mark Leone at the University of Maryland, College Park (UMD), has produced some of the most studied assemblages ever recovered in the field of historical archaeology. These assemblages have provided the research basis for training and the scholarly work of many graduates who are now leaders in the field.

The AiA program has detailed the lives of many Annapolitans as well as peoples on the Eastern Shore. The program has studied the lives of immigrants, free Blacks, wealthy Whites, and enslaved and indentured people. Yet the program has not thoroughly addressed diversity in the production of knowledge and meaning, especially with regard to Black authorship and representation. In this chapter, I explore how this omission can begin to be corrected through the application of a critical approach to the next stage of AiA program—digital humanities.

The AiA research program is committed to continuing to explore and address the modern world through critical archaeology as well as partnering with and sharing authority in its archaeological research. Critical archaeology seeks to use critical theory in archaeological research to challenge current structures of inequality (Leone, Potter, and

Shackel 1987). As the AiA program evolves, the program has sought to embrace the role that current technology can play in presenting a more complete picture of the past and making that past accessible. The need for Black authorship and authority can begin to be addressed through this expansion of digital technology. The future relevance of archaeology and the AiA program lies in its ability to share the material of the past in a meaningful and available manner and through a wider engagement in the digital humanities.

This chapter outlines the beginning of these efforts. First, a brief overview of critical theory and the digital humanities is provided, followed by a background history of the AiA program and its engagement with critical theory. The chapter then discusses the program's current efforts in the digital humanities and the limitations of legacy collections. With this overview, the chapter finally presents plans for moving forward with the critical digital initiatives including the relational database.

Critical Theory and the Digital Humanities

Digital humanities encompass the intersections of disciplines of computing and humanities (Kirschenbaum 2010). While archaeologists have used digital or computational archaeology since the 1950s, the full potential of digital approaches has not been exploited, and its analytical and data storage capabilities have not been universally applied (Watrall 2016: 346). The humanities must better engage with the digital, critically and materially, instead of just integrating technology into current practices (Svensson 2016: 1).

Since the 1990s, digital archives as sources of archaeological data have grown rapidly. These archives are more than just digital storage: archaeology's involvement in the digital humanities has meant an expansion in the preservation of records, accessibility of gray literature, comparative studies, e-publishing, and free and publicly accessible data (Davies 2020: 232). All of these capabilities provide an avenue for the recontextualization and democratization of knowledge about the past. This aspect of digital humanities is vital because it ultimately allows for critical reevaluations of the past and its use. One example of an archaeological database that accomplishes many of these goals is the Digital Archaeological Archive of Comparative Slavery (DAACS), a publicly accessible archaeological archive representing enslaved Africans and their descendants living in the Chesapeake, Carolinas, and Caribbean during the colonial and antebellum periods. Similarly, the Digital Archaeological Record (tDAR) presents and synthesizes archaeological data that is archived and searchable. These examples demonstrate only two of an unlimited number of ways that archaeological information can be shared via digital platforms.

The goals of a digital humanities approach—accessibility, democratization, and reinterpretation—fit the mission of critical archaeology. Archaeologists have challenged the notion of the objective construction of knowledge and instead have questioned and/or called for a decolonization of the process of deriving meaning (Atalay 2006; Franklin 1997). While the AiA program has to sought to address structures of oppression in its archaeological practice, one of the most significant omissions has been the need for more diverse scholarship, especially Black scholarship, within the program. The program has worked with Black communities, descendants, and scholars, but the practitioners of the AiA, whether graduate students or staff, have been largely middle-class and white. As Michael Blakey (2020: S194) describes, the voice of Black authors (whether as scholars or the general public) in this research has been missing.

According to Mark Leone, the program has engaged and involved different communities and scholars. For a decade, Mark Leone worked with Gladys-Marie Fry, a folklorist, curator, and expert on the WPA (Works Progress Administration) *Slave Narratives* and African American textiles, and they coauthored several papers (Leone and Fry 1999; Leone, Fry, and Ruppel 2001; Ruppel et al. 2003). Leone also worked with Laurence Hurst, a curator and the exhibit designer of the Banneker Douglass Museum, for several years including three different exhibits on African American life such as an exhibit titled *The Maryland Black Experience as Understood through Archaeology* and an article exploring whether African American historical archaeology could be an alternative voice (see Leone et al. 1995). Leone has also collaborated with historian and archaeologist Cheryl LaRoche (Leone, LaRoche, and Babiarz 2005) and historian and historic preservationist Dale Green in Easton, Maryland. More recently, the program has collaborated and worked with more diverse groups of students to broaden authorship and professional training. There is a still a great need to include Black voices, ownership, and control of the archaeological narrative. The expansion of the AiA program further into the digital humanities provides an opportunity to foster decolonization.

Archaeology in Annapolis Background

To understand how the AiA plans to decolonize its critical archaeological practice through the digital humanities, we must first understand the AiA program and its sustained research in Annapolis. Annapolis, Maryland, founded as the capital of the colony of Maryland in 1695, remains the capital today. The city is small—home to only roughly 38,000 people—and serves as the permanent home of the US Naval Academy. Annapolis is historically important for several reasons. The city has always been a seat of power as Annapolis was home to all four Maryland signers of the Declaration of Independence, was the capital of the United States from November 1783 to June 1784, and was where General George Washington resigned his position as commander-in-chief of the Continental Army before returning to civilian life, demonstrating the primacy of civilian rule in the new country (Leone 2005). Annapolis was a center of free Black culture with a large free Black community before 1865 and has had a population that has been at least one-third Black since 1750. Annapolis continued to play a role in Black life in the twentieth century, for it was in Annapolis that Thurgood Marshall took up and won the right of Black public school teachers to receive equal pay in 1939 (Mills v. Board of Education of Anne Arundel County).

Unlike other cities, the historic core of Annapolis has remained largely extant. Annapolis has never been burned or raided and urban renewal has bypassed much of the city. Thus, the city has more than fifty eighteenth-century buildings and a thousand nineteenth-century buildings. Additionally, below-ground archaeological remains and historical documents dating to the early eighteenth century are also well preserved.

To study this history, the Archaeology in Annapolis program was created in 1981 by St. Clair Wright, founder and longtime president of Historic Annapolis, Inc./Foundation, and Mark P. Leone of the Department of Anthropology at the University of Maryland, College Park, (Leone 2005). The goal of Archaeology in Annapolis was to understand the past of the city through archaeology, to make it available immediately to residents and to visitors to the city, and to train students (Leone 2005). To date, Archaeology in Annapolis has excavated nearly sixty sites in Annapolis, Maryland, and several sites on Maryland's Eastern Shore. The program's archaeologists opened the first sites to the public in Maryland using an early National Endowment for the Humanities (NEH) grant. This early effort at public interpretation introduced visitors to the idea that the past is created, not just excavated. For example, the archaeologists showed the ideological nature of seventeenth- and eighteenth-century planned landscapes. They also conducted the first archaeology of Black Annapolitans in the city and reconstructed the earliest parts of African heritage to be found within Afro-Christianity (Leone, personal communication).

Within its localized context, the AiA program provides an important perspective on the birth and development of part of the United States, Maryland's history, and slavery and conditions of freedom. The program also provides a wide perspective on the city's political leaders, free African Americans, enslaved people, wage workers, crafts people, and children. Spanning more than three hundred years of history, the AiA collection serves to answer questions on the unequal holding of wealth, concepts of citizenship, survival under Jim Crow, racialization through rules of public health and safety, and gender through workspaces and family conditions—questions of interest to fields such as historical archaeology, modern material culture studies, historic preservation, and American history (for example, see Jopling 2015 or Mullins 1999). Through this work, the archaeological research program has produced some of the most important and widely studied assemblages in historical archaeology, and these in turn have provided the research basis for many scientific publications as well as dozens of graduate degrees in the discipline, including doctorates (see Little 1987; Shackel 1987; Potter 1989; Kryder-Reid 1991; Mullins 1996; Matthews 1998; Warner 2015; Ernstein 2004; Larsen 2004; Palus 2010; Knauf 2013; Tang 2014; Deeley 2015; Pruitt 2015; Skolnik 2019).

Critical Theory at Archaeology in Annapolis

The program was and continues to be grounded in critical archaeology. Drawing from the failure of historical awareness at places like Colonial Williamsburg in their presentation of current ideology and using the theoretical perspectives of the Frankfurt School and French Structural Marxism, Leone was challenged to build a program that could raise public consciousness through the sharing of historical knowledge (Leone 2010; Palus, Leone, and Cochran 2006). Based on the writings of Georg Lukács and Louis Althusser, Leone devised public tours and talks believing that by exposing dominant ideologies that masked social hierarchies, the program could raise an awareness that would make challenges to these hierarchies possible. The program attempted to show how material played an active role in creating and sustaining that false consciousness (Leone 2005). By 1990, Leone realized that democracy was subject to capitalism and public consciousness could not be changed in this manner (Leone 2010: 151–52). Therefore, Leone examined Jürgen Habermas's theory of communicative action focusing on the history of those were alienated and exploited and created alternative histories. Starting in the 1990s, the program began to examine African Americans in Annapolis and worked with community members to better understand these alternative histories. Using this theoretical perspective based on Habermas, Leone believes that a dominant ideology can be pierced with such alternatives (Leone 2020: 291).

The AiA program is but one effort (see Funari 2001; Saitta 2007) that has sought to recognize the structures of power in which historical archaeology is embedded and the use of the past in the present (see Palus et al. 2006). Over the last forty years, the AiA program has sought to understand the social and material practices that have allowed the overwhelming inequality of the modern world to persist and be tolerated (Mullins 1998: 12). Although the program's methodology has evolved over time, the AiA program continues to study the development of this inequality and draw connections between artifacts, inequality, and current conditions (Leone 2010). As the AiA looks to the future, we believe that digital humanities offer a new opportunity and platform from which to pursue these critically derived objectives.

Digital Humanities and Archaeology in Annapolis

AiA's efforts are driven by critical theory and the need of the program to better address fundamental limitations. The original perspective and purpose adopted by Leone from Habermas continues to drive the program, including in its new digital effort. For the AiA collections, a need exists to expand the narrative and reach of these collections and to cede authority in the construction of knowledge. Universal and free access is essential for providing the dissemination of these histories and the alternatives to modern capitalism that they present. Giving access to more data and to tools to present original interpretations reduces the boundaries between researcher and audience (Joyce and Tringham 2007: 329).

The project seeks to broaden the scope and relevance of this information in two ways. First, the AiA initiatives continue the construction of critical historical narratives that counter the present racist and exclusionary history of Annapolis and the Eastern

Shore. These narratives are grounded in material culture, allowing for a counter to history derived from documents and allow for a material, tangible although still digital connection. The critical narratives serve as alternative narratives that can challenge traditional histories. As Camille Westmont (chapter 6, this volume) highlights, the directed narrative has public appeal and can be persuasive.

The second goal is the presentation of data in its many forms with the ability to easily navigate through search features in an attempt to decolonize the data. The capability to search multiple sites at once and draw meaning and identity from a larger set of data is an effort to expand critical dialogues. This process of researching and querying the data allows researchers and the public to examine and use these sources to devise their own interpretations. The recent 2021 Society for Historical Archaeology Conference presentation by archaeologist Garrett Fessler and his analysis and reinterpretation of spirit bundles from Annapolis illustrates the ability of researchers to do just that. The extension of the analysis to other archaeological databases further broadens the context outside of Annapolis and the Eastern Shore. Providing the data directly to the public allows people to draw their own interpretation, thereby removing anthropologists' bias and preventing invented identities (Friedman 1992).

At the same time, the ability for individuals to study and navigate the data themselves fulfills a call in critical archaeology (Wilke and Bartoy 2000) to reconceptualize the relationship between researchers and the public; it also prioritizes the agency of the individuals who lived at these archaeological sites by providing a direct link to their material culture less obscured by archaeologists' interpretations. Providing the contextualization of the data within the global, capitalist process prevents the data from being completely subjective and disarticulated. Further, the use of specific key words is an effort to serve the first goal and more easily link the data to critical narratives for the user while still giving the user control, similar to Monika Stobiecka's (this volume) description of the role of a critical museum.

While the AiA program is determined to pursue and achieve these goals, the program's long tenure has presented some challenges. Just as museum curators have raised alarms about the "curation crisis," AiA, with its forty years of continuous research, now faces similar challenges related to artifact and data storage, outdated methods and materials, and outmoded software. Tackling these problems is essential to ensuring the future and accessibility of the collection. As excavations have ceased, the AiA program is using the opportunity to curate and digitize its collections as an opportunity to achieve its critical goals.

The Challenges of Legacy Collections

As the AiA program begins to work toward critical goals on diversity, the program must contend with the challenges of its legacy collections. To make the full collection available online, including overcoming major scale, ownership, and usability concerns,

the program must work toward addressing its problems with authorship and representations. Creating digital collections from physical collections and paper records presents a host of challenges; however, addressing these challenges can also articulate with
the goals of democratization and decolonization. AiA is beginning the process to deal
with the material reality of this work and growing its reach while identifying the problem of authorship and representation.

Over forty years, the AiA project has accumulated a large and valuable data set
that can be used to better understand the people of Annapolis and Maryland's Eastern
Shore as well as larger trends in US history and historical institutions such as slavery.
However, the curation of these assemblages has not kept up with changing standards
or preservation politics. The result is an artifactual collection of over 1,850 boxes,
currently stored across three different repositories, the bulk of which do not meet current archaeological collection standards. The collections must be updated prior to their
acceptance and storage at the Maryland Archaeological Conservation Laboratory; this
update is also imperative to ensure their preservation and future accessibility. Given the
size of the collection, the effort is a major financial and labor undertaking.

The problem of ownership further complicates this preservation effort. AiA does not
own the collections; rather, some objects are owned by individuals, others are owned by
institutions in Annapolis, and still others belong to the City of Annapolis. Having multiple owners complicates the ability to secure the financial backing necessary to carry out
the above-mentioned work and to achieve the project's goals. Although Historic Annapolis and the city agreed in the 1980s to house the collections in Annapolis and provide
for their curation, as needs and priorities have changed, the collections have been shifted
in and out of the city,[1] further putting them at risk for theft or damage and increasing
the need to secure permanent storage for the entire collection.

Another issue pertaining to the usability of the physical collections and archival
records is the coding of artifact catalogs. The AiA program made use of early computer
spreadsheet software to tabulate and catalog artifacts. Artifacts were assigned numeric
codes based on different classifications. This coding system had a six-digit master code
for the artifact type (e.g., earthenware, oyster shell, or brick) and a four-digit form
code for the form description (e.g., bowl or plate) of each artifact. The coded catalogs
are indecipherable without a sheet of master codes, and many of the catalogs were
finalized with the artifacts solely listed by code.

While managing archaeological collections presents its own challenges, even making basic documents available digitally can be complicated. Since 2010, information
about the excavations, including site reports and artifact catalogs, has been made available to the public via the Digital Repository at the University of Maryland (DRUM).
In total, DRUM holds 119 unique documents pertaining to thirty-eight archaeological
sites in the AiA program. While this format has shown some success in increasing the
accessibility of the documents,[2] the presentation of this digital data is problematic for
other reasons. The major flaw with the presentation of data on DRUM is that it presents
text-laden information that is not necessarily easy to navigate or organized for con-

sumption by the general public. The format of the reports, their density, and technical writing can be an obstacle for outside readers who lack insider knowledge. Further, the reports provide no means for the presentation of a critical dialogue. Instead, the report assumes people will be able to digest the information, make comparisons, and draw their own informed critical assessments.

Critically Moving Forward

Engagement with the digital humanities provides an avenue for the AiA program to move its efforts at critical archaeology forward. The decolonization of the scholarship is an essential component of this work, especially in terms of the inclusion and perspectives of diverse scholars and students. This effort and the expansion of the website, DRUM, and other digital resources add value, usability, and utility to the collections. Furthermore, the formulation of a relational database will make the AiA collections comparable with sites across Annapolis and outside of Annapolis, expanding the research potential of the collections and number of people who can access the collections.

Creating a Resource for the Future

The AiA program is committed to not just the more democratic dissemination of knowledge but to involving, ceding authority to, and training the next generation of scholars. First, the program will seek the partnership of a diverse base of scholars in the making and formulation of the digital database and all aspects of the digital program moving forward. This collaboration will provide for diverse voices to set the terms and the structure of the public platform. Using Susan Dion's (2009) idea of braiding histories, many voices are essential in the creation and formulation of many forms of knowledge. Involvement of a diverse group of scholars is essential even at this initial process of formatting the data.

Equally important for decolonization is the involvement of diverse groups of students in terms of collaboration and pedagogical practice. Critical race theory demands that archaeologists foster and support the work and voices of minority scholars (see Epperson 2004). Pedagogical practice allows for the instillment of value and learning through doing. Involving students will teach this digital literacy and create further new tools for collaboration and diverse interpretations. Thus, this involvement allows for self-expression that will enrich the interpretations as well as the learning of skill sets for the next generation of scholars (Morgan and Eve 2012: 529). In this way, the boundaries between the teacher and learner can be blurred and hierarchical positions more easily challenged through multivocality (Cook 2020: 123). The democratization of the data allows the sharing of access, meaning, and the ability to challenge traditional positions of privileged authority.

Increasing the digital access of the AiA collections adds utility and value to the program and to its existing collections, both for professional archaeologists and the public. Making the AiA collections accessible, researchable, and comparative will increase the value of these collections for other archaeologists. This is particularly important because digital repositories of archaeological collections often focus more on accessing and collecting data than on data reuse (Faniel et al. 2013). Once the AiA collections are online, other scholars will be able to identify and extract the forms of data that are of value for their own projects. Archaeologists have already used the artifact collections and associated records to reevaluate and reinterpret archaeological sites excavated by Archaeology in Annapolis (Beaudry, Cook, and Mrozowski 1991; Clifton 2017; Galke 2000), resulting in new interpretations; we expect this trend to continue as more data is made available and accessible.

Additionally, making the data accessible to the public will increase its utility as a teaching tool. Currently, the lack of readily accessible comparative data severely limits archaeological research and relevancy (Galle, Bollwerk, and Neiman 2019: 56). Organizing and increasing the accessibility of these collections will provide a useful and comprehensive comparative resource for teaching, thereby increasing the utility of a resource that has generally been underappreciated and underutilized (Agbe-Davies et al. 2014; Barker 2004; Marquardt, White, and Scholtz 1982; Sonderman 2004).

Increasing access to the data not only helps increase the utility and value of the existing collections, better access also helps address systematic problems within archaeology. Archaeology in Annapolis will help with the current curation crisis in archaeology (Childs and Sullivan 2004; McDavid 2002; Swain 2007; Trimble and Marino 2003; Voss 2012; Witze 2019), a crisis created by the increasing numbers of excavated collections, dwindling curatorial space, and limited online access to information. Making these collections accessible online will expand their research capability and allow archaeologists to reanalyze artifacts that are already excavated rather than excavate new sites, which further compounds the crisis.

Confronting Current Challenges

These efforts to expand authorship and authority and to pursue new forms of critical archaeological engagement are being combined with the current needs of the collection. Before the AiA collections can be resources for critical scholarship moving forward, AiA must address its current limitations, particularly those related to updating the artifact housing, making documents readable, and making all of it accessible.

Over the last several years, the Archaeology in Annapolis project has been working on a curation project and a related digital expansion project. The large-scale curation and consolidation project has reboxed, rebagged, and labeled more than two hundred boxes in preparation for the permanent storage of the artifactual collections at the MAC (Maryland Archaeological Conservation) lab. Unfortunately, only small amounts of funding have been procured for this work, and large-scale funding efforts have not been successful nor were other scholars involved.

Although the AiA program is aware of the limitations of DRUM, because of DRUM's accessibility, content continues to be uploaded to the server, including updated site forms, catalog, and visual documents, like maps and photographs. As more content is added, efforts are being made to improve the navigability of the AiA's DRUM account paired with an updated website. To improve the navigability of the AiA resources on DRUM, the collection description page will be as used as a table of contents for the documents available on DRUM. This table of contents will list all of the archaeological site names and numbers and links to documents related to those sites. The project also aims to link these sites to the dissertations based on the Archaeology in Annapolis project. Thus, DRUM could connect the various online resources together so that when people visit one resource, they can be directed to the other associated resources. This effort attempts to make the data more navigable, discoverable, and centralized.

The AiA program is also working to make the artifact catalogs that characterize the collections readable on DRUM. While the artifact catalogs were written with a coding system that was meant as a time saving effort, as technology has improved, it has become easier to quickly write out the descriptions and filter data. To decode the catalogs, a script was created in R-Studio by graduate student Madeline Laub to replace numerical codes with textual descriptions. These text-based descriptions are being uploaded to DRUM, making it much easier for both archaeologists and the general public to utilize the data. The decoded catalogs provide greater ease of access and allow more people to quickly see and analyze the information available in the catalogs, which is essential for democratizing the data.

Increasing accessibility also means locating and digitizing documents that are currently only available in paper form. Several of the catalogs and site reports are missing or were only available on paper. In December 2019, these paper catalogs were digitally scanned into PDF format. The digitization and reformatting work will continue to push forward the efforts to update DRUM and provide access to sites that were not previously available, beyond what is currently accessible on DRUM.

Moving forward, the new AiA website will be key to helping people navigate the work of the program. Other scholars will help formulate what this website will contain and how the information will be ordered and presented. For instance, they will help craft a summary of each site while also including the links to the site reports and catalogs available on DRUM. These links make it even more important that the information made available on DRUM is up to date and comprehensive. The act of navigating through the data and text allows for independent choices in accessing different pages of data and is a step in the independent creation of knowledge (Joyce and Tringham 2007: 329).

A Relational Database

The current efforts to make the AiA collections more readable is one step of a larger effort to provide a means to synthesize and query the data, make it accessible and comparable, and allow for outside analysis and interpretation. The work of Archaeology in Annapolis represents a sample of the archaeology of an entire city and its many facets, from the 1720s through the 1990s. While the assemblages can be compared with each other over spans of time, the addition of a comparative digital database will also more easily allow comparisons with digital materials available through other digital databases, such as DAACS. This project will follow models such as the data publishing platform *Open Context* by the Alexandria Archive Institute. The greater accessibility of data on Black lives offers further potential for integration with other digital projects focused on the lives of enslaved peoples, such as the Mellon Foundation-funded Enslaved project based at Michigan State University.

The digital resource produced through this project will have two main components: a relational database, primarily built from the artifact catalogs, and a full-text search application and archive, primarily built from project site reports and other documents. These components will both be accessible through the expanded project website, which will serve as the user interface. This database will transform the extensive collections into a powerful analytical tool that can return relevant information from multiple AiA sites, a key functionality that the current project lacks. The linkage of the web interface to the database will allow for functionality such as searching one archaeological site or multiple sites, the filtering of search results by controlled vocabularies, and export of specific data extracts for download in open formats such as comma-separated value (CSV) files. Search results from both the relational database and full-text search will also provide links back to original project documents hosted on DRUM for all results. The nomenclature for searches will be standardized archaeological terms that are comparable to other databases and agreed upon by a host of scholars.

The formulation of the database and its design has been a long consultative process that begins a new partnership with other scholars. Initially, the AiA program talked with researchers in the field on the strengths and limitations of different database designs and functions. A survey was conducted on the use of existing archaeological databases by students, researchers, and the public to understand how people navigated these databases and which components were seen as the most valuable by the different groups. From this research, a model website design was constructed that provides some wayfinding tools and additional indexing of material in the underlying documents. An example of the currently available methods for finding comparable bodies of data from more than one catalog, can be seen on the page dedicated to African American bundles.[3] True analytical work that would allow any user to compare data on bundles, or on the earliest cutlery or spoons and forks, or the first use of water pipes or sewage drains, will depend on the completion of the website and database.

This effort at designing the database was limited by a lack of involvement by a diverse audience, student body, and scholarly body. To correct this omission, the AiA program is applying for funding to support and involve a wide range of partners in designing the goals, format, and actual database. While the original authorship of the archaeology work cannot be expanded, how it is interpreted, seen, and used can be set by more diverse scholarship.

Data curation of Archaeology in Annapolis material will go beyond transforming the digital materials of the project from a collection of documents into a data resource. These efforts will also serve to make this data more interoperable by aligning it to common standards and creating the basis for linkages with related work such as databases like DAACS and Colonial Encounters.

Project-specific vocabularies will focus searching and browsing. For example, users will be able to search by types of artifact or materials, such as in the Colonial Encounters database. However, to increase the usability of the data, the team will identify select terms for alignment with broader vocabularies and ontologies such as those published by tDAR or CIDOC-CRM (International Committee for Documentation-Conceptual Reference Model) or Conceptual Reference Model, which has greater adoption for museum collections. Making the assemblages comparable with other databases extends the analysis and the ability of others to produce knowledge.

The list of thematic and subject terms will be expanded to be most productive for users of the database. Keywords may include theoretical concepts, artifact types, interpretive conclusions, and other data that can be foreseen as anticipated search terms. These subject terms will also be cross-linked to vocabularies such as Library of Congress subject headings and potentially Wikidata entries where appropriate to aid researchers in discovering related materials across multiple collections. Subject terms will be incorporated in faceted browsing functionality of the project database and particular terms may be made available as "canned" searches to highlight particularly rich subsets of the collection. These subsets can be further connected to established critical narratives. The overall selection of these terms will be accomplished working with a wider community of scholars.

Conclusion

The critical archaeological data and scholarship remain a referenced resource for the field and further research. Web traffic to the existing online content demonstrates the worldwide use of the AiA material while recent publications and conference presentations show that scholars continue to use and reevaluate the data, especially in relation to other sites. The overall example of the program's focus on critical archaeology is another source archaeologists and related fields continue to draw from. The recent translation of articles by Mark Leone and the AiA program into Portuguese (see *Vestígos: Revista Latino-Americana de Arqueologia Historica* 2021, Volume 15[2]) is a current illustration of the continued global engagement and utility of this scholarship.

From this scholarship, the lives of many Annapolitans as well as peoples on the Eastern Shore have been detailed archaeologically, but the program has not addressed diversity in the production of knowledge and meaning, especially ensuring Black authorship and representation. Success and decolonization is dependent on correcting this omission. Partnership and collaboration and ultimately, the ceding of authority over these digital initiatives and their creation is a step toward more inclusive, representative, and critical productions of knowledge.

The current efforts of the Archaeology in Annapolis program provide an example of how technology can be applied to expand the use of archaeological collections and scholarship in continued engagement with the present and the modern world. The program seeks to curate the existing collection at the Maryland state curation facility to ensure its long-term preservation and availability for the future. The program also seeks to expand digital access and use of the collections and the critical narrative. The reformatting, decoding, and correction of data and the utilization of previously available online mediums such as the Digital Repository of the University of Maryland provide greater access to digital data. Expanding linkages and adding more visual data allows a more user-friendly digital database and easier consumption of the data. The creation of a relational database will facilitate making the data comparable across AiA-excavated sites and beyond. Through a broader partnership and collaboration, these initiatives in combination can create a powerful and critical research tool for researchers and the public.

The goals of Archaeology in Annapolis to document the formation of the modern world and its inequalities and understand the lives of the people who were most marginalized can be expanded through the democratization of data and its analysis. Through the use of technology and partnership with a wider field of scholars, the AiA program hopes to extend and expand the life and authorship of critical narratives and ultimately highlight alternatives to the inequities produced by the modern world, and archaeology itself.

Acknowledgments

This chapter is drawn from many efforts including the work of Master of Applied Anthropology student Madeline Laub and several recent NEH grant proposals to fund these efforts. Mark Leone and Paul Shackel graciously read drafts of this chapter and provided comments. Camille Westmont patiently encouraged the writing of this chapter and offered a wealth of constructive feedback.

Adam Fracchia is a historical archaeologist and associate research professor at the University of Maryland who studies the processes of urbanization and industrialization and their impact on the modern world and everyday life. His research has focused on labor and the material and spatial evolution of the Baltimore metropolitan region and the role and responsibility of archaeology for present communities. He also directs forensic aviation recovery excavations for the Defense POW/MIA Accounting Agency.

Notes

1. The bulk of the collections are currently being stored in a public storage facility rented by the City of Annapolis.
2. The site reports on DRUM have been downloaded for searchability over 65,000 times as of 2019. The Library system at UMD has also tracked a large number of downloads from internet addresses in Annapolis, Israel, and Japan.
3. "African American Bundles." *Exploring Archaeology in Annapolis*. Retrieved 6 March 2022 from http://aia.umd.edu/explore/critical/bundles.html.

References

Agbe-Davies, Anna S., Jillian E. Galle, Mark W. Hauser, and Fraser D. Neiman. 2014. "Teaching with Digital Archaeological Data: A Research Archive in the University Classroom." *Journal of Archaeological Method and Theory* 21(4): 837–61.

Atalay, Sonya. 2006. "Indigenous Archaeology as Decolonizing Practice." *American Indian Quarterly* 30(3/4): 280–310.

Barker, Alex W. 2004. "Stewardship, Collections Integrity, and Long-Term Research Value." In *Our Collective Responsibility: The Ethics and Practice of Archaeological Collections Stewardship*, ed. S.T. Childs, 25–41. Washington, DC: Society for American Archaeology.

Beaudry, Mary C., Lauren J. Cook, and Stephen Mrozowski. 1991. "Artifacts and Active Voices: Material Culture as Social Discourse." In *The Archaeology of Inequality*, ed. Randall H. McGuire and Robert Paynter, 150–91. Oxford: Blackwell.

Blakey, Michael L. 2020. "Archaeology under the Blinding Light of Race." *Current Anthropology* 61 (Supplement 22): 183–97.

Childs, S. Terry, and Lynne P. Sullivan. 2004. "Archaeological Stewardship: It's about Both Collections and Sites." In *Our Collective Responsibility: The Ethics and Practice of Archaeological Collections Stewardship*, ed. S.T. Childs, 3–21. Washington, DC: Society for American Archaeology.

Clifton, Ellis. 2017. "Close Quarters: Master and Slave Space in Eighteenth-Century Annapolis." In *Slavery in the City: Architecture and Landscapes of Urban Slavery in North America*, ed. Clifton Ellis and Rebecca Ginsburg, 69–86. Charlottesville: University of Virginia Press.

Cook, Katherine. 2020. "Re-Coding Collaborative Archaeology: Digital Teaching and Learning for a Decolonised Future." In *Communicating the Past in the Digital Age: Proceedings of the International Conference on Digital Methods in Teaching and Learning in Archaeology*, ed. S. Hageneur, 115–26. London: Ubiquity Press.

Deeley, Kathryn Hubsch. 2015. "Double 'Double Consciousness': An Archaeology of African American Class and Identity in Annapolis, Maryland, 1850 to 1930." Ph.D. dissertation. College Park, MD: University of Maryland.

Davies, Peter. 2020. "Historical Archaeology and Technology." In *The Routledge Handbook of Global Historical Archaeology*, ed. Charles E. Orser, Jr., Andrés Zarankin, Pedro Paulo A. Funari, Susan Lawrence, and James Symonds, 231–46. London: Routledge.

Dion, Susan D. 2009. *Braiding Histories: Learning from Aboriginal Peoples' Experiences and Perspectives*. Vancouver: University of British Columbia Press.

Epperson, Terrence W. 2004. "Critical Race Theory and the Archaeology of the African Diaspora." *Historical Archaeology* 38(1): 101–8.

Ernstein, Julie H. 2004. "Constructing Context: Historical Archaeology and the Pleasure Garden in Prince George's County, Maryland, 1740–1790." Ph.D. dissertation. Boston, MA: Boston University.

Faniel, Ixchel, Eric Kansa, Sarah Whitcher Kansa, Julianna Barrera-Gomez, and Elizabeth Yakel. 2013. "The Challenges of Digging Data: A Study of Context in Archaeological Data Reuse." In *Proceedings of the 13th ACM/IEEE-CS Joint Conference on Digital Libraries*, 295–304. JCDL'13. Indianapolis, IN: Association for Computing Machinery.

Franklin, Maria. 1997. "'Power to the People': Sociopolitics and the Archaeology of Black Americans." *Historical Archaeology* 31(3): 36–50.

Friedman, Jonathan. 1992. "The Past in the Future: History and the Politics of Identity." *American Anthropologist* 94(4): 837–59.

Funari, Pedro Paulo A. 2001. "Public Archaeology from a Latin American Perspective." *Public Archaeology* 1(4): 230–43.

Galke, Laura J. 2000. "Did the Gods of Africa Die?: A Reexamination of a Carroll House Crystal Assemblage." *North American Anthropologist* 21(1) 19–33.

Galle, Jillian E., Elizabeth Bollwerk, and Fraser D. Neiman. 2019. "The Digital Archaeological Archive of Comparative Slavery: A Case Study in Open Data and Collaboration in the Field of Archaeology." In *New Life for Archaeological Collections*, ed. Allen Rebecca and Ford Ben, 54–90. Lincoln: University of Nebraska Press.

Jopling, Hannah. 2015. *Life in a Black Community: Striving for Equal Citizenship in Annapolis, Maryland, 1902–1952*. Lanham, MD: Lexington Books.

Joyce, Rosemary A., and Ruth E. Tringham. 2007. "Feminist Adventures in Hypertext." *Journal of Archaeological Method and Theory* 14(3): 328–58.

Kirschenbaum, Matthew. 2010. "What Is Digital Humanities, and What's It Doing in English Departments?" *ADE Bulletin* 150: 55–61.

Knauf, Jocelyn Elaine. 2013. "Brought up Carefully: The Archaeology of Women, Race Relations, Domesticity, and Modernization in Annapolis, Maryland, 1865–1930." Ph.D. dissertation. College Park, MD: University of Maryland.

Kryder-Reid, Elizabeth. 1991. "Landscape as Myth: The Contextual Archaeology of an Annapolis Landscape." Ph.D. dissertation. Providence, RI: Brown University.

Larsen, Eric. 2004. "Situating Identity: An Archaeology and Representation of Race and Community in Annapolis, Maryland." Ph.D. dissertation. Buffalo: State University of New York at Buffalo.

Leone, Mark P. 2005. *The Archaeology of Liberty in an American Capital: Excavations in Annapolis*. Berkeley, CA: University of California Press.

———. 2010. *Critical Historical Archaeology*. Walnut Creek, CA: Left Coast Press.

———. 2020. "Critical Theory." In *The Routledge Handbook of Global Historical Archaeology*, ed. Charles E. Orser, Jr., Andrés Zarankin, Pedro Paulo A. Funari, Susan Lawrence, and James Symonds, 289–97. London: Routledge.

Leone, Mark P., and Gladys-Marie Fry. 1999. "Conjuring in the Big House Kitchen: An Interpretation of African American Belief Systems Based on the Uses of Archaeology and Folklore Sources." *Journal of American Folklore* 112(445): 372–403.

Leone, Mark P., Gladys-Marie Fry, and Timothy Ruppel. 2001. "Spirit Management among Americans of African Descent." In *Race and the Archaeology of Identity*, ed. Charles E. Orser, Jr., 143–57. Salt Lake City: University of Utah Press.

Leone, Mark P., Cheryl Janifer LaRoche, and Jennifer J. Babiarz. 2005. "The Archaeology of Black Americans in Recent Times." *Annual Review of Anthropology* 34(1): 575–98.

Leone, Mark P., Paul Mullins, Marian C. Creveling, Laurence Hurst, Barbara Jackson-Nash, Lynn Jones, Hannah Kaiser, George Logan, and Mark Warner. 1995. "Can an African American Historical Archaeology Be an Alternative Voice?" In *Interpreting Archaeology: Finding Meaning in the Past*, ed. Ian Hodder, Michael Shanks, Alexandra Alexandri, Victor Buchli, John Carman, Jonathan Last, and Gavin Lucas, 110–24. London: Routledge.

Leone, Mark P., Parker B. Potter, Jr., and Paul A. Shackel. 1987. "Toward a Critical Archaeology." *Current Anthropology* 28(3): 283–302.

Little, Barbara J. 1987. "Ideology and the Media: Historical Archaeology of Printing in Eighteenth-Century Annapolis, Maryland." Ph.D. dissertation. Buffalo: State University of New York at Buffalo.

Marquardt, William, Antaa Montet-White, and Sandra C. Scholtz. 1982. "Resolving the Crisis in Archaeological Collections Curation." *American Antiquity* 47(2): 409–18.

Matthews, Christopher N. 1998. "The Making of the Annapolis Landscape: An Archaeology of History and Tradition." Ph.D. dissertation. New York: Columbia University.

McDavid, Carol Ann. 2002. "Archaeologies that Hurt; Descendants that Matter: A Pragmatic Approach to Collaboration in the Public Interpretation of African-American Archaeology." *World Archaeology* 34(2): 303–14.

Mills v. Board of Education of Anne Arundel. 1939. Mills v. Board of Education of Anne Arundel. United States District Court for the District of Maryland. 30 F. Supp. 245, No. 170. Justia US Law. Retrieved 1 July 2019 from https://law.justia.com/cases/federal/district-courts/FSupp/30/245/1378476/.

Morgan, Colleen, and Stuart Eve. 2012. "DIY and Digital Archaeology: What Are You Doing to Participate?" *World Archaeology* 44(4): 521–37.

Mullins, Paul R. 1996. "The Contradictions of Consumption: An Archaeology of African America and Consumer Culture, 1850–1930." Ph.D. dissertation. Amherst: University of Massachusetts.

———. 1998. "Expanding Archaeological Discourse: Ideology, Metaphor, and Critical Theory in Historical Archaeology." In *Annapolis Pasts: Historical Archaeology in Annapolis, Maryland*, ed. Paul A. Shackel, Paul R. Mullins, and Mark S. Warner, 12–34. Knoxville: University of Tennessee Press.

———. 1999. *Race and Affluence: An Archaeology of African America and Consumer Culture*. New York: Kluwer Academic/Plenum Publishers.

Palus, Matthew. 2010. "Materialities of Government: A Historical Archaeology of Infrastructure in Annapolis and Eastport, 1865–1961." Ph.D. dissertation. New York: Columbia University.

Palus, Matthew, Mark P. Leone, and Matthew D. Cochran. 2006. "Critical Archaeology: Politics Past and Present." In *Historical Archaeology*, ed. Martin Hall and Stephen W. Silliman, 84–104. Oxford: Wiley-Blackwell.

Potter, Parker B. 1989. "Archaeology in Public in Annapolis: An Experiment in the Application of Critical Theory to Historical Archaeology." Ph.D. dissertation. Providence, RI: Brown University.

Pruitt, Elizabeth. 2015. "Reordering the Landscape: Science, Nature, and Spirituality at Wye House." Ph.D. dissertation. College Park: University of Maryland.

Ruppel, Timothy, Jessica Neuwirth, Mark P. Leone, and Gladys-Marie Fry. 2003. "Hidden in View: African Spiritual Spaces in North American Landscapes." *Antiquity* 77(296): 321–35.

Saitta, Dean J. 2007. *The Archaeology of Collective Action*. Gainesville: University of Florida Press.

Shackel, Paul A. 1987. "A Historical Archaeology of Personal Discipline." Ph.D. dissertation. Buffalo: State University of New York at Buffalo.

Skolnik, Benjamin A. 2019. "'The Real Distance Was Great Enough': Remapping a Multivalent Plantation Landscape Using Historical Geographic Information Systems (hGIS)." Ph.D. dissertation. College Park, MD: University of Maryland.

Sonderman, Robert C. 2004. "Before You Start that Project, Do You Know What to Do with the Collection?" In *Our Collective Responsibility: The Ethics and Practice of Archaeological Collections Stewardship*, ed. S. T. Childs, 107–20. Washington, DC: Society for American Archaeology.

Svensson, Patrik. 2016. "Introducing the Digital Humanities." In *Debates in the Humanities*, ed. Matthew K. Gold and Lauren F. Klein, 1–35. Minneapolis: University of Minnesota Press.

Swain, Hedley. 2007. *An Introduction to Museum Archaeology*. New York: Cambridge University Press.

Tang, Amanda. 2014. "'Fried Chicken Belongs to All of Us': The Zooarchaeology of Enslaved Food-ways on the Long Green, Wye House (18TA314), Talbot County, Maryland." Ph.D. dissertation. College Park: University of Maryland.

Trimble, Michael K., and Eugene A. Marino. 2003. "Archaeological Curation: An Ethical Imperative for the Twenty-First Century." In *Ethical Issues in Archaeology*, ed. L. J. Zimmerman, Karen D. Vitelli, and Julie Hollowell-Zimmer, 99–112. Lanham, MD: AltaMira.

Voss, Barbara L. 2012. "Curation as Research: A Case Study in Orphaned and Underreported Archaeological Collections." *Archaeological Dialogues* 19(2): 145–69.

Warner, Mark S. 2015. *Eating in the Side Room: Food, Archaeology, and African American Identity*. Gainesville: University Press of Florida.

Watrall, Ethan. 2016. "Archaeology, the Digital Humanities, and the 'Big Tent.'" In *Debates in the Humanities*, ed. Matthew K. Gold and Lauren F. Klein, 345–58. Minneapolis: University of Minnesota Press.

Wilkie, Laurie A., and Kevin M. Bartoy. 2000. "A Critical Archaeology Revisited: A Critical Archaeology Revisited." *Current Anthropology* 41(5): 747–77.

Witze, Alexandra. 2019. "Disappearing Digital Data." *American Archaeology* 23(1): 40–45.

Part III

Situating Critical Archaeology

CHAPTER 8

Public Archaeology through the Lens of Historiography

Torgrim Sneve Guttormsen

Introduction

Public archaeology studies the complex relationship between archaeology and the wider world (Guttormsen and Hedeager 2015; Moshenska 2017: 3), a definition that emphasizes archaeology's many uses in society. Nevertheless, despite increasing academic support for this research field, there is a need to understand how to analyze the complex interplay between archaeology and the public. A major theoretical concern in the literature is to examine what it means for archaeology as a profession, a discipline, and a practice to interact with the public(s) in multiple ways; and vice versa, what defines archaeology when the latter is interpreted and used by a diverse public (for an overview, see Richardson and Almansa-Sánchez 2015; see also Matsuda 2016; Varghese 2017). However, in the discourses on public archaeology, less attention has been given to the processes of heritagization in the history of archaeology—that is, how archaeological heritage is being created in a close relationship between archaeologists and a diverse public. Investigating said processes of heritagization is the topic of this chapter.

Historiographical studies of archaeology emphasize the biography of archaeologists and how their singular achievements have contributed to increasing the knowledge of the discipline (e.g., Klindt-Jensen 1975). This is sometimes referred to as an internalistic or rationalistic, or even an evolutionistic, approach, whereby the (internal) development of the discipline—that is, the history of the world within archaeology—is emphasized based on a historiographic approach to archaeology as continuous and intensifying knowledge production that steadily uncovers more "truth" about the past (Olsen 1997: 46–47; Brattli and Svestad 1991).

At the same time, a social constructivist (or contextual and externalistic) approach is concerned with how mentalities, concepts, and knowledge regimes in the present society have shaped the discipline and how archaeology pertains to contemporary public discourse about the past (e.g., Rowley-Conwy 2006; Schnapp 1996; Thomas 2004; Trigger 1989). In the constructionist approach, an archaeologist's biography is examined in relation to the conditions of their society, with a focus on the history of archaeology in the wider world (e.g., museum exhibitions, national commemorations, tourism industry, school programs, immigration politics, etc.). This approach focuses on the history of archaeology and heritage production from a public perspective rather than the history within the archaeological discipline. Such a focus raises the question of whether the public dimension of a historiographical approach can enrich the knowledge, theory, and analysis of the relationship between archaeology and the public.

Historiographical theory provides access to the relational historical aspects behind the people who are involved in history writing and heritage making—that is, to the complex relationships that archaeology and archaeological expertise have with the wider world. It seems to me that in historiographical scholarship, scholars have tried to apply easy labels and place each other, research traditions, and discourses into categorical boxes or branches with historiographical origins. However, rather than viewing archaeology as a "tree of knowledge" with a common "trunk" (the tree metaphor), the growing historical literature on archaeology has demonstrated that archaeology is a network of many "trunks" and "branches" (the rhizome metaphor); in other words, "that its history and development [has] always involved multiple strands—in essence the existence of other possibilities and practices" (Murray and Evans 2008: 3). Historiography entails versatile uses of the past; or, expressed more profoundly, "You could say that the most distinguished feature about history is that in reality, it never occurs alone, it always gives rise to other histories. The ideology shaping function of histories becomes undisguised when they are compared with other stories on the same subject—when you do not just read one story but several. This is what critical researchers within the humanities do, and which is in its true sense the educational function of the humanities" (Hedeager and Schousboe 1989: 10, my translation). Reading several stories on the same topic involves examining how archaeologists and their statements are included in the wide and diverse processes of history writing and heritage production in the public domain, where other stakeholders also participate in interpreting and using the past.

In this chapter, I will examine the wide and diverse processes of history writing and heritage production by focusing on the involvement of archaeology and archaeologists in the establishment of the Norwegian Museum of Technology (Norsk Teknisk Museum) in 1914. I will use "public historiography" as a theoretical and methodological lens to understand the relationship between archaeology and the public, thus hopefully stimulating a debate about the purpose of public archaeology as an analytical research field. An epistemological framework for this approach is critical theory (Horkheimer [1937] 1982): a nonreductive, interdisciplinary, and holistic approach that acknowledges the relational conditions between text(s), exhibition practices, and society. In other words, an epistemic (critical) realism where parts and totality are connecting as an integrated whole and examined in a hermeneutic, historically situated, and socially complex contextual and critical perspective.

The study of public archaeology through the lens of "public historiography" caters an example of the three criteria uttered by Horkheimer when he states that critical theory "must be explanatory, practical, and normative" (Horkheimer [1937] 1982). In our context it means when public archaeology, thereby the relationship between archaeology and the public, adequately manages to explain the social problems that exist in society, offers practical solutions for how to respond to them and make changes, and clearly adheres to the norms of criticism established by the field. To study this historiographically means to open up for an interdisciplinary approach that connects a number of different research topics (narratives in fiction and factual prose, societal changes, trends and grand concepts in wider society etc.).

I will employ the following method: first, I will analyze the types of history writing and hence the literary genres that form the basis of the museum's educational content; and second, I will focus on the relationships between the museum's collections and the contemporary exhibitions on technology in the early twentieth century. As I derive much of my theoretical framework about the relational aspects of history writing and heritage making from the Soviet linguist and philosopher Mikhail Mikhaîlovich Bakhtin (1895–1975), I will explain in more detail his perspectives and my use of his ideas for my "public historiographical method."

Bakhtinian Theory and Historiography

Bakhtin's primary interest was to examine the principles of language use and historical poetics, with an emphasis on the emergence of the realist novel tradition in European literature. His innovative ideas are presented in his historical analyses of, for example, the chronotopes (*xronotop*, "time-space") in the novel tradition, the polyphony (*mnogojazyčie*, *polyglossia*, "many-voices") of characters in Fyodor Dostoyevsky's works, and the carnivalesque in François Rabelais and his world (Bakhtin 1984, [1981] 2008). The dialogical principle is a master concept that guided Bakhtin throughout his works. The dialogical principle, also called "dialogism" (*dialogizm*) in Bakhtinian scholarship (Holquist [1990] 2002: 15), defines an epistemological position—a mode of perceiving the world—and is a basic position in his study of historical poetics (107–48).

Dialogism is a literary theory used to analyze the contact zone between two points of view or speech positions in a situation of communication (e.g., speaker vs. listener or writer vs. reader). Bakhtin's main contribution to linguistic theory was his attention to the non-authorial and transcendental character of utterances. According to Bakhtin, an utterance, or "my voice," is relatively constituted by "the voices of others" (the presence of the other's otherness); this dialogical situation is intersubjective, trans-linguistic, and contextually situated in history and culture (a position that linguist Julia Kristeva used in the 1960s for her theory of intertextuality). In Bakhtin's literary theory, the polyphonic multiplicity of voices in utterances and texts is also called heteroglossia (*raznorečie*, *raznojazyčie*, *raznorečivost*, see Bakhtin [1981] 2008: 263). Bakhtin further explained how centripetal (*centrostremitel'nyj*, centralizing) and centrifugal (*centro-bežnyj*, decentralizing or decentering) forces of any language or culture are represented in utterances, whereby the dialogical heteroglossic position, when subjugated by verbal-ideological (centripetal) forces, turns into monologization, conceptualized by the phrase monoglossia (*odnojazyčie*, Bakhtin [1981] 2008: 270–72). A dialogue, unlike a monologue, is multivocal (the presence of at least two distinct voices). Monologization describes how authoritative voices in utterances, texts, and literature result in unanimity, canonized meaning, and power. However, the monologic centripetal forces are under constant pressure from heteroglossic centrifugal forces that are characteristic of dialogue. Consequently, knowledge is a relative, constantly open, and never-ending process of dialogical communication involving tensions between dialogues and monologues.

For Bakhtin, dialogism represented and exposed real human conditions, reaching far beyond literary theory. As a form of language use, dialogism became a framework for conceptualizing human consciousness, ideology, beliefs, worldviews, and sociopolitical systems (Holquist [1990] 2002: 21). Today, dialogism covers several disciplinary fields: from philosophy and psychology (the communicative or hybrid self) to cultural and social science (social diversity and power relations). Not surprisingly, dialogism has also been used in the theory of ethics and politics (e.g., as a theory of transhumanism and democracy/totalitarianism). Dialogism has become a strong foundation for postmodern ideas, not least for structuralist and post-structuralist theory (Gardiner and Mayerfeld Bell 1998). Dialogism is used as a theoretical approach to analyze the construction of utterances and texts as well as discourses, narratives, cultures, and society. Therefore, we could benefit from a Bakhtinian approach when analyzing how archaeological utterances are dialogically constructed within various situations of communication (within texts, social milieus, and societies). To understand what public archaeology is and how archaeology has been shaped throughout history implies studying the situations of communication where archaeology is dialogically positioned in relation to "the voices of others" in discourses of the past. Below, I will describe in more detail how two of Bakhtin's core concepts, chronotopes and the carnivalesque, can be understood as conceptual tools for a historiographical analysis of the relationship between archaeology and the wider world (in history writing and discourses of heritage; for example, in museology).

Chronotopes in Multivocal Biographies

The chronotope (in ancient Greek *kronos* = time, *topos* = space) is a concept for narrating place and landscape, developed by Bakhtin in his historical poetics, which he introduced to describe how "time-space" relationships are represented in narrative genres (Bakhtin [1981] 2008: 84–258). According to Bakhtin, a chronotope is not strictly an image or a visual metaphor but a narrative tool used by writers and readers (interpreters) to make a story unfold and become a physical reality. Chronotopes are important sites in a story where "spatial and temporal indicators are fused into one carefully thought-out, concrete whole" (84). According to Bakhtin, from antiquity onward, various genres of European literature have contained different and interrelated chronotopes by which changing historical relations of humans and their surroundings interact. Specific chronotopes and combinations of chronotopes correspond to distinct literary genres; in other words, to stabilize forms of language use that express social discourses (distinct practices, worldviews, ideologies, and mentalities within a society). Therefore, the chronotope is an idea, a historical concept, and a literary or narrative concept.

In history writing, the idea of the chronotope is a tool for understanding how historians organize a storied time-space, or a "history space" (Munslow 2007: 58). Every history space created in history writing has its own chronotopes, which are based on literary choices and different political, ideological, and ethical worldviews. "Thus, a historian can create a Whig chronotope, a Marxist chronotope or a gender chronotope. Or . . . a geographical chronotope" (59), such as the chronotope of "going West" in US history writing. History writing and its genres extend disciplinary boundaries with their storied chronotopes (various unfolding historical time-spaces, for instance based on the idea of "progress" vs. the idea of a mythic "golden age" in the past), reflecting contemporary regimes of history writing and heritage production in society and thus becoming a fundamental tool for broader social and historical analysis (Holquist [1990] 2002: 112).

Chronotopes are resistant over time (transhistorical) but also "highly sensitive to historical change: different societies and periods result in different chronotopes both inside and outside literary texts" (Holquist [1990] 2002: 112). A vital aspect of this chronotopic dynamism is that it involves the production of historic narrative worlds (storyscapes) defining a shared heritage that is both representational (symbolic, visionary, cartographic, etc.) and phenomenologically explored by people's senses of place and landscape. Therefore, chronotopes are also strategies applied by observers for interpreting the materiality of the real world. According to the anthropologist Keith Basso, heritage landscapes, including the place names of the American Apache Indians, "have served the people for centuries as indispensable mnemonic pegs on which to hang the moral teaching of their history. Accordingly, such locations present themselves as instances of what Mikhail Bakhtin calls *chronotopes*" (Basso 1984: 44, italics in the original; for a similar perspective, see Brink 2008; Ingold 2000: 205; Clifford 1997: 25n7). The semiotic-material chronotopes are "points in the geography of a community where time and space intersect and fuse. Time takes on flesh and becomes visible for human contemplation; likewise, space becomes charged and responsive to the movements of time and history and the enduring character of a people . . . . Chronotopes thus stand as monuments to the community itself, as symbol of it, as forces operating to shape its members' images of themselves" (Basso 1996: 62). Similar approaches to archaeological sites as chronotopic entities are evident in, for instance, the archaeologist Jim Barrett's (2008) examination of Stonehenge as a "real-life chronotope" participating in various historical and contemporary narratives with supplementary meanings or as a means for heritage struggles. Barrett used Bakhtin's term heteroglossia to explain the chronotopic elements in the biography of Stonehenge as a multi-voiced narrative phenomenon (see also Bruner and Gorfain 1984; Lawson 2011).

The Carnivalesque in Popular and Public Culture

Bakhtin's analysis of the medieval carnival tradition defined a distinct Rabelaisian chronotope in the form of folk culture and laughter culture (the wag, the jester, and the fool in the novel) (see Bakhtin [1981] 2008: 167–206). A central element in Rabelaisian literature is the notion of grotesque realism, a cultural transformation of culture associated with the ordinary people's everyday life (realism). Whereas realism depicts a practical embodied reality, grotesque realism in the carnival tradition becomes an ecstatic hyperrealism perceived from the perspective of the masses and the common man. The carnivalesque transforms "the language of the marketplace"—where ordinary life unfolds with all its physical gestures, outbursts, smells, colors, games, and plays—into a staged, humorous, frivolous, comic, ridiculous, absurd, and dreamlike world (Bakhtin 1984).

Cultural theory has used Bakhtin's notion of the carnivalesque to analyze the history of popular culture and public culture (people-centered culture from below) in premodern and modern times and how such culture is expressed in a vast range of interconnected domains (see Stallybrass and White 1986: 19; Featherstone 1991: 22, 81; Gardiner 1992): from counter-political cultures and utopias (such as squatting communities and protest movements with carnivalesque/grotesque elements of expressions) to consumer culture commercially situated as mass culture, low culture, or pulp culture (such as dreamlike real fantasies, for example Disney World or the World Fair) and as an educational and aesthetical ideal (*bildung*) related to staging or exhibiting the grotesque body (dance movements, art exhibitions, horror films, etc.).

The characteristic elements of carnivalesque culture have been used in historiographical studies to understand specific forms of public space and the transformative nature of different exhibition traditions in public space (Stallybrass and White 1986; Bennett [1995] 2009). The change in the carnivalesque from frivolous grotesque realism to a tamer or a more controlled emotional performance with the rise of the middle class in modern times shows that carnivalesque culture is a historical phenomenon undergoing transformation. As argued by the sociologist Mike Featherstone, "The civilizing process . . . involved an increasing control of the emotions, sense of disgust at bodily betrayal, the smells, sweating, and noises of the lower body, and sensitivity to one's own bodily space. It involved the middle class in a process of complex distancing from the popular, the grotesque other . . . . Hence we have the attractions of the forest, fair, theatre, circus, slum, savage, seaside resort for the bourgeois" (Featherstone 1991: 81). Carnivalesque culture has been transformed into modern places and landscapes, expressed by "dream-worlds" such as carnivals, festivals, bazaars, fairs, exhibitions, amusement parks or theme parks, holiday resorts, sport arenas, and department stores (Featherstone 1991: 79–89). One could add to this list museums, heritage places, and landscapes, where popular (e.g., medieval) culture and (e.g., fierce) public debates are performed today (Bennett [1995] 2009; Guttormsen and Taylor 2019).

Keeping the above discussion in mind, examining the emergence of archaeology as an academic discipline and expert culture in institutional domains (universities, museums, and heritage-management sectors) will involve a relational historiographical approach that takes into account the role that archaeology plays in different public spheres—for instance, in popular literature and exhibitions such as the World Fair—and how these public spheres disseminate the relationship between the "high," expert, or academic culture versus the "low," the popular, or folk culture. The institutional and the popular spheres are relational and connected to the cultural movements, ideologies, and societal processes of a specific historical period. A dialogic historiographical approach that considers chronotopes as analytical concepts in genres and the cultural form of the carnivalesque allows examining archaeology and the public as interconnected practices that are expressed in the literacy, cultural life, and societal ideas of a period.

The Material Chronotopy of the Oseberg Grave Mound

In this section, I will use the Bakhtinian theoretical approach described above as a method to analyze how technology was defined in history writing and as heritage at the beginning of the twentieth century in Norway. The Oseberg grave mound in Vestfold County, Norway, excavated in 1904, was one of the most distinguished archaeological locations at the time. The mound uncovered a Viking ship with a variety of travel equipment, showcasing both sea- and land-travel technology of the Viking period (Nordeide 2011). Much like Jim Barrett's (2008) analysis of Stonehenge, the Oseberg archaeological site and its findings can be comprehended as a complex chronotopic material ensemble that disseminated multiple histories of technology and participated in different genre distinctions and heritage production in the early twentieth century.

Oseberg Archaeology in History Writing:
Chronotopes, Genres, and the Author's Environment

The first distinction in terms of technology history regarding the rich archaeological material from Oseberg is that between sea travel and land travel. The stories about Norse ship-crafting technology emphasized how technological innovation laid the foundation for the histories of explorers and conquerors associated with Viking journeys to foreign shores (see, e.g., Guttormsen 2018 about the Viking Leif Eriksson in modern myth making). At the beginning of the twentieth century, the technology history of Viking ships was interwoven with the grand European and national technology history of the time, involving a chronotopic arsenal that combined stories of discovery, technological progress, colonization, and conquest. This chronotopic content referred to a transcending, steadily increasing, reforming, and forward-looking time-space that various "histories of progress" have used to create a space of action (Joyce and Preucel 2002: 34–36). Histories of technology as progress—for example, ideas of cultural evolution—promoted a world of speed and progression (in literature, for example, via technological science fiction, visual arts, etc.) that also relied on real historical changes caused by technological and industrial revolution in the early twentieth century. The pervasive technological developments of the period were manifested in these ideas and physical processes as a continuously unfolding (evolutionary, teleological, and futuristic) time-space of technologically advanced societies.

The perspective of technology history through which the stories of the Oseberg ship were conveyed resonates with the technology historical genre of the interwar period that was advanced by engineers such as Georg Brochmann (1930) and Edgar B. Schieldrup (1934). The main concern in these "internalistic" studies of technology history was the long-term development of construction principles and invention designs for technological artifacts. Scholars have called such internalistic studies the "nuts-and-bolts" form of history writing, in contrast to the later "contextual" and "externalistic" technology history writing, which emphasized the interrelated function of technology in the various parts of society at different periods (Berg 1996). In the "internalistic" history writing on technology, whose popularity peaked at the beginning of the twentieth century, traditional vehicles and their origins (such as the wheeled cart in the Oseberg archaeological repertoire; see Figure 8.1.) were the starting point for elaborating the world history of technological progress, a teleological history of predetermined technological development in constant evolution leading from the most advanced vehicles and roads represented by the great ancient civilizations (i.e., Egyptian and Roman roads) to the industrial nations of the world (a case of Eurocentrism that highlighted, for example, the roads of the British Empire, Napoleon's royal roads, and the German's autobahns). Technology history was a history of gradual technological improvement, societal progress, and cultural advancement, pronounced in evolutionary statements such as "from sledge to car travel" or "from tracks to motorways" (see Adas 1989).

The perspective of technology history through which the stories of the Oseberg Viking ship and the Oseberg cart were conveyed produced a distinct chronotope. The emergence of "adventurous time" in European literature revealed, according to Bakhtin, a historiographical distinction that introduced historical time into storytelling, with time (and speed) taking precedence over space, in contrast to the idyllic chronotope where space dominated time (Bakhtin [1981] 2008: 243–45). The objects associated with land travel in the Oseberg material repertoire belonged to a history of technological progress based on an adventurous time advanced by a chronotope that signified a narrative structure of time-space in sequences and plots, following the progressive outlook of engineers. The story evolves just as the characters travel on the road. The road not taken is an untold story—an empty (uncultivated) space of narrat-

Horses on carpet

Horse-driven wagon

Land Technology/Travel

Museum

Grave Mound and landscape

Sea Technology/Travel

Ship

Figure 8.1a–e. The chronotopic complex at the Oseberg site includes all the archaeological remains, the actual grave mound, and the museum that contains all the archaeological artifacts from Oseberg. Collage by Torgrim Sneve Guttormsen. (a) The Oseberg ship under excavation. Photo by Olaf Væring (1837–1906)/Kulturhistorisk museum, UiO (Museum of Cultural History, University of Oslo, Norway), CC BY-SA 4.0. (b) The Oseberg ship in the Viking Ship Museum in Oslo. Photo by Petter Ullcland, CC BY-SA 1.0. (c) The Oseberg grave mound. Photo: unknown, CC BY-SA 3.0. (d) Reconstructed woven wall carpet from the Oseberg grave mound, Mary Storm. Photo by Eirik Irgens Johnsen/Kulturhistorisk museum, UiO, CC BY-SA 4.0. (e) The Oseberg wagon from the Oseberg grave mound. Photo by Jac Brun, National Library of Norway, Wikimedia Commons, public domain.

ing action. This chronotope is a significant feature in adventure literature (e.g., in the road-movie genre), where the "road" defines a linear timeframe involving the progressive achievements of heroes on their way to conquering the world. This narrative stereotype is based on a chronotope that resembles a technology historical approach that elaborates the progressive history and outlook of the "modern" world by constructing an adventurous landscape led by future-oriented heroic engineers. In this landscape, genuine culture, advancement of civilization, and the future world are represented by the growing cities and urban life rather than the traditional rural countryside.

The adventurous chronotope associated with technological progress and heroic engineers was an integral part of the intertextual discourse about technology in the interwar period. For instance, the previously mentioned engineer and technology historian Georg Brochmann was a popular novelist, writing on the border between fiction and science (Weium 2001). He translated Aldous Huxley's science fiction novel *Brave New World* in 1948 and wrote several novels in which scientists and engineers were the leading characters. In his criminal/adventure novel *Dødståken* (*The Fog of Death*), the main character is a sunburnt and rational engineer who solves mysteries (Figure 8.2.). The intertextuality in the proliferation of the engineer as a narrative hero across academic texts and fiction is evident here.

The early twentieth century also saw the emergence of a culture historical genre produced by writers such as the archaeologists Haakon Shetelig (1910) and Sigurd Grieg (1928) and the historian Sverre Steen (1929; see the book covers in Figure 8.3. and Figure 8.4.) that emphasized the importance of traditional land travel due to the ethnographic and archaeological discoveries of vehicles and travel equipment and the significance of travel in medieval texts. The archaeological materiality of Oseberg associated with land travel (roads and "hollow ways" for horse riding) also made an appearance in this form of history writing. The chronotopic features in this genre resembled Bakhtin's definition of "folkloristic time," which he identified in various forms of literature written in ancient and modern times. The simplicity of everyday life expressed by folkloristic time is a narrative structure that depicts a chronotope of pastoral idyll, a narrative time-space that takes place in a practical working landscape dominated by crafts. The characteristic elements of this idyll are "an organic fastening-down, a grafting of life and its events to a place, to a familiar territory with all its nooks and crannies, its familiar mountains, valleys, fields, rivers and forests, and one's own home. . . . defined by the *unity of place*, by the age-old rooting of the life of generations to a single place, from which life, in all its events, is inseparable" (Bakhtin [1981] 2008: 225, emphasis in original). Folkloristic time is characterized by the rhythmical cycles of time, which nourished the pastoral idyll chronotope: a time-space that is filled with stable traditional habits; in other words, where space dominates time (as well as speed and the adventurous elements characteristic of engineers), a common feature of pastoral societies worldwide.

Similar to the technology historical genre, the culture historical genre also belonged to the intertextual discourse of the chronotope of the pastoral idyll. For instance, this

Figure 3.2. "The engineer-protagonist" of the interwar literature, as depicted on the cover of the science fiction novel *Dødståken* (The Fog of Death) by the engineer-historian Georg Brochmann (1st edition in 1931, new edition by Ponnibok in 1950, shown here). Reprinted by permission of Fredrik Oftebro/Norsk Teknisk Museum (the Norwegian Museum of Science and Technology).

is evident in the antimodern rhetoric in utterances of collective memories and material heritage in which the chronotope of the pastoral idyll signified the sense of a disappearing past and the loss of traditional values in a rapidly changing modern world. The previously mentioned archaeologist Haakon Shetelig, for example, published a wide range of academic texts on technological narratives (traditional crafts/art, i.e., land travel and maritime technology), modernism, and heritage. He translated the prose of Charles Baudelaire, which, according to Shetelig, represented a criticism of moder-

Figure 8.3. The medieval idyll on the cover of the historian Sverre Steen's book from 1929 illustrates the culture historical genre's narrative of land travel as an idyllic chronotope. Reprinted by permission of Aschehoug publishing.

nity, a philosophical mentality of decay, and the idealization of the medieval lifeworld and the poetic past (Shetelig 1943, see Figure 8.4). Shetelig published his translation during the Nazi occupation of Norway (1940–45), with the reference to Baudelaire for Shetelig becoming a metaphor for the destruction brought about by modern military technology, inhumanity, and totalitarianism. Shetelig's "Baudelairean" perspective corresponded with his nostalgic portrayal of traditional land-travel technology emanating from the chronotope of the pastoral idyll, which, during the interwar period, was opposed to the processes of modern urbanism and increased automobility, alienating forces that represented the loss of intimacy, emotion, and multiplicity in relation to people, places, and local landscapes (Shetelig 1910: 7–8). The landscape of the medieval road (Figure 8.3, illustrated by the book cover of the historian Sverre Steen's *Ferd og Fest* from 1929) and the horse-track roads from previous times represented a traditional time-space concretized by the pastoral idyll, which still could be experienced

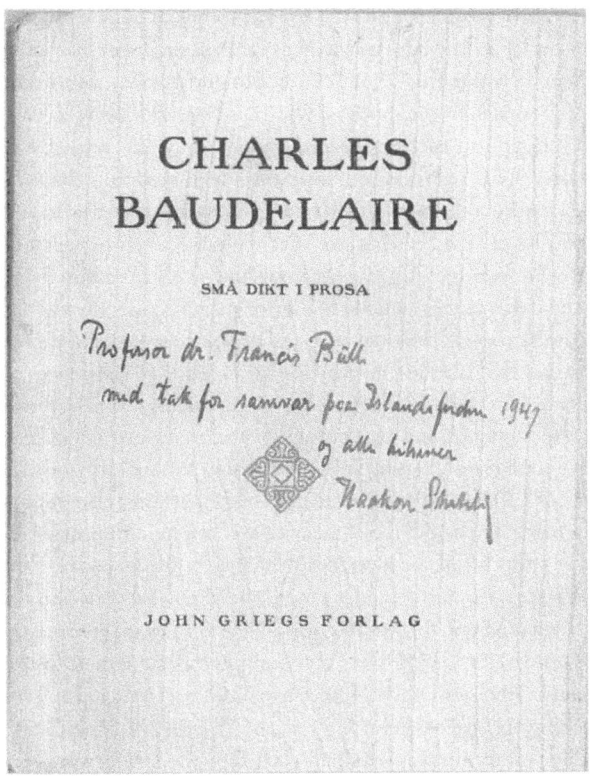

Figure 8.4. Contemporary intertextuality and interdiscursivity. Archaeologist Haakon Shetelig's translation of Baudelaire's prose poem (published in 1943), with the cover signed by Shetelig and addressed to the literary historian Francis Bull as a thank you note. Reprinted by permission of the Norwegian Directorate of Cultural Heritage.

via relict traces of heritage and traditional folklore untouched by modern industrial landscapes.

The Establishment of the Norwegian Museum of Technology

The historiography of technology that the Oseberg archaeological ensemble was part of in the early twentieth century was interwoven with broader societal discourses about technological change and societal progress. The focus on technological heritage and a materialist conception of history (historical materialism) paved the way for an educational ideal that focused on instrumental knowledge (the world of matter: the outer, physically present, perceivable, and, therefore, measurable reality) associated with craftsmanship and technological skills, representing the values derived from the common experience of people's practical uses of things in their daily lives. Technology studies (and consequently the natural sciences) and an engineer-like mentality became popular concepts when thinking about the world and society, representing the ideals associated with the wealth of the modern world, whose driving force was based on the common man's function in the development of history. The engineer-based histories involved a cognitive shift from the romanticized ideal, based on the knowledge of the individual and exceptional human qualities of historic kings and warlords with a focus on the history of a highly educated upper-class culture, to an experience-based realist ideal, built on the knowledge of histories associated with the knowledge of "the practical hand" and the experiences of daily life among the broader strata of the population with a focus on the history of craftmanship and popular inventions, thereby focusing on what is common and that is influenced by the knowledge of the crowd.

The adventurous chronotope associated with technological progress and heroic engineers, which the engineer and technology historian Georg Brochmann introduced via his aforementioned novel, was broadly received in the society of the early twentieth century (Dalbak and Dahl 1994). The heroic engineer was also represented by, for instance, the engineer Michael Nicolai Leegaard when he emphasized the importance of preserving "the memory of the pioneers who have built the country generation after generation" for these personalities had formed "the historical consciousness of our people and provide the backbone for finding our own way forward in the future" (Leegaard 1927: 3–4, my translation). However, technology was subject to more than unconditional enthusiasm. Archaeologists, historians, and engineers also promoted ethical humanism regarding the use of technology in the "Age of Machines" and warned about the "dehumanizing technicalization of Man" caused by the modern abuses of destructive technology (war technology and the mechanical exploitation of Nature). Antimodern sentiments, as shown above by the archaeologist Shetelig's "Baudelairean" perspective, were prominent in the texts of the historian Sverre Steen (1929: 1–2, 5) and the engineer and technology historian Georg Brochmann (1939: 10–12). Oseberg's archaeological ensemble was thus part of an ambiguous modern project; or expressed more profoundly, "both progress and longing for stability were an essential part of modernity, even if the latter may be seen as a consequence of the former. As a socio-political enterprise, archaeology became linked to both" (Olsen 2001: 43).

The role of archaeology in the history of technology (including Thomson's three-period system for categorizing prehistoric artifacts into stone, bronze, and Iron Age objects), as evidenced by the Oseberg ship, gained them large audiences at the World Fairs that became popular during the second half of the nineteenth century. The World Fairs were popular public arenas that "promoted enlightenment, progress, and education and helped shape a new economy and a new social order" (Brenna 2002: 52, my translation). The World Fairs were staged arenas of reality that transformed contemporary society into a hyper-real setting that promoted a blend of national exhibitions. With reference to the carnivalesque as a cultural expression, the World Fairs can be understood as a concept of popular culture, a popular hyper-real social setting in which the carnivalesque life of play, laughter, and absurdities was allowed to unfold. In the Bakhtinian sense, the exhibitions were arenas of hybridization that conveyed many the "voices" of contemporary society: low/high culture, broad/narrow culture, mass/elite culture, supranational/national, and universal/particular.

The World Fairs, highly resonant and popular in the society of the early twentieth century, provided a historical and cultural framework for showcasing technology and progress, inspiring many museum exhibitions in Europe (Wiwjorra 2009: 43). For example, the inspiration for the Norwegian theologian and sociologist Eilert Sundt's (1817–1875) effort to establish a workers' museum in Norway came from his experience at the exhibitions of industry, crafts, art, and innovation during his visit to the World Fair in Paris in 1867. The national 1914 Jubilee Exhibition that took place from 5 May to 11 October in Kristiania (today Oslo), Norway, marked the centennial anniversary of Norway's 1814 constitution. A central focus at the exhibition was technology and industry. The 1914 Jubilee Exhibition also became a platform for archaeologists and engineers to create a dialogic forum for establishing the Norwegian Museum of Technology, which indicates how the hybrid and transformative character of exhibitions, from fairs to museums, disseminated a systematic message about technology as an educational value for society.

The complex material chronotope of the Oseberg archaeological ensemble consisting of the Oseberg grave mound, the Viking ship, and land-travel artifacts also included the Viking Ship Museum at Bygdøy, Oslo (built in several stages during the 1930s), where the archaeological objects were exhibited. The museum was part of a larger exhibition tradition during the first half of the twentieth century. At the sixth national technology meeting, held in conjunction with the 1914 Jubilee Exhibition at Frogner (see the poster in Figure 8.5), contemporary ideas about technology as history and heritage were formalized with the founding of the Association for the Norwegian Museum of Technology (Brochmann 1939: 38–39). The aforementioned Michael Nicolai Leegaard, a politician, engineer, and chairman of the Polytechnic Association, was the driving force behind the establishment of the association. The members of the Supervisory Board included Hans Aall, the director of the Norwegian Folk Museum, and the board of the Association for the Norwegian Museum of Technology included Anton W. Brøgger, politician and archaeologist, in addition to politicians, engineers, and others with similar areas of expertise. The archaeologist Brøgger was a key figure in establishing the Norwegian Museum of Technology. Brøgger's efforts are evidenced by the fact that he managed to subsume the Viking Ship Museum at Bygdøy in 1932, which was subsequently transformed into a national center for older sea- and land-travel technology history and for technology history in general.

The founding of the Association for the Norwegian Museum of Technology in 1914 and its establishment at the Viking Ship Museum in 1932 illustrates that there were close relationships between museum exhibitions and national exhibitions in terms of how technological cultural heritage was communicated in the early twentieth century. Technology, crafts, and industry became common concerns for archaeologists and

Figure 8.5. The poster for the 1914 Jubilee Exhibition at Frogner, in which the "Age of Machines" is illustrated by wheel hubs (technology), elevator cranes (industry), forests (natural resources), and a lighthouse and sailing ships (Norway, the nation of ships). Poster made by Brynjulf Larsson (Norwegian, 1881–1920), Wikimedia Commons, public domain.

engineers due to the popularity of ideas regarding the function of technology as an educational value for society, which the archaeologists and engineer-historians were a part of. During the interwar period, the recognition of the past as technological and industrial heritage became a central issue in Norwegian heritage debates. Archaeologists, the new Cultural Heritage Directorate established in 1912, and museums were all profoundly engaged with the responsibility to protect past technological cultures in the rapidly changing society in the "Age of Machines."

The example discussed in this chapter shows that the emergence of the Viking Ship Museum at Bygdøy in Oslo was part of the chronotopic complex of the excavated Oseberg archaeological ensemble, which, at the beginning of the twentieth century, was part of the grand narrative about technology in society. The Oseberg archaeological complex found its main audience at the popular histories and exhibitions, where the knowledge of technical skills and craftsmanship, the humanistic educational and aesthetic values, and the ideas of scientific and cultural progress became a framework for evaluating the past. Therefore, when the archaeologist Brøgger suggested that the Norwegian Museum of Technology should be located in the Viking Ship Museum at Bygdøy in Oslo, this proposal was very much in accordance with the general mentality of the time. In 1932, the multifaceted intellectual environment involving both archaeologists and engineer-historians was further strengthened by the opening of the Norwegian Museum of Technology (see Figure 8.6.). The Oseberg archaeological complex, in-

Figure 8.6. Crowds gathered outside the entrance to the Norwegian Museum of Technology in 1934, located in the cellar of the Viking Ship Museum at Bygdøy, Oslo. The picture is from Georg Brochmann (1939: 78). Reprinted by permission of Norsk Teknisk Museum (the Norwegian Museum of Science and Technology).

cluding the museum, became a real-life chronotope that participated in the literary genres, environments, mentalities, and ideologies of the period. As such, the museum became a material chronotope, where "spatial and temporal indicators are fused into one carefully thought-out concrete whole" (Bakhtin [1981] 2008: 84), that facilitated "multivocal" public relationships, with archaeologists being one of many stakeholder groups.

What Is Public Archaeology through the Lens of Historiography?

Public archaeology is a research field that engages with other related research fields, such as heritage studies, memory studies, and studies of public history. What distinguishes public archaeology from these related fields is the very starting point—that is, the relationship of the archaeologist and the archaeological discipline to a wider world—and the binary opposite, or how "they"/"the others" interact with the domain of archaeologists. If one divides public archaeology into different types (Moshenska 2017: 6, Figure 1.1), then the example in this chapter, the enthusiasm for technological histories and heritages at the beginning of the twentieth century, will cover several types. However, rather than sorting public archaeology into various boxes, it would be more important to examine how the archaeologically situated spheres in society are contributing to the production of history and heritage at large and to investigate what happens in heritage processes (heritagization); in other words, we should focus on the dynamic spheres where dialogues about the past take place between different stakeholders. This means examining the relational aspects of how archaeology is being negotiated and forms a part of a world with many interests where archaeologists do not have a privileged position but belong to larger societal contexts.

This chapter used historiography as a lens to understand the relationships between archaeology and the public. This approach is based on the idea that the relationship between archaeology and the public is best understood retrospectively. The first insight that has emerged from this historiographical approach is the need for theoretical discussions that would allow us to understand the essence of public archaeology as a research field. Here, Bakhtin's theoretical universe is useful, allowing us to understand the interconnection between archaeology and the public as a relational, dialogic, and multivocal domain, where archaeology finds its voice while interacting with the voices of others. Bakhtin's historical concepts of the chronotope and the carnivalesque are worthwhile analytical resources for understanding history writing as a field composed of many histories and genres about the same phenomenon and for viewing heritage production via the hybrid and transformative nature of the exhibition tradition and the emergence of museums (e.g., the Norwegian Museum of Technology).

I advocate a relational dialogical approach to archaeology and the public that can capture the nuances and interconnections between the various utterances, discourses, persons, and milieus engaged with the past. This diversified knowledge enables study-ing the relationships within public archaeology using multiple approaches. First, a dialogical approach will provide access to understand complex archaeology-public re-lationships that go beyond the disciplinary outlook of archaeology, reflecting how ar-chaeologists define their profession in the contemporary world shared with many other stakeholders. The utterances of archaeologists are intertextually and interdiscursively linked with other discourses in society (e.g., the popular discourse of technology). Second, a dialogical approach allows examining societal issues or the ideological and political discourses in society as manifold and varied phenomena that are created via a synthesis of conflicting interpretations and oppositional knowledge. In retrospect, it is far too easy to categorize scholars into various camps or crystallize distinct ideologies on their behalf. Finally, if archaeology, as I suggest, is the result of a constant dialogue whereby archaeologists or heritage practitioners create their statements in, and on the basis of, a world shared with other voices, the question arises regarding how archae-ological identity is defined, both as a (biographical) knowledge domain and a fluent (non-biographical) voice in the public realm. Dialogisms as a theoretical stand implies the recognition of academics or professional archaeologists as producers of more than just "academic facts"; they are political and societal entrepreneurs, or in the case of most archaeologists, minor wheels in the production of history writing and heritage making constantly at work in and for society.

When using Bakhtin's theoretical perspective to define public archaeology, the fol-lowing characteristics will be crucial: public archaeology is relationally and dialogically situated in the wider world that consists of a variety of stakeholders. Such complexity of the relationship between archaeology and the public deserves increased attention in future studies. Transferred to a "post-truth" reality, where the past is used for promot-ing intolerance, fear, and xenophobia, one future line of inquiry could involve investi-gating the Bakhtinian approach as a tool for uncovering the complexity of multivocality, including hegemonic conformity of public archaeology, and thus questioning the mo-nologic statements about the past in the public and the epistemic populism (normative usages of "people" as always representing the good) in order "to face social reality as it is: complex, in that communities are extremely diverse and not always progressive" (González-Ruibal, González, and Criado-Boado 2018: 510). Analyzing the role of the archaeological expert (Hølleland and Skrede 2018; Fredheim 2020), thereby gaining knowledge about the tensions between dialogues and monologues, would in this case give empirical access for advancing theories on dialogism within public archaeology. New theories that resonate with the field of public archaeology would, by looking back on its past, open the way for discovering new intricacies for the archaeology of the future, thereby guaranteeing the field's legitimacy in a constantly changing world with new public complexities.

In this chapter, I am suggesting that public archaeology through the lens of "pub-lic historiography" is an example of critical theory where the explanatory, practical, and normative criteria described in my introduction fits the requirements of how the application of chronotopes and historical fixations on technological progress, inter-connected in literature and in the real world's social discourses, comes to exposure in the Norwegian Museum of Technology display. This conclusion also hits on another key aspect of critical theory, which is the role of reflexivity in understanding relational aspects of knowledge systems and processes, including subjective process (e.g., psychological) and social behavior/relationships. Reflexivity in social sciences points to how parts and totality are connected and affect each other as a complex interplay in an overall self-reflective process (e.g., Bourdieu and Wacquant 1992). Since archaeology is relationally and dialogically situated in the wider world, I am calling for a greater recognition and engagement with the fact that archaeological interpretations are at least in part the outcomes of the prevailing social trends. Within critical theory, theorists have repeatedly argued that in order to achieve a liberatory or emancipatory goal, we must first recognize the systems that we are embedded in and reveal those systems explicitly. The chapter highlights the fact that public archaeology is perhaps not reflexive or critical enough in the ways it channels the views of its stakeholders.

Torgrim Sneve Guttormsen is an archaeologist and research professor at the Norwegian Institute for Cultural Heritage Research (NIKU). He is also the Head of his institute's Department of Heritage and Society. From the 1990s and onwards he has participated in and been directing numerous archaeological excavations and field surveys in Norway, as well as participated at archaeological and heritage-based projects in Greece, Italy, Oman and USA. His previous and on-going research and publications comprises studies related to theory of heritage, heritage politics and management, heritage routes, commemorations and memorials, difficult heritage, urban heritage and immigrant heritage, as well as public archaeology and historiography.

References

Adas, Michael. 1989. *Machines as the Measure of Men: Science, Technology, and Ideologies of Western Dominance.* Cornell Studies in Comparative History. Ithaca, NY: Cornell University Press.

Bakhtin, Mikhail Mikhaîlovich. 1984. *Rabelais and His World*, trans. Hélénè Iswolsky, foreword by Krystyna Pomorska, prologue by Michael Holquist. Bloomington: Indiana University Press.

———. (1981) 2008. *The Dialogic Imagination: Four Essays by M. M. Bakhtin*, ed. Michael Holquist, trans. and intro. by Caryl Emerson and Michael Holquist. Austin: University of Texas Press.

Barrett, Jim. 2008. "Stonehenge as Chronotope (The Struggle for the Sign in Dialogic Reality)." *Strategies for Golden Realities.* Accessed 23 October 2020. https://goldenrealitystrategies.wordpress.com/stonehenge-as-chronotope-the-struggle-for-the-sign-in-dialogic-reality/.

Basso, Keith H. 1984. "'Stalking with Stories': Names, Places, and Moral Narratives among the Western Apache." In *Text, Play, and Story: The Construction and Reconstruction of Self and Society*, ed. E. M. Bruner, 19–55. Long Grove, IL: Waveland Press.

———. 1996. *Wisdom Sits in Places: Landscape and Language among the Western Apache.* Albuquerque: University of New Mexico Press.

Bennett, Tony. (1995) 2009. *The Birth of the Museum: History, Theory, Politics.* London: Routledge.

Berg, Bjørn Ivar. 1996. "Norsk teknologihistorie i dag: Tendenser og utviklingslinjer" [Norwegian technology history today: Trends and lines of development]. *Volund* 1996: 7–28.

Bourdieu, Pierre, and Loïc J. D. Wacquant. 1992. *An Invitation to Reflexive Sociology*. Chicago: University of Chicago Press.

Brattli, Terje, and Asgeir Svestad. 1991. "Forskningshistoria og den arkeologiske praksisen" [Research history and the archaeological practice]. *Viking* 1991: 105–12.

Brenna, Brita. 2002. *Verden som ting og forestilling: Verdensutstillinger og den norske deltakelsen 1851–1900* [The world as object and performance: World Fair exhibitions and Norwegian participation 1851–1900]. Oslo: Unipub.

Brink, Stefan. 2008. "Landskap og plats som mentala konstruktioner" [Landscape and place as mental constructions]. In *Facets of Archaeology: Essays in Honour of Lotte Hedeager on Her 60th Birthday*, ed. Konstantinos Chilidis, Julie Lund, and Christopher Prescott, 109–20. Oslo: University of Oslo.

Brochmann, Georg. 1930. *De store opfinnelser: Forskning og fremskritt*, Bind IV, Jordens utnyttelse [The great inventions: Research and progress, vol. 4, Utilization of the Earth]. Oslo: Nasjonalforlaget.

———. 1939. *Per aspera ad astra: Et skrift om Norsk teknisk museum gjennom 25 år og et gløtt inn i framtida* [Per aspera ad astra: A publication about the Norwegian Technology Museum through 25 years and a glimpse into the future]. Oslo: Norsk Teknisk Museum.

———. 1950. *Dødståken (Den store ødelegger)*. [The Fog of Death: The Great Destroyer]. Oslo: Nasjonalforlaget.

Bruner, Edward M., and Phyllis Gorfain. 1984. "Dialogic Narration and the Paradoxes of Masada." In *Text, Play, and Story: The Construction and Reconstruction of Self and Society*, ed. Edward M. Bruner, 56–79. Long Grove, IL: Waveland Press.

Clifford, James. 1997. *Routes: Travel and Translation in the Late Twentieth Century*. Cambridge, MA: Harvard University Press.

Dalbak, Tom H., and Grete Dahl, eds. 1994. *Ingeniøren som helt, skurk og elsker: Et knippe ingeniørportretter i norsk litteratur fra 1879 til vår egen tid* [The engineer as hero, villain and lover: A selection of engineering portraits in Norwegian literature from 1879 to our own time]. Oslo: Norske sivilingeniørers forening.

Featherstone, Mike. 1991. *Consumer Culture and Postmodernism*. London: Sage.

Fredheim, Harald. 2020. "Decoupling 'Open' and 'Ethical' Archaeologies: Rethinking Deficits and Expertise for Ethical Public Participation in Archaeology and Heritage." *Norwegian Archaeological Review* 53(1): 5–22. https://doi.org/10.1080/00293652.2020.1738540.

Gardiner, Michael. 1992. "Bakhtin's Carnival: Utopia as Critique." *Utopian Studies* 3(2): 21–29.

Gardiner, Michael, and Michael Mayerfeld Bell. 1998. "Bakhtin and the Human Sciences: A Brief Introduction." In *Bakhtin and the Human Sciences*, ed. M. Mayerfeld Bell and M. Gardiner, 1–12. London: Sage Publications.

González-Ruibal, Alfredo, Pablo Alonso González, and Filipe Criado-Boado. 2018. "Against Reactionary Populism: Towards a New Public Archaeology." *Antiquity* 92(362): 507–15. https://doi.org/10.15184/aqy.2017.227.

Grieg, Sigurd. 1928. "Kongsgaarden" [The Kings Farm]. In *Osebergfundet, Bind II*, ed. Anton Wilhelm Brøgger and Haakon Shetelig. Oslo: A. W. Brøøgers Boktrykkeri.

Guttormsen, Torgrim Sneve. 2018. "Valuing Immigrant Memories as Common Heritage: The Leif Erikson Monument in Boston." *History & Memory* 30(2): 79–115.

Guttormsen, Torgrim Sneve, and Lotte Hedeager. 2015. "Introduction: Interactions of Archaeology and the Public." *World Archaeology* 47(2): 189–93.

Guttormsen, Torgrim Sneve, and Joel Taylor. 2019. "Using Contestation to Elicit Values for Heritage Planning: The Case of the Urban Park at Ekeberg in Oslo, Norway." In *Cultural Heritage*, ed. Adriana Campelo, Adam Lindgreen, Laura Reynolds, and Michael Beverland, 39–58. London: Routledge.

Hedeager, Lotte, and Karen Schousboe. 1989. "Indledning" [Introduction]. In *Brugte historier: Ti essays om brug og misbrug af historien*, ed. Lotte Hedeager and Karen Schousboe, 7–10. Copenhagen: Akademisk forlag.

Hølleland, Herdis, and Joar Skrede. 2019. "What's Wrong with Heritage Experts? An Interdisciplinary Discussion of Experts and Expertise in Heritage Studies." *International Journal of Heritage Studies* 25(8): 825–36. https://doi.org/10.1080/13527258.2018.1552613.

Holquist, Michael. (1990) 2002. *Dialogism: Bakhtin and His World*. London: Routledge.

Horkheimer, Max. (1937) 1982. *Critical Theory*. New York: Seabury Press.

Ingold, Tim. 2000. "The Temporality of the Landscape." In *The Perception of the Environment: Essays on Livelihood, Dwelling and Skill*, ed. Tim Ingold, 189–208. London: Routledge.

Joyce, Rosemary A., and Robert W. Preucel. 2002. "Writing the Field of Archaeology." In *The Languages of Archaeology: Dialogue, Narrative, and Writing*, ed. Rosemary A. Joyce, 18–38. Oxford: Blackwell.

Klindt-Jensen, Ole. 1975. *A History of Scandinavian Archaeology*. London: Thames and Hudson.

Lawson, James. 2011. "Chronotope, Story, and Historical Geography: Mikhail Bakhtin and the Space-Time of Narratives." *Antipode* 43(2): 384–412.

Leegaard, Michael. 1927. *Norsk Teknisk Museum: Hvorfor og hvorledes skal vi verne om de kulturskatter, som vidner om utviklingen innen teknikk og industri?* [Norwegian Technology Museum: Why and how should we protect the cultural heritage that testifies to developments in technology and industry?] Oslo: Teknisk ukeblad.

Matsuda, Akira. 2016. "A Consideration of Public Archaeology Theories." *Public Archaeology* 15(1): 40–49. https://doi.org/10.1080/14655187.2016.1209377.

Moshenska, Gabriel. 2017. "Introduction: Public Archaeology as Practice and Scholarship where Archaeology Meets the World." In *Key Concepts in Public Archaeology*, ed. Gabriel Moshenska, 1–13. London: UCL Press.

Munslow, Alun. 2007. *Narrative and History*. Basingstoke: Palgrave Macmillan.

Murray, Tim, and Christopher Evans 2008. "Introduction: Writing Histories of Archaeology." In *Histories of Archaeology: A Reader in the History of Archaeology*, ed. Tim Murray and Christopher Evans, 1–12. Oxford: Oxford University Press.

Nordeide, Sæbjørg Walaker. 2011. "Death in Abundance—Quickly! The Oseberg Ship Burial in Norway." *Acta Archaeologica* 82(1): 7–15.

Olsen, Bjørnar. 1997. *Fra ting til tekst: Teoretiske perspektiv i arkeologisk forskning* [From things to text: Theoretical perspectives in archaeological research]. Oslo: Universitetsforlaget.

———. 2001. "The End of History? Archaeology and the Politics of Identity in a Globalized World." In *Destruction and Conservation of Cultural Property*, ed. Robert Layton, Peter G. Stone, and Julian Thomas, 42–54. London: Routledge.

Richardson, Lorna-Jane, and Jaime Almansa-Sánchez. 2015. "Do You Even Know What Public Archaeology Is? Trends, Theory, Practice, Ethics." *World Archaeology* 47(2): 194–211.

Rowley-Conwy, Peter. 2006. "The Concept of Prehistory and the Invention of the Terms 'Prehistoric' and 'Prehistorian': The Scandinavian Origin, 1833–1850." *European Journal of Archaeology* 9(1): 103–30.

Schieldrop, Edgar B. 1934. *Teknikkens vidundere: I fartens tidsalder*, Første bind [The wonders of technology: In the age of speed, vol. 1]. Oslo: Gyldendal.

Schnapp, Alain. 1996. *The Discovery of the Past: The Origins of Archaeology*. London: British Museum Press.

Shetelig, Haakon. 1910. *Gammelt kjøre- og ridetøi* [Old driving and riding equipment]. Bergen: Bergen Museum.

———. 1943. *Charles Baudelaire: Små dikt i prosa* [Charles Baudelaire: Small poems in prose]. Bergen: John Griegs forlag.

Stallybrass, Peter, and Allon White. 1986. *The Politics and Poetics of Transgression*. London: Methuen.

Steen, Sverre. 1929. *Ferd og fest: Reiseliv i norsk sagatid og middelalder* [Travel and feast: Travelling life in the Norwegian saga period and the Middle Ages]. Oslo: Aschehoug.

Thomas, Julian. 2004. *Archaeology and Modernity*. London: Routledge.

Trigger, Bruce G. 1989. *A History of Archaeological Thought*. Cambridge: Cambridge University Press.

Varghese, Rachel A. 2017. "Archaeology and Its Public(s): Thinking Through the Archaeology - Public Relationship." *Heritage: Journal of Multidisciplinary Studies in Archaeology* 5: 56–68.

Weium, Frode. 2001. "Fra teknokrati til teknikkens humanisering: Georg Brochmanns studier av forholdet mellom teknikk og samfunn" [From technocracy to the humanization of technology: Georg Brochmann's studies of the relationship between technology and society]. *Volund 2001*: 69–106.

Wiwjorra, Ingo. 2009. "Arkaisme og krisen i det moderne: Ideen om 'Ahnenerbe'" [Archaism and the crisis of modernity: The idea of 'Ahnenerbe']. In *Jakten på Germania: Fra nordensvermeri til SS-arkeologi*, ed. Terje Emberland and Jorunn Sem Fure, 35–59. Oslo: Humanist forlag.

CHAPTER 9

Public Perceptions of Archaeology in the Museum

Chiara Zuanni

Introduction

This chapter explores the emergence of interpretations and values about archaeology during a museum visit and their impact on visitors' experiences in the galleries. It aims to unpack the perceptions of the past and of cultural institutions as mediators of it, and it discusses how these perceptions contribute to shape the understanding of archaeology during a museum visit. Thus, it will contribute to a better understanding of public meaning-making of archaeology, highlighting how curatorial aims are unpacked and repurposed in the museum setting through the background and individual experience of each visitor.

Visitors come into museums with their own identities shaped by their social, cultural, educational backgrounds, as well as their ideas and opinions on society and its histories. In the case of archaeological exhibitions, audiences will have expectations in terms of what archaeology is and what an archaeology series of exhibits look like, they will have some knowledge of the specific culture on display, and they will have anticipations of possible museum narratives. Their perspectives on the past will have been shaped by a range of situations: from school memories to identity questions, from popular media to current political opinions, and more. At the same time, museums might enter into a dialogue with contemporary society, by proposing narratives that critique society and challenge power structures. However, in order to understand how critical museum interpretations impact on visitors, it is necessary to first investigate more in-depth the way museum narratives intersect with, and impact, visitors' experiences and understanding.

The chapter draws on research in the *Ancient Worlds Galleries* of the Manchester Museum aimed at investigating the impact of public perceptions of archaeology on the museum (Zuanni 2016). The study of visitors' experiences in the galleries drew on un-obtrusive and participant observations, interviews, and mental mapping. The research considered the museum an institutional middle ground, caught up in a juxtaposition of interpretations, perceptions, and practices, in which people negotiated their narrative of the past and of the museum itself.

This chapter will begin with a short review of literature on the contexts and under-standing of visitors in museums and on the public representations and understanding of the past and of archaeology, and it will then introduce the case study and subsequently present some insights on the factors affecting the visitor experience that emerged during the research. Two subsequent sections will focus more in detail on the emer-gence of public perceptions of archaeology and of museums, respectively, in order to highlight how experiences in the galleries were influenced by, and framed within, ex-isting expectations of archaeological displays and heritage institutions. Ultimately, the chapter argues that while visitor experiences are informed by many variegated, vari-able, and personal factors, museums are also widely recognized as trustworthy sources of knowledge about the past.

Toward an Empowerment of the Public in Museums

The identification of a public for archaeology, the discussion on the limits and possibil-ities of the public understanding of the past, and the attitudes toward a better dissem-ination of the discipline are some of the main themes that both public archaeologists and museum professionals have approached. Both public archaeology and museology developed throughout the twentieth century and have hugely expanded since the early 1990s. It is beyond the scope of this chapter to unpack the origins of public archae-ology. For the purposes of this text, it is sufficient to mention the work of Mortimer Wheeler, who introduced archaeology to a broader public, and the appearance of the term "public archaeology" in Charles McGimsey (1972), followed by the slow con-figuration of public archaeology as a discipline throughout the 1980s and early 1990s (e.g., Merriman 1991), its growth throughout the first decade of the twenty-first cen-tury (e.g., Merriman 2004), the emergence of a digital public archaeology (Bonacchi 2012b; Richardson 2013), and its current evolution (Moshenska 2017).

Conversely, in the context of this chapter, it is more relevant to briefly introduce key perspectives on museums, institutions that have also developed complex relation-ships with society at large, and their visitors in particular, throughout the last two centuries. Eilean Hooper-Greenhill (1992), drawing on Michel Foucault, pointed out how the construction of knowledge and the definition of museums have been shaped throughout history by different models of socially constructed ideals, which reflected the current dominant power. Tony Bennett examined how, in the nineteenth century, museums were reconceptualized as "cultural resources" (Bennett 1995: 28) and "an exemplary space" (Bennett 1995: 28), involving "both the education and the entertainment of the working classes" (Barrett 2012: 49). However, at the beginning of the twentieth century, this "civilizing role" diminished in favor of increased attention to collection management, with curators attempting "to establish museums as places where important objects were collected and cared for" (Hooper-Greenhill 1999: 259). Education was then considered to be limited only to school groups, and it gradually became a sub-specialization within the museum, "with different categories of staff, and different objectives and values from the rest of the institution" (Hooper-Greenhill 1999: 259). In the second half of the century, the ecomuseums proposed first by Hughes de Varine and Georges Henri Rivière in France (Davis 1999) and the New Museology (Vergo 1989) in the English-speaking world led to increased attention to social justice and inclusion, drawing also on postcolonialism, postmodernism, and social sciences frameworks, especially after the first English translation of Pierre Bourdieu and Alain Darbel's *L'amour de l'art* (Bourdieu, Darbel, and Schnapper 1969) in 1991.

Throughout the 1990s, museums increasingly focused on community engagement, social inclusion, and audience diversification programs. This process of opening up museums to new audiences and including different voices and communities has its counterpart in museums challenging their own authority by combining their views and interpretations with those from audiences and communities. With the advent of the Web 2.0—websites that prioritize user generated content—Nina Simon proposed the adoption of participatory cultures in museums (2010), suggesting that they also allowed reconciling "the data about visitors' self-generated contexts with the rigid form of the stories and experiences traditionally offered in a history museum" (Simon 2011: 20). However, the often-claimed dilution of the museum authority (as a result of this opening up) has also been contested and debated (Ross 2004; Janes 2009; McCall and Gray 2013). Despite these criticisms to New Museology and participatory theories, it is clear that they contributed—alongside political and economic pressures to demonstrate museums' relevance—to a repositioning of museums within society (Sandell and Dodd 2001; Knell 2007) and to increasing attention to social justice themes (Sandell and Nightingale 2012; Janes and Sandell 2019).

Museum education and relationships with visitors have also been reframed, moving from a formal model of learning to a constructivist one (Hein 1998), and to the aim of offering valuable experiences, while recognizing the diversity and diverse needs of the audiences. As Hooper-Greenhill argued, museums were "no better at imparting information than other places" but their strength was in giving "people an experience of the real thing such that a desire to know more ensues" (Hooper-Greenhill 1999: 1). This process was paralleled by a reconsideration of visitor studies methods. Museum researchers argued that quantitative data, such as the surveys that had driven much of the research until the 1990s, and observations of visitor movements in the galleries were not sufficient to understand their interpretations and experiences of the museum (Hooper-Greenhill 2006: 372–373), and there was a need for more qualitative methods. Sharon Macdonald highlighted how visitors had an active role in the meaning-making process, which can lead to original interpretations of the displays encompassing visitors' own experiences (Macdonald 1992, 2002). John Falk and Lynn Dierking researched the individual factors influencing visitors besides the design of the exhibition (what they call the physical context), such as their motivations, preconceptions and feelings toward museums (personal context), or the occasion of the visit (social context; see Dierking and Falk 1995; Falk and Dierking 1992, 2000, 2013; Falk, Dierking, and Foutz 2007; Falk 2009).

During the last few decades, museums have therefore evolved from institutions presenting more severe curatorial interpretations strongly rooted in the European bourgeoise and often responding to the interest of political leaders while aiming to educate the public to more open and flexible institutions. Museums' attention turned to the public, first in order to better acknowledge its needs and then as a potential collaborator and co-author in developing more nuanced and culturally sensitive interpretations. In parallel, researchers have also investigated archaeological audiences and the role of museum displays in the public understanding of the past.

Archaeological Audiences and Museums

A series of surveys on the public perception of archaeology have been conducted since the 1980s. Initial studies called also for a deeper investigation into the diverse modes of engagement with the past emerging in the public sphere (Merriman 1991; Stone 1994); however, most of the successive research has focused on a quantitative evaluation of the public understanding of, and support for, the discipline (Pokotylo and Mason 1991; Pokotylo and Guppy 1999; MORI 2000; Ramos and Duganne 2000; Pokotylo 2002; Feder 2006; Almansa Sanchez 2006; IPSOS 2011; Kajda et al. 2018; Marx, Nurra and Salas Rossenbach 2017). Despite the different methodologies and contexts, printed press and television have consistently been identified as the major sources of information on the past, while education and social interaction (i.e., family, friends) are also mentioned. The Internet was first cited as a source of information in the 1999 survey (Pokotylo and Guppy 1999), but it was then absent in the 2000 survey and the 2006 Spanish survey (Almansa Sanchez 2006). It reappeared in the French preliminary survey of 2006 (IPSOS 2011), whose data are directly comparable with those of 2010. The 2006 French survey and the 2010 survey witnessed a huge increase of Internet use (from 14 percent to 41 percent) in the face of a decrease both of television (75 percent to 66 percent) and press (both generalist and specialized, from 56 percent to 44 percent). However, in all these surveys, museums have had a limited presence. This could be partially explained by looking at the design of the questionnaires, for example, museums were notably absent both in the mid-1980s survey coordinated by the Cambridge Archaeology Department and in the 2000 US survey. In this sense, the research by Nick Merriman on public attitudes to the past and archaeological collections, conducted in the 1980s, still stands out as a positive exception (Merriman 1991).

Another strand of research on archaeological audiences has focused on analyzing the impact of specific archaeological media on the public. However, research on archaeological content in various media has often focused exclusively on a single medium and its representation (e.g., on television, Ascherson 2004; Kulik 2006, 2007), rather than on its relationships with other media and narratives (Holtorf 2005b, 2007a). Angela Piccini and Don Henson analyzed the socio-demographic characteristics of heritage viewers in the UK, observing TV audience data for the most successful programs in a year and highlighting how these failed to attract a younger audience (Piccini and Henson 2006). Chiara Bonacchi analyzed the visions and experiences of archaeology of *Time Team* audiences, comparing it with that of other heritage audiences (Bonacchi 2012a, 2013). Her results showed how the program had prompted in its fans a greater interest in visiting heritage sites, alongside an increased understanding of archaeology practices and approaches to the past. However, there is still a lack of research on the reciprocal impact and influences of popular images of archaeology and museum interpretations. Although museums and public archaeology initiatives carry out regular evaluations of their programs, they tend to focus on the immediate needs of the institution and funders. Thus, the impact of different media and museum initiatives has often been evaluated independently, although it has been acknowledged that such narratives reach the public and contribute to its perception of archaeology (e.g., Hooper-Greenhill 1994).

Besides researching archaeological audiences, scholarship on the image of archaeology in the public sphere has also focused on popular representations of the discipline, including the agencies, media, and impact of these different approaches to the past. The study of archaeological representation examines "how non-academic representations of the past have contributed to the construction of knowledge about ancient societies and cultures" (Moser 2009: 1048). Histories and analyses of archaeological representations have covered various types of media: museums (Moser 2003, 2006, 2010), television and magazines (Smiles and Moser 2005; Nichols 2006; Brittain and Clack 2007; Kulik 2007), newspapers (Finn 2001), literature (Evans 1993), science fiction (Russell 2002), computer games (Reinhard 2018), souvenirs, and so on, offering substantial insight into the origins and forms of various perceptions of archaeology. Researchers, such as Neal Ascherson (2004) and Cornelius Holtorf (2007a), have also discussed different representations of archaeologists and the themes most used to introduce archaeology in the media. In this context, museum representations have been discussed, highlighting how developments in the discipline of archaeology and in curatorial practices contribute to inform public perceptions of the past (Merriman 1999; Moser 1998, 2003, 2006, 2010). Increasingly, critiques of archaeology representations in museums have exposed the influence of nationalist and colonial ideologies in these displays. Stephanie Moser has emphasized how "ideas about ancient culture were conveyed through the spatial arrangement of selected objects in particular settings, and although aesthetic concerns were often of primary importance, a 'scientific' meaning was still conferred upon the objects through such arrangements" (Moser 2009: 1064).

Undoubtedly, the major contribution of these studies lies in exposing how different media select narratives about the past and portray archaeology. However, the dialectical relations between these representations, their media, their producers, and their publics often seem lost in this type of study. In her research on the display of Ancient Egypt in the British Museum, Moser includes a study of popular reception of these displays, but the discussion is only partially connected to a discussion of other popular representations of Egypt that may have also influenced the British Museum's visitors (Moser 2006). An exception to this trend is a chapter by Monique Scott (2005), who investigated how representations of human origins stemming out of Africa influenced visitors in three London museums, therefore grounding her research in visitor studies. Holtorf, departing from a study of representations to explore the construction of heritage knowledge, researched the presence of archaeology in popular culture, examining cinema, music, television, and printed media and objects of everyday life (Holtorf 2005a, 2005b, 2007a, 2007b) and emphasized that these media represent "the main opportunities where people who are not archaeologists themselves and go about their ordinary lives can hear or see something that strikes them as being 'archaeological'" (Holtorf 2007a: 13). Therefore, he expanded its analysis to the social groundings and impact of these representations, arguing that different views of the past are significant as "different manifestations of a widespread fascination with both the past and archaeology" (Holtorf 2005a: 549).

In conclusion, museums have been mentioned in a series of studies on the sources of archaeological information for the public, but their impact on the formation of archaeological knowledge has not yet been fully unpacked. Similarly, while archaeological representations, including those at museums, have been widely researched, these studies tended to focus either on selected media (e.g., cinema, videogames, museums) or on selected themes (e.g., the representation of the figure of the archaeologist). Both these trends, one drawing on histories of archaeology and media and the other drawing on heritage studies, aim to explore how aspects of the past have been represented in the public sphere. The study I will discuss in the following sections aims to contribute to this broader field by focusing on the museum, but highlighting how the impact of different media and personal characteristics came into play during a museum visit to contribute to the understanding of the displays. As such, this research is therefore trying to focus on the interaction and reciprocal influences of various types of representations and their effect on museum experiences.

The Case Study: The Ancient Worlds Galleries

The Manchester Museum, an interdisciplinary University Museum with both an academic and a public mandate, represented an ideal setting for researching tensions between different representations of—and approaches to—archaeology in the public sphere. The paper draws on a visitor study I conducted in the Ancient Worlds Galleries

in 2013, shortly after their opening. The methodology of the visitor study included un-
obtrusive observations, participant observations, interviews, and mental maps, while
longer interviews with curatorial staff facilitated my understanding of the genesis and
messages of the galleries. Research participants were aware of a wide set of narratives
of the past that influenced their itineraries in the galleries. These narratives prompted
them to move toward objects they recognized and that fit within their background
knowledge, their meaning-making processes, and their appreciation of the same displays. Mental maps highlighted how previous definitions and concepts are highly resilient and appeared to be rarely challenged by new narratives encountered in the
museum, unless these new ideas had been developed in a conversation during the visit,
highlighting the importance of face-to-face active engagement.

The Ancient Worlds Galleries opened in October 2012, following a major redevelopment of the archaeology and Egyptology displays of the Manchester Museum; they
were closed to the public in the autumn of 2018 in order to undergo another major
redevelopment. The Ancient Worlds Galleries comprised three sections that showcase
a range of design solutions (Merriman 2012). The first part, Discovering Archaeology, introduced the collections, practices and peoples in archaeology: the objects belonged to different chronological and geographical contexts, from Ancient Egypt to
cave dwellings, from Roman Manchester to Ancient Greece, and so on, while the space
was articulated around three large, low glass cases, with panels highlighting meta-
narratives of archaeology and its practice (Sitch 2012). Egyptian Worlds was an in-
depth exploration of a single civilization, with a focus on objects from daily life arranged
chronologically within few thematic subsections, and it included three mummies (Asru
in the main gallery and two wrapped mummies in an annexed smaller room, alongside
the Graeco-Roman portraits from Hawara). This gallery aimed to highlight the con-
tacts between Ancient Egypt and its neighbors and the continuity of Egyptian history,
from prehistory to the Islamic period, thus challenging the "traditional" space- and
temporal-borders of Ancient Egypt (Price 2012). Finally, Exploring Objects, arranged
around a balcony and not in direct contiguity with the other two galleries, explored the
richness and variety of the archaeological collections, reflected on museum practices,
and included a range of hands-on interactives.

The visitor study took place between September and November 2013, about a year
after the opening of the galleries. The study relied on four main methods: unobtrusive
observation, semi-structured interviews, participant observation, and mental maps.
Unobtrusive observation, gathered across the galleries, allowed an insight into visitors'
pattern of movements across the galleries and the collection of many unprompted
comments on the displays. Interviews were collected both on the first floor at the
end of the Egyptian Worlds Gallery (when visitors were about to continue to the natural history section of the museum) and on the second floor in the Exploring Objects
Gallery (where visitors could arrive from multiple directions). These semi-structured
interviews consisted of two parts: a first part investigating visitors' experiences in the
galleries and a second part exploring visitors' perceptions and attitudes to archaeol-

ogy and archaeological displays (also in comparison to other sources of information about the past). Participant observation allowed further investigation of visitors' meaning-making processes during their museum visit. In this case, participants were either recruited beforehand or invited to take part in the study at the beginning of their visit. When participants allowed me to follow them during their time in the galleries, the visitors dictated the itinerary and timings of the visit. Visitors also chose how much they commented or discussed the displays with me. Finally, I also asked research participants to quickly sketch a map of the gallery highlighting the main features (whether objects or themes) they remembered. Thus, instead of using the map as a tool to prompt the conversation (although sometimes the maps triggered more comments), I utilized it primarily as a further source of information on visitors' experiences, as a way "to convey knowledge and experience in a different form" (Gieseking 2013: 722). Sketching the map after the interview also revealed how—just a few minutes after the end of their visit—previous perceptions and understanding of archaeology were already informing participants' maps. In the analysis of the maps, the most relevant analytical categories among those identified by Jen Jack Gieseking (2013: 717–18) were: scale (of spaces and objects, implying which exhibits caught most of their attention), labeling (terminology used to define archaeological artifacts), number of items included (to represent their attention and memory), and edges (which revealed what participants considered part of the "archaeology and Egyptology galleries").

Overall, the study involved 302 visitors and around 80 children who came to the museum on a school visit. The research received ethical approval from the University of Manchester's Research Ethics committee. Informed consent was received from all the research participants and permission from carers was sought when minors were involved, school groups were contacted in advance to gain carers' permission to follow the guided activities in the museum. Data has been anonymized.

The Visitor Experience

The triangulation of the different data collected led to an examination of the meaning-making processes of the research participants and of the impact of public perceptions of archaeology and museums on their visit. The analysis drew on Falk and Dierking's framework of personal meaning-mapping in visitors' museum experiences (Falk 2009; Falk and Dierking 1992, 2000, 2013; Dierking and Falk 1995; Falk, Dierking, and Foutz 2007). They suggested a "contextual model of learning," recognizing three overlapping contexts affecting the museum visit: the personal, the socio-cultural, and the physical. They argued that free-choice learning in museums "can be conceptualized as the integration and interaction of these three contexts" (Falk and Dierking 2000 13). The personal context includes "the visitor's prior knowledge, experience and interest"; the physical context involves "the specifics of the exhibitions, programs, objects, and labels they encounter"; the socio-cultural context involves "the within-

and between-group interactions that occur while in the museum and the visitor's cultural experiences and values" (Falk 2009: 159). This model has subsequently been updated by Falk to highlight that the museum experience is "an ephemeral and constructed relationship that uniquely occurs each time a visitor interacts with a museum" (158) and that "the long-term meanings created by visitors from their time in the museum are largely shaped by short-term personal, identity-related needs and interests" (35). This framework allows addressing the impact of the design, the social context of the visit, and the personal context of the visitor while not designating visitors' socio-cultural background a priori as done in the cultural approach (for the definition of the psychological and cultural approaches, see Hooper-Greenhill and Moussouri 2002: 11). While I also observed the impact of the physical context, which led to different appreciations of the displays, this context is not relevant for the purposes of this chapter and is not included here.

Another significant aspect was the social context of the visit. Individual visitors chose their own path in the galleries, depending on their interests and motivations to visit, while couples and groups of friends influenced each other. For example, the jewelry section appeared very successful with couples, whose itineraries tended to differ so as to include this section more often than the itineraries of individual visitors or groups of people. Couples often used the exhibits as a springboard to speak about themselves, introducing the partner to their interests (Lehn, Heath, and Hindmarsh 2001; Galani 2005). The presence of children also significantly altered adult visitors' paths and experiences: in these cases, children took up the leading role in the visit influencing the itinerary and the adults' attitude to the displays (Hooper-Greenhill and Moussouri 2002). On one side, the design of the cases in Discovering Archaeology allowed children to get a closer view of the objects because the cases were at their eye-level so that they were often the ones pointing out an artifact to their carers and asking for explanations. Adults tended to neglect their own interests in favor of the perceived learning needs of the youngest visitors and tried to engage them with the exhibits by highlighting some of the features, such as the age or provenance of certain objects or their similarities with modern ones.

The social context emerged as a key factor in influencing the way visitors remembered and evaluated their experiences. One example illustrates how the personal interests of the visitors shaped their experiences. Two international students were prompted by the mass display of shabtis to discuss the status of their owners ("Did poor people have them?"). This conversation had such an influence that their mental maps of this gallery identified a section focusing on "status" (where the shabtis case is located) and "a model showing people in different classes" (referring to an interactive model interpreting an Egyptian stele). Thus, their conversation and interest in social structures led to an unexpected interpretation of these exhibits.

Personal background, motivations, and interests supported the meaning-making processes of research participants. Visitors were re-contextualizing objects within their everyday experiences; using them as gateways to recall their own culture, stimulated by similarities in appearance, materials, or functions; remembering their school experiences; or drawing on personal interests (see also Dicks 2016). In the case of jewelry, for example, there was a difference in interest between individual visitors and couples, in addition this display prompted research participants to proudly discuss their ethnic origins ("[these are similar to] traditional motives, still worn in India and Pakistan"), to reaffirm their personal interests (e.g., crafters discussed decorations or techniques), or their political stances at large (e.g., fashion in relation to society). It is worth remembering here Laurajane Smith's emphasis on the fact that "the social impact of museums may be more usefully characterized by the role they play in affirming and reinforcing identity and belief, rather than as primarily educational resources" (2017: 70).

Groups of friends considered the visit as just as much a social occasion as a learning opportunity, and therefore they often went through the galleries browsing the displays while engaging with each other: their shared conversations in the galleries had a notable influence on the way they remembered the visit. The case of three university students is illustrative of the effects of the social context of the visit on itineraries in the galleries and meaning-making processes. The three friends, originally from Cheshire and Wales, shared an interest in local history and archaeology, though these were not the subjects they were studying at university. They began their visit in Discovering Archaeology together, but then they continued their exploration of this gallery independently, although often pointing out to each other a particular exhibit; they then re-grouped at the Roman Manchester section of the display. After having followed the three friends during their visit, I asked them which were their favorite objects and, in Discovering Archaeology, they all pointed to the section on Roman Manchester. The choice of the Roman Manchester display was rare in visitors' answers. It could be argued that these three students had appreciated it so much because they had discussed it together, reading all the labels, the two nearby panels, and commenting upon it; therefore, they could remember it as a significant element of their visit. However, they did not acknowledge the narrative suggested by the museum, that is, rescue archaeology as an example of archaeologists' work in the context of the history of Manchester, and were instead led in their interpretation by their interest in local history. In front of the same case, another visitor was led by her personal interests to a completely different reaction. This visitor commented that she was happy to see "Stuff from Greece and Rome," since she preferred materials from other countries rather than British ones. Therefore, her preference for the classical world had led her to confuse the origins of these materials, and she did not notice that they were indeed from Manchester. Her narrative of this case was about classical antiquities and not about the history of the city (as most of other visitors interpreted it) or the role of rescue archaeology (the curatorial intent). As Macdonald noted, "explicit or intended messages may be ignored or not seen by visitors where they are at odds with visitors' cultural preconceptions" (Macdonald 2002: 55).

Similarly, educational background also influenced the itinerary of the visit, the attention of the visitors to certain topics or objects, and their interpretation and evaluations.

Notably, previous education on a topic could also lead visitors to ignore the museum narratives and even the objects themselves, in favor of reinforcing previous knowledge. A woman visiting with two adult children spent a few minutes in front of the case with Demotic, Greek, and Latin Papyri, explaining to them the ancient Egyptian writing system of "hieroglyphs, ieratic, and demotic." However, they were looking at papyri from the Hellenistic age, which were mostly written in ancient Greek. For this mother, the gallery was about Ancient Egypt and her background interest in hieroglyphs led her to overlook the other messages the museum aimed to convey in this display—the continuity of Egyptian life in the Hellenistic and Roman period. This example recalls Hooper-Greenhill and Moussouri's (2002:15) observation that parents "expected to see things related to a particular theme or subject (subject-specific agenda) and intended to influence their children's educational experience and enjoyment."

Additionally, in this context numerous media and popular representations of the past and of museums emerged. For example, the Iron Age chain reminded a young woman both of the history of the anti-slavery movement in the United States and of "the movies about the Romans." It is these particular mentions of popular images of archaeology that are most of interest for this chapter, and they will be presented and further unpacked in the following section.

Public Perceptions of Archaeology

This section focuses on those data concerning the impact of public perceptions of archaeology in informing the experience, understanding, and appreciation of the displays. Boon (2011: 422), discussing Michel de Certeau in relation to visitors' experiences, has argued that: "These [displays] will often be related to stories and narratives that are already familiar to them. If we accept this argument, it is clear that the kinds of sense-making that visitors enter into in museums may also be thought of as the construction of narratives, as they incorporate what they encounter into how they already think." This study shows that the impact of previous knowledge and information affected visitors' itineraries in the galleries. The example of a young man is particularly indicative, since his passion for Christian Jacq's books prompted him to focus his visit around objects connected to Ramses II. Despite a declared interest in Ancient Egypt and his acknowledgment that Jacq's books should not have been taken seriously, only two objects seemed to capture his attention during the visit: a bust of Ramses II in the Egyptian Worlds gallery and the replica of Nefertiti's bust in Exploring Objects. In the latter case, he recognized the iconic bust as "Nefertiti," but he added "Ramses's wife," thus confusing two iconic Egyptian queens Nefertiti and Nefertari. His interest was therefore key in directing his attention toward those objects but did not lead to further engagement with the exhibits.

A second group of research participants cited media representations as a way to engage with the objects and their narratives. The association of an exhibit with a popular image prompted visitors to find common ground between the objects and their personal experiences. Visitors' comments were inspired by the features of the objects on display, for example, the haircut on the facial reconstruction of Worsley Man was compared with "Tom Cruise's one," or by the theme and the historical figures themselves, for example the facial reconstruction of Philip II prompted a comparison between two different movies about Alexander the Great (and between Richard Burton's and Colin Farrell's acting). The range of citations was also varied, from the more expected ones, like *The Mummy*, to more culturally specific ones, like the Romanian movie *The Immortals* (*Nemuritorii* 1974). In this sense, popular images of archaeology fostered the social experience of the visit, contributing to the previously mentioned identity-affirming processes and enabling a creative engagement with the displays connecting themes across archaeology, popular culture, and media productions.

For a third group of visitors, the impact of popular representations on the understanding and evaluation of the displays was more substantial. A woman commented how a documentary about mummy portraits she had recently watched had allowed her to "appreciate them more now than what I would have done before." Another research participant explicitly acknowledged the impact of television programs on his fascination for certain objects; for example, looking at the facial reconstruction of Worsley Man, he commented "the beheaded [man] . . . this is the story I like, if I close my eyes I can almost see it." He seemed to frame the story of Worsley Man in a context of ancient violent societies and warfare, thus reinforcing his fascination for this aspect of the past; he did not engage with the information presented by the museum in this display such as the technique of facial reconstructions or the phenomenon of bog bodies. Another participant, while watching the unwrapped mummy of Asru, asked "is this script under her head?," and he commented that it might have been a "will, something for the Gods." He seemed to expect the presence of some "secret script" near the mummy, emphasizing the popular perception of mystery surrounding Egyptian mummies.

As in the examples discussed in the previous section, the exhibits of jewelry was also particularly interesting in this case because it prompted quite stereotypical discussions on gender (the jewels could have belonged to "a princess") as well as a variety of comments on the material and age of the artifacts, which conferred them further value ("it is amazing people could do these things 4,000 years ago"). In this case, personal perspectives and prejudices were again subduing the curatorial intents. For example, a visitor observed repeatedly that at the time of some of the Egyptian artifacts "5000 years ago" there was "nothing British," and he continued by commenting that "people think it's like the British Empire, but it lasted 5000 years this, though." On one side, he was criticizing what he thought was a common comparison (i.e., Ancient Egypt and the British Empire); on the other side, he was also revealing how he considered Ancient Egypt to be frozen in time, despite the fact that Egyptian Worlds aimed to argue exactly the opposite by highlighting the continuity of Egyptian history.

The mental maps used in the research were a key method for uncovering the connections between most remembered objects and themes, frameworks used to understand them, and the impact of popular representations of the past. For example, most of the maps include the section on facial reconstructions in Discovering Archaeology, but the words used to label it reveal the different narratives constructed around it. For example, a young man—remembering a nearby panel on the battle of Chester—described it as "skeleton of men [died] in violent attacks," while a woman marked the area as focusing on "skeleton stereotypes"—considering the display to be a tool to challenge racial prejudices. The attempt to define objects by drawing on their ancient function led another visitor to mark the Roman lamps in Exploring Objects as "candle holders," demonstrating some confusion on their operating principles. Public perceptions of archaeology also clearly emerged in the confusion between the Manchester Gallery (an adjacent gallery of local history) and the Ancient Worlds Galleries. For example, popular perceptions of archaeology and paleontology notoriously confuse the two fields of study. In my research, a visitor included the skeleton of Maharaja, an elephant that died in the 1880s and is now on display in the Manchester Gallery, in her map of the "archaeology galleries," marking it as a "dinosaurus." Her interpretation was shared by other visitors; one visitor even indicated Maharaja as his favorite object in the "archaeology galleries," commenting that "the extinct animal is unique." Similarly, the popularity of certain periods, themes, or terms in archaeology influenced the labeling of the objects on the mental maps. The Neolithic skulls from northern Wales displayed in Discovering Archaeology were marked "Neanderthal skulls" by a research participant; in the sketches of Egyptian Worlds, the label "mummy" referred not only to the actual mummy of Asru, but also to the Two Brothers' coffins, the animal mummies, and—in one case—the (u)shabtis in the Exploring Objects area, which were labeled by a visitor as "massive tiny mummys!" [sic]. The (u)shabtis were indeed one of the more appreciated objects and were photographed for their aesthetic qualities. Another visitor noted them on the map as "blue stattuettes" [sic]; however, a few visitors noted the panel and hands-on interactive display describing them and their function in Ancient Egypt.

In conclusion, public perceptions of archaeology shaped visitors' itineraries, their engagement with the objects and their fellow visitors, and influenced their meaning-making processes, appreciation, and (at least) short-term memories of the visit. At the same time, visitors also often mentioned their perceptions and expectations of museums, as will be discussed in the next section.

Public Perceptions of Museums

Perceptions of museums had a crucial role in framing visitors' words in the interviews and in their recollections of the Ancient Worlds Galleries. A section of the interviews, in particular, directly investigated visitors' evaluation of museum displays in comparison to other sources of information about archaeology. While the influence of popular representations of the past has already been noted above, this section explores how conscious these influences were and to what extent the museum visit was responding to a different need than a TV program or an online source.

Museums are now embedded into discourses of participatory practices, public engagement and community participation. Still, most of the visitors seemed to consider the museum primarily an educational site and were acting accordingly both in the galleries and when answering my questions. They felt compelled to praise the "instructive" or "informative" character of the galleries, though they did not always engage with it because of a lack of interest. In particular, the idea of museums as sites of learning was often mentioned in relation to children, who were sometimes considered the primary audience of museums. For example, a woman argued that the museum should be "trying to raise their [children's] interest and help them connecting [to the objects], capture their attention," while a father even suggested—only partially joking—that museums were intrinsically positive for children's knowledge because "they can't turn away [from the displays]," as they would do in front of a television or a book.

Some visitors further negotiated their position in the interview by remarking that though they already knew the topic, they appreciated certain features as "very helpful for visitors." This type of comment revealed that some interviewees not only considered the museum to have primarily an educational purpose, but they also considered themselves to have higher cultural capital (Bourdieu 1984) than the average museum audience. Additionally, a few interviewees remarked how they worked in other museums, reclaiming the role of experts that, in turn, enabled them to evaluate their experience properly. However, it should be noted that museum professionals and archaeologists who visited the galleries also tended to rely on their background knowledge to the detriment of the Manchester Museum's own narrative. A visiting curator commented that the typology and Wentworth cases in Exploring Objects contributed "to show that typology is the main topic in archaeology," despite the fact that the Manchester Museum was prompting a reflection on collecting practices and challenging typological classification of artifacts with these displays. Similarly, a museum educator who was evidently expecting a more traditional display criticized the lack of information on flints in Exploring Objects. She completely ignored the museum messages about fakes and authenticity (even when I asked explicitly about it and pointed out those flints were fakes) and advocated for an educational display showing the uses of these objects in the past.

Furthermore, local visitors frequently remarked on the positives of having such collections in Manchester, praising the value of the museum for the local community. In contrast, international visitors tended to be more critical. Some international students directly compared the museum with the British Museum, which seemed to inform their expectations for all archaeological displays. As a consequence, while remarking that the Ancient Worlds Galleries had value for education since it was "easier to get access," they also noted how the galleries were smaller and had fewer objects on display. This evaluation of the Manchester Museum's collections highlights the different perceptions linked to the provenance of visitors: while city pride shaped local visitors' comments, outsiders tended to judge the museum according to their previous experiences with bigger museums.

A section of the interviews asked about television or online documentaries as a source of information. Some visitors immediately discarded TV programs: one considered them "boring" and repetitive, while another found them "frustrating, either [they are] patronizing or they are showing off" and consequently, he preferred to read about topics he wanted to know more since reading allows you to "follow your own path." Conversely, others appreciated television since its bigger audience implied a wider impact and, therefore, they argued that a good documentary could also influence people's decision to visit a museum. Children's education was also referenced in this section of the interviews by an interviewee who noted that "not everybody goes to the museum, you see the children come with school trips, maybe they even don't want to be here"; instead, the interviewee suggested that these same children might stop to watch a documentary.

When asked to directly compare their experience of the past in museums and with television, research participants unanimously argued that museums offered a better experience due to the direct relationship with the objects they allow and the presence of more trusted and detailed information. One interviewee argued that museums offer "more time to study" the objects and the visitor participates directly in "the process": he could choose his own path, how much time to focus on an object, and therefore "construct" his own narrative with the instruments the museum offers rather than passively following a documentary. Another participant commented that when comparing archaeological displays with *Time Team*, museums allowed seeing "many more things than one dig, and a wide range of panels and explanation and context." She appreciated *Time Team* but also criticized it for showing "all the processes, but sped up." Furthermore, in a participant's words, an object in a museum case has "more impact live." As another visitor specified, on television one gets "just an image" while in a museum "you can see the details, the scale, and get an explanation." The rhythm and speed of images on television does not allow viewers to clearly perceive the context in which objects are filmed. For example, looking at an Egyptian relief, a visitor argued that a documentary would have zoomed onto the figures and the hieroglyphs, and he would not have noted how the relief was carved from a "long chunk of stone."

While these visitors highlighted the more informative character of museum displays, others praised the different type of experience enabled by museums. The value of a different sensory engagement with objects is exemplified by a discussion among two women. One of them was criticizing her friend for trying all the interactives in Exploring Objects, to which the second one answered "you like seeing them in the media, I like touching [them]." Museums were therefore considered more immersive environments: as one visitor said, they are "more tactile and visually more inspiring," a characteristic that led her to focus mainly on the objects during her visit, drawing on the written interpretation only sporadically.

Museums were more trusted sources of knowledge and their authority and expertise was largely cited as a reason in favor of learning about the past in this setting. Interviewees declared that "in museums you have the facts" and their presentation was "more objective" than television. This is evident from the quote of a participant who, seeing the toys in Egyptian Worlds, asked, "when the fathers give toys to children in the movie, it's real?" implying that the museum had a greater authority as a source of knowledge and served to validate the information she had acquired from the media. The direct relationship with the objects enabled by museums was again a key motivation for this trust: as one interviewee said, in museums "you know more and get to touch, and there are more proofs," for example, the "real" objects on display. Therefore, not only can you "see the size, colors and technique much better," but you can also "see the reality" because there are "many real objects from ancient times." This argument about the value of "real" objects in museums also emerged in a discussion on the facial reconstruction of Philip II when a man concluded that "it's not the same face that media can show us, it's more real." The reason for the greater authenticity was the presence of facial features ("this reconstruction is more real because of the hair and the scar"), the same features that had prompted another visitor to draw a comparison between the reconstruction and Val Kilmer's portrayal of Philip II in the 2004 movie *Alexander*. The first visitor, though declaring his ignorance of archaeology, applied the same reasoning to the small image of Philip in the label, adding that "the picture is different from the media" because the "clothes in the media look like Romans," and instead here the representation was more accurate in showing "the ancient Greek style."

Finally, despite the vast majority of the interviewees praising museums' presentation of archaeology in comparison to other media's presentation, there were also some dissenting voices. For example, a couple appreciated the possibility of seeing "the real thing" in museums, but they preferred the "huge graphics" of television. Similarly, one interviewee was a keen viewer of "The Brain Scoop" YouTube channel based at the Field Museum in Chicago (at the time of the research, in 2013, it had already gained more than 9 million views). This channel was described by the interviewee as showing "the backstage of museum work." As a consequence of his fascination with the web series, he thought that "the display is fun, but not as interesting as seeing how they get to it" and he was thus disappointed by the displays, which did not stand up to the expectations he had of the museum.

Conclusion

This chapter has unpacked the impact of previous knowledge and perceptions of the past during a museum visit. It has framed visitors' experiences in the Ancient Worlds Galleries of the Manchester Museum within the framework developed by Dierking and Falk and by utilizing an original use of mental maps to gather research data. However, this choice does not intend to overlook also other beneficial outcomes of a museum visit. The absence of a discussion of the other benefits of a museum visit for visitors' enjoyment, health, and more, is due to the purposes of my research, and it should be highlighted that visitors reported positive outcomes beside those discussed here.

The chapter discussed how the personal and social contexts of visitors are crucial for understanding the performative and identity-affirming interpretations and narratives that emerge during a museum visit. It has been evidenced that research participants tended to draw on previous knowledge and perceptions in shaping their itineraries across the galleries, in interpreting the displays, and in evaluating them. The chapter has also highlighted how, in order to understand visitors' experiences during a museum visit, it is not sufficient to consider the impact of public perceptions of the subject at hand (Egyptology and archaeology in this case); public perceptions of museums should also be investigated. Museum objects have agency in attracting visitors to a museum first (to see the "real" objects more "in detail") and then directing their steps in the galleries. Expectations and previous encounters with archaeology and with archaeological displays shaped visitors' itineraries, meaning-making processes, and evaluation. Indeed, expectations about a museum visit and the "type" of representations of the past a visitor could find there emerged as crucial in shaping the experiences of my research participants' visits to the Ancient Worlds Galleries.

Previous perceptions tended to overcome the museum narrative and, moreover, they also often prevailed in informing visitors' memories of the galleries, even when visitors had read the supporting material and attentively observed the displays. Therefore, the impact of previous knowledge and public perceptions seems highly resilient and visitors appeared to seek confirmation of their preconceived interpretations rather than allow their interpretations to be challenged by the museum. This might be partially explained by the effort needed to digest and re-contextualize the newly acquired information within previously held frameworks; for example, visitors' habit of seeing arrangements focusing on specific civilizations or "traditional" themes (e.g., dresses, warfare, housing, etc.) appeared to underlie many narratives that emerged from Discovering Archaeology, whose innovative and challenging narratives might have demanded a significant effort by visitors.

At the same time, expectations about museums also played a key role in motivating visitors and shaping their understanding. On the one hand, visitors commented positively on the museum as a source of authoritative knowledge, valuing the direct contact with the objects enabled by this environment. On the other hand, though, visitors seemed to perceive the museum as a primarily educational space, ignoring recent developments and debates on inclusivity, co-production and participatory practices within the museum field.

Certainly, more research on visitors' experiences and meaning-making processes is needed, especially in a moment in which audiences have access to many competing representations of the past thanks to digital media. This chapter has contributed to this evolving area across the fields of public archaeology and museum studies by highlighting the interplay of personal and social factors with perceptions of archaeology and museums, and their reciprocal impacts in shaping public understanding of archaeological displays.

Both public archaeology and museum studies have been increasingly critically engaging with modern social issues, drawing attention on the contemporary power structures that have traditionally shaped museum collections and interpretation. This chapter has emphasized how innovative displays can be challenging for visitors, whose experience is significantly shaped by engrained understandings of the past and museums' role in mediating it. A better understanding of visitors' understanding is therefore necessary, in order to broaden the space for critical conversations about contemporary society enabled by archaeological collections.

Chiara Zuanni is assistant professor in Digital Humanities at the Centre for Information Modelling – Austrian Centre for Digital Humanities, University of Graz. She studied Classics (BA) and Archaeology (MA) at the University of Bologna, and has a PhD in Museology from the University of Manchester. Her research focuses on data practices and digital media in the heritage sector, on social media and digital cultures in memory institutions, and on the creation and mediation of knowledge in museums.

References

Almansa Sanchez, Jaime. 2006. "La imagen popular de la arqueología en Madrid" [The Popular Image of Archaeology in Madrid]. *ArqueoWeb* 8(1).

Ascherson, Neal. 2004. "Archaeology and the British Media." In *Public Archaeology*, ed N. Merriman, 145–58. London: Routledge.

Barrett Jennifer. 2012. *The Museums and the Public Sphere*. Hoboken, NJ: Wiley-Blackwell.

Bennett, Tony. 1995. *The Birth of the Museum: History, Theory, Politics*. London: Routledge.

Bonacchi, Chiara. 2012a. "Communicating Archaeology: From Trends to Policy. Public Perceptions and Experience in the Changing Media Environment." Ph.D. dissertation. London: University College London.

———. 2012b. *Archaeology and Digital Communication: Towards Strategies of Public Engagement*. London: Archetype Publications.

———. 2013. "Audiences and Experiential Values of Archaeological Television: The Case Study of *Time Team*." *Public Archaeology* 12(2): 117–31. https://doi.org/10.1179/1465518713Z.0000 0C00035.

Boon, Tim. 2011. "A Walk in the Museum with Michel de Certeau: A Conceptual Helping Hand for Museum Practitioners." *Curator: The Museum Journal*, 54: 419-429. https://doi.org/10 .1111/j.2151-6952.2011.00107.x

Bourdieu, Pierre. 1984. *Distinction. A Social Critique of the Judgement of Taste*. Abingdon: Routledge.

Bourdieu, Pierre, Alain Darbel, and Dominique Schnapper. 1969. *L'Amour de l'art les musées d'art européens et leur public [par] Pierre Bourdieu et Alain Darbel avec Dominique Schnapper* [The love of art: European art museums and their public]. 2 edn. Paris: Les Éditions de minuit.

———. 1991. *The Love of Art: European Art Museums and Their Public*. Cambridge: Polity.

Brittain, Marcus, and Timothy Clack 2007. *Archaeology and the Media*. Walnut Creek, CA: Left Coast.

Davis, Peter. 1999. *Ecomuseums: A Sense of Place*. London: Continuum.

Dicks, Bella. 2016. "The Habitus of Heritage: A Discussion of Bourdieu's Ideas for Visitor Studies in Heritage and Museums." *Museum and Society* 14(1): 52–64. https://doi.org/10.29311/mas .v14i1.625.

Dierking, Lynn D., and John H. Falk 1995. *Public Institutions for Personal Learning: Establishing a Research Agenda.* Washington, DC: American Association of Museums.

Evans, Christopher. 1993. "Digging with the Pen: Novel Archaeologies and Literary Traditions." In *Interpretative Archaeology*, ed. C. Tilley, 417–47. Oxford: Berg.

Falk, John. H. 2009. *Identity and the Museum Visitor Experience.* Walnut Creek, CA: Left Coast.

Falk, John H., and Lynn D. Dierking 1992. *The Museum Experience.* Washington, DC: Whalesback Books.

———. 2000. *Learning from Museums: Visitor Experiences and the Making of Meaning.* Walnut Creek, CA: AltaMira Press.

———. 2013. *The Museum Experience Revisited.* Washington, DC: Whalesback Books.

Falk, John H., Lynn D. Dierking, and S. Foutz. 2007. *In Principle, in Practice: Museums as Learning Institutions.* Lanham, MD: Altamira Press.

Feder, Kenneth. 2006. "Skeptics, Fence Sitters, and True Believers: Student Acceptance of an Improbable Prehistory." In *Archaeological Fantasies: How Pseudoarchaeology Misrepresents the Past and Misleads the Public*, ed. G. G. Fagan, 71–95. London: Routledge.

Finn, Christine. 2001. "Mixed Messages: Archaeology and the Media." *Public Archaeology* 1(4): 261–68.

Galani, Areti. 2005. "Far Away Is Close at Hand: An Ethnographic Investigation of Social Conduct in Mixed Reality Museum Visits." Ph.D. dissertation. Glasgow: University of Glasgow. Retrieved 7 March 2020 from http://theses.gla.ac.uk/3918/.

Gieseking, Jen Jack. 2013. "Where We Go from Here: The Mental Sketch Mapping Method and Its Analytic Components," *Qualitative Inquiry* 19(9): 712–24. https://doi.org/10.1177/1077800413500926.

Hein, George E. 1998. *Learning in the Museum.* London: Routledge.

Holtorf, Cornelius. 2005a. "Beyond Crusades: How (Not) to Engage with Alternative Archaeologies." *World Archaeology* 37(4): 544–51. http://www.jstor.org/stable/40025090.

———. 2005b. *From Stonehenge to Las Vegas: Archaeology as Popular Culture.* Walnut Creek, CA: Altamira Press.

———. 2007a. *Archaeology Is a Brand! : The Meaning of Archaeology in Contemporary Popular Culture*, ed. Q. Drew. Oxford: Archaeopress.

———. 2007b. "Can You Hear Me at the Back? Archaeology, Communication and Society," *European Journal of Archaeology* 10(2–3): 149–65. https://doi.org/10.1177/1461957108095982.

Hooper-Greenhill, Eilean. 1992. *Museums and the Shaping of Knowledge.* London: Routledge.

———. 1994. *Museums and Their Visitors.* London: Routledge.

———. 1999. *The Educational Role of the Museum.* 2 edn. London: Routledge.

———. 2006. "Studying Visitors." In *A Companion to Museum Studies*, ed. S. Macdonald, 362–76. Hoboken, NJ: Blackwell.

Hooper-Greenhill, Eilean, and Theano Moussouri. 2002. *Researching Learning in Museums and Galleries 1990–1999: A Bibliographic Review.* Leicester: RCMG.

IPSOS. 2011. "Image de l'archéologie auprès du grand public." Retrieved 10 February 2020 from https://www.inrap.fr/sites/inrap.fr/files/atoms/files/ipsos-archeologie.pdf.

Janes, Robert R. 2009. *Museums in a Troubled World: Renewal, Irrelevance, or Collapse?* London: Routledge.

Janes, Robert R., and Richard Sandell, eds. 2019. *Museum Activism.* London: Routledge.

Kajda, Kornelia, Amala Marx, Holly Wright, Julian Richards, Arkadiusz Marciniak, Kai Salas Rossenbach, Michal Pawleta, et al. 2018. "Archaeology, Heritage, and Social Value: Public Perspectives on European Archaeology." *European Journal of Archaeology* 21(1): 96–117. https://doi .org/10.1017/eaa.2017.19.

Knell, Simon J. 2007. *Museums in the Material World*, ed. S. J. Knell. London: Routledge.

Kulik, Karol. 2006. "Archaeology and British Television." *Public Archaeology* 5(2): 75–90.

———. 2007. "A Short History of Archaeological Communication." In *Archaeology and the Media*, ed. M. Brittain and T. Clack, 111–24. Walnut Creek, CA: Left Coast.

Lehn, Dirk Vom, Christian Heath, and Jon Hindmarsh. 2001. "Exhibiting Interaction: Conduct and Collaboration in Museums and Galleries." *Symbolic Interaction* 24(2): 189–216. https://doi.org/10.1525/si.2001.24.2.189.

Macdonald, Sharon. 1992. "Cultural Imagining among Museum Visitors: A Case Study." *Museum Management and Curatorship* 11(4): 401–9. https://doi.org/10.1016/0964-7775(92)90079-K.

———. 2002. *Behind the Scenes at the Science Museum*. Berg: Oxford.

Marx, Amala, Federico Nurra, and Kai Salas Rossenbach, eds. 2017. *Europeans & Archaeology: A Survey on the European Perception of Archaeology and Archaeological Heritage*. Paris: NEARCH. https://doi.org/10.5284/1043770.

McCall, Vikki, and Clive Gray. 2013. "Museums and the 'New Museology': Theory, Practice and Organisational Change." *Museum Management and Curatorship* 29(1): 19–35. https://doi.org/10.1030/09647775.2013.869852.

McGimsey, Charles R. 1972. *Public Archaeology*. New York: Seminar Press.

Merriman, Nick. 1991. *Beyond the Glass Case: The Past, the Heritage and the Public in Britain*. Leicester: Leicester University Press.

———. 1999. *Making Early Histories in Museums*. London: Leicester University Press.

———, ed. 2004. *Public Archaeology*. London: Routledge.

———. 2012. "Introduction." In *The Manchester Museum: Window to the World*. Manchester: The Manchester Museum.

MORI, Ipsos. 2000. "What Does 'Heritage' Mean to You?" *Ipsos*, 26 September. https://www.ipsos.com/en-uk/what-does-heritage-mean-you.

Moser, Stephanie. 1998. *Ancestral Images: The Iconography of Human Origins*. Ithaca: Cornell University Press.

———. 2003. "Representing Archaeological Knowledge in Museums: Exhibiting Human Origins and Strategies for Change." *Public Archaeology* 3(1): 3–20.

———. 2006. *Wondrous Curiosities: Ancient Egypt at the British Museum / Stephanie Moser*. Chicago: University of Chicago Press.

———. 2009. "Archaeological Representation: The Consumption and Creation of the Past." In *The Oxford Book of Archaeology*, ed. B. Cunliffe, C. Gosden, and R. A. Joyce, 1048–77. Oxford: Oxford University Press.

———. 2010. "The Devil Is in the Detail: Museum Displays and the Creation of Knowledge." *Museum Anthropology* 33(1): 22–32. https://doi.org/10.1111/j.1548-1379.2010.01072.x.

Moshenska, Gabriel, ed. 2017. *Key Concepts in Public Archaeology*. London: UCL Press.

Nichols, Stephen. 2006. "Out of the Box: Popular Notions of Archaeology in Documentary Programmes on Australian Television." *Australian Archaeology* (63): 35–46.

Piccini, Angela, and Don Henson. 2006. "Survey of Heritage Television Viewing, 2005–2006." Retrieved 7 March 2022 from http://hc.english-heritage.org.uk/content/pub/eh_tvcounts_report_final.pdf.

Pokotylo, David. 2002. "Public Opinion and Canadian Archaeological Heritage: A National Perspective." *Canadian Journal of Archaeology* (26): 88–129.

Pokotylo, David, and Neil Guppy. 1999. "Public Opinion and Archaeological Heritage: Views from Outside the Profession." *American Antiquity* 64(3): 400–16.

Pokotylo, David L., and Andrew R. Mason. 1991. "Public Attitudes towards Archaeological Resources and Their Management." In *Protecting the Past*, G. S. Smith and J. E. Ehrenhard, 9–18. Boca Raton: CRC Press. http://www.nps.gov/seac/protectg.htm.

Price, Campbell. 2012. "Living and Dying under the Pharaohs." *The Manchester Museum: Window to the World*. Manchester: The Manchester Museum.

Ramos, Maria, and David Duganne. 2000. "Exploring Public Perceptions and Attitudes about Archaeology." *Society for American Archaeology*. Retrieved 7 April 2022 from https://documents.saa.org/container/docs/default-source/doc-publicoutreach/harris_poll1999.pdf

Reinhard, Andrew. 2018. *Archaeogaming: An Introduction to Archaeology in and of Video Games*. New York: Berghahn Books.

Richardson, Lorna. 2013. "A Digital Public Archaeology?" *Papers from the Institute of Archaeology*, 23(1). http://doi.org/10.5334/pia.431.

Ross, Max. 2004. "Interpreting the New Museology." *Museums and Society* 2(2): 84–103.

Russell, Miles, ed. 2002. *Digging Holes in Popular Culture: Archaeology and Science Fiction*. Oxford: Oxbow Books.

Sandell, Richard, and Jocelyn Dodd. 2001. *Including Museums: Perspectives on Museums, Galleries and Social Inclusion*. Leicester: RCMG.

Sandell, Richard, and Eithne Nightingale. 2012. *Museums, Equality and Social Justice*. London: Routledge.

Scott, Monique. 2005. "'We Grew up and Moved on': Visitors to British Museums Consider Their 'Cradle of Mankind.'" In *Envisioning the Past: Archaeology and the Image*, ed. S. Smiles and S. Moser, 29-50. Hoboken, NJ: Blackwell.

Simon, Nina. 2010. *The Participatory Museum / by Nina Simon*. Santa Cruz, CA: Museum 2.0.

———. 2011. "Participatory Design and the Future of Museums." In *Letting Go? Sharing Historical Authority in a User-Generated World*, ed. B. Adair, B. Filene, and L. Koloski, 18–33. Walnut Creek, CA: Left Coast Press.

Sitch, Bryan. 2012. "Tales from Ancient Worlds." *The Manchester Museum: Window to the World*. Manchester: The Manchester Museum.

Smiles, Sam, and Stephanie Moser, 2005. *Envisioning the Past: Archaeology and the Image*. Malden, MA: Blackwell.

Smith, Laurajane. 2017. "'We are we are everything': The Politics of Recognition and Misrecognition at Immigration Museums." *Museum & Society* 15(1): 69–86.

Stone, Peter G. 1994. "Interpretations and Uses of the Past in Modern Britain and Europe: Why Are People Interested in the Past? Do the Experts Know or Care? A Plea for Further Study." In *Who Needs the Past?: Indigenous Values and Archaeology*, ed. R. Layton, 195–206. London: Routledge.

Vergo, Peter, ed. 1989. *The New Museology*. London: Reaktion Books.

Zuanni, Chiara. 2016. "Mediating the Past: Museums and Public Perceptions of Archaeology." Ph.D. dissertation. Manchester: University of Manchester.

CONCLUSION

Critical Public Archaeology in Context

Suzie Thomas

Introduction

The public's engagement with archaeology is a topic that has attracted a lot of attention for many decades. This has been the case whether through the efforts of archaeologists themselves to open up their processes and projects to a wider audience, archaeology's (and archaeologists') involvement in political and activist issues, or through non-professional groups and individuals creating their own motivations and methods for archaeological interventions. This is not least due to the discipline's own origins primarily as an amateur pastime of the privileged in Western Europe from the fifteenth century onward. In addition to archaeology's evolution from an elite activity to an established (albeit still multidisciplinary) science, the relationship between archaeological research, access to archaeology, and the wider public has never been straightforward. This is especially true on the global scale as different legislation, governmental regimes, societies, and cultures have influenced professional and community relationships with archaeology and, more broadly, heritage.

V. Camille Westmont notes in the introduction, and indeed it forms a common thread through many of the chapters, that critical theory although not exactly new to archaeological thinking has a lot to offer for approaching public archaeology in particular. In this *Critical Public Archaeology* volume, we have seen perspectives from authors working primarily in Western countries, albeit with a range of different and diverse communities, audiences, and publics. The goal of the book as a whole is to advance our understanding and analysis of public archaeology by elevating case studies and projects as opportunities for critical reflection and developing new ways of thinking about methods, whether for practice and delivery of public archaeology or for its study and evaluation. Furthermore, authors have worked to develop and enhance the theoretical frameworks within which we seek to conceptualize archaeology as a whole, not only the public's response to it and archaeologists' responses to the public. In this short concluding chapter I aim to respond and react to the authors of this book while also bringing in my own perspectives, situating this volume within the context of archaeology and its engagement with communities over time.

The Development and "Value" of Public Archaeology

The professional discipline of archaeology sprang from the interests of amateur antiquarians who were active in Western Europe from the fifteenth century (Trigger 1989: 14) but especially from the eighteenth century in connection with the "philosophical turn toward empiricism and a greatly increased confidence in the explanatory power of observation and experiment" (Seymour 2014: 2220; also Immonen and Taavitsainen 2011: 140). Early researchers in what could be said to be archaeology typically came from the nobility and, later, from the clergy (Taylor 1995: 502). Michael Seymour (2014: 2221) notes that, certainly in northern Europe, excavation work in the eighteenth century was mostly carried out as a hobby. The activities of clergymen and other amateur antiquarians, usually people situated in a particular locale with sufficient education and free time, often led to the foundation of antiquarian and local history societies (Taylor 1995: 504; Thomas 2014: 1513–14).

Archaeology itself, then, has its roots in amateur (although mostly privileged, educated, and white European) activity. It is hardly surprising that non-professional interests in archaeology have endured to the present period, although its form and relationship with professional archaeology has changed over time. At the same time, Western perspectives on what counts as (archaeological) heritage, and how best to handle it, have dominated the work and debates within international heritage management (Byrne 1991). Archaeological heritage sites have been seen as places to be appreciated, managed, and protected—sometimes resulting in exclusion, even by force, of (usually Indigenous) communities that might have other uses and understandings, as well as needs, of those places (Chirikure and Pwiti 2008: 468). Similarly, other forms of heritage, including but not only intangible forms, have not been recognized by decision-makers as legitimate forms of heritage until relatively recently, with their inclusion into discussion arguably "accelerated since the adoption of the UNESCO Convention for the Safeguarding of the Intangible Cultural Heritage, 2003" (Smith and Campbell 2017: 27). Alternative cosmologies that might give quite a different understanding of archaeological sites, cultural landscapes and other heritage elements have not always been considered in the academy despite several important studies (e.g., Ingold 2000).

Valuation of archaeology and heritage have also become central considerations for many public-oriented archaeological studies (e.g., Jones 2017). Margarita Díaz-Andreu (2016) has noted that while numerous values, such as aesthetic and historical, have been associated with heritage (particularly archaeological heritage), the notion of social value attached to heritage, and hence its "value" to communities—especially within Indigenous and other non-Western cultures—has emerged only relatively recently. This social value has implications also for understanding different power structures affecting and influencing how archaeological heritage is used and by whom, core considerations for this emerging critical public archaeology, as it is also for critical heritage studies (Smith 2006) and critical museology (Shelton 2013; also Stobiecka in this volume). Within this context, the relationships between different communities to both archaeology and heritage have been complex and have changed over time.

Although archaeology can claim "amateur" roots, the early non-professional practitioners were rarely from a background other than white, male, and educated and/ or of the nobility. In non-Western contexts, local people have in the past (and even sometimes in current times) been assumed to be less knowledgeable about their local history and certainly not proficient in archaeological field skills. The history of archaeological excavation in regions such as the Middle East shows a long tradition of hiring local laborers to carry out the "heavy" work, with the expert (and Western) archaeologists taking a directorial role. In most cases, especially in the nineteenth century, the rationale for and results of the excavations were not shared with these local people (Mickel 2019: 184). Hence, while members of the local community in such projects were technically engaging with the local heritage, this was done as a business transaction—paying locals to do the physical labor. Not only was there no information-sharing from the Western site directors, but often there was no space given to incorporate local knowledge and interpretations of archaeological sites and the material culture.

Increasing community engagement over the years has provided fascinating perspectives—perspectives that previously would have been ignored or not even noticed—on how archaeological heritage is understood in the present. Collaborative community archaeology research at Laetoli in northeastern Tanzania has been recently applied by scientists documenting early hominin footprints left in Pliocene volcanic deposits. Despite earlier projects, most notably led by the Leakeys, engaging local Maasai people as laborers on site, it is only relatively recently that archaeologists have taken the time to document the narratives of Maasai. This work has revealed rich folkloric layers that shed light on how local communities perceive these footprints, not only enriching knowledge about how they have been taken into local cultural heritage but also allowing community understandings of these remarkable footprints a place at the table alongside scientific interpretations (Ichumbaki et al. 2019). Such work is not only multivocal but also multidisciplinary, tapping into rich folkloristic and ethnographic layers and bringing interesting methodological combinations to archaeological fieldwork. Combining archaeological methods with other approaches is also a thread through the chapters of this volume.

In the United States, too, strategies employed within public archaeology look not only to engage the wider community, but in some cases also to seek to engage sectors of society that have been less involved with archaeology previously, whether for economic, cultural, or social reasons. These types of community engagement strategies seek to involve people not only in the physical fieldwork (or other work, such as post-excavation processes), but also increasingly in the development of research agendas and goals. Jodi Skipper (2014) for example gives an account of increasing the agency of an African American church community in Dallas, Texas, in relation to a culturally relevant excavation project. Here giving a voice to this particular community in relation to their cultural heritage was significant not only for the general goal of increasing participation in the archaeological past, but also to equip communities— particularly those that may be underrepresented or otherwise marginalized—with the tools and knowhow to preserve and lobby for historic sites that are important to them.

In his chapter, Torgrim Sneve Guttormsen acknowledges the possibility of utilizing Bakhtin to consider the different voices present in the interactions between archaeology and the public. While still identifying "archaeology" as one "voice," he notes that the public can consist of various other voices and viewpoints. Critical public archaeology as expressed in much of this book requires for the voices and knowledge of non-archaeologists to be heard and valued, in stark contrast to the knowledgeable but silenced laborers revealed in Allison Mickel's research. Yet, multivocality in and of itself is not necessarily the same thing as critical public archaeology; or at least it is not so on its own, as Westmont's introduction to this volume reminds us.

Not all archaeologists have expressed satisfaction with multivocality or indeed with the relinquishment of even some of their role as trained experts. In a Debate piece for the journal *Antiquity*, Alfredo González-Ruibal, Pablo Alonso González, and Felipe Criado-Boado (2018) have pushed back, to some extent, against the multivocality common in much archaeological practice that encourages participation, multiple perspectives, and the defocalization of the role of the expert. They warn that the public archaeology agenda as currently envisaged leaves professional archaeologists "politically and theoretically disempowered" (2018: 507). Their concerns relate to the wider challenges brought to society by the growth of populism in the early twenty-first century and the apparent rejection of expert opinion, a concern echoed by others (e.g., Schlanger 2017). Yet it also reveals a deeper issue in the current identity of archaeology as a professional pursuit, and its exaction of power over management of, access to, and interpretation of the past. A recent book met with strong opposition, including several high-profile anthropologists and archaeologists calling for its withdrawal from publication.[1] The authors of that book adopt an extreme perspective presumably intended as a reaction to arguments that scientific results should be considered on par with other versions of the past, in their case those derived from traditional Native American knowledge. Naturally this is an extreme version of the view that particularly positivist archaeologists and anthropologists may hold, but it is a reminder that even within the sector "we" do not all speak with one voice.[2]

Within this volume, the authors have demonstrated the importance of allowing a voice to non-archaeologists, especially in situations where equal treatment and respect for views and wishes have not always been a given. Mary Furlong Minkoff, Terry Brock, and Matthew Reeves address this issue head on in their chapter, as they describe their efforts to make the Montpelier Foundation an "anti-racist" organization. Applying Critical Race Theory, they aim to go beyond "superficial incorporation" of African Americans into archaeological work, tackling this challenge at policy level. This is also much more sophisticated than a basic multivocality without critical reflection, and allowed for change at a more fundamental operational level.

Work with Communities: Which Communities? Which Experts?

There are implications for the ways present and future archaeologists consider public engagement in their work. A core question to ask may be which communities we are considering when we talk about community engagement. Are there certain biases inherent in the ways communities are enticed to work with archaeologists? And what are the processes behind the decision-making that goes into public archaeology projects?

The terms "public archaeology" and "community archaeology" are common in the present time, both in archaeological practice and scholarship. Whole volumes (e.g., Moshenska 2017a), and journals such as *Public Archaeology* and *Journal of Community Archaeology and Heritage* have been dedicated to the discussion of these terms, with different definitions offered at various times by different authors (e.g., quoted in Moshenska 2017b: 1). These terms have some overlap, although public archaeology arguably takes a broader stance on what falls within its purview, with community archaeology seen as a category within public archaeology (Bollwerk, Connolly, and McDavid 2015: 179).

The expansion of understanding of "values" attached to archaeological heritage to include also social values (sensu Jones 2017) has helped heritage scholars in particular to recognize that "scientific" understandings of the past can fail to identify or acknowledge how particular groups or communities may understand their heritage. Archaeology itself as an inherently colonial practice brings its own problems even when it tries to engage with local communities. Shatha Abu-Khafajah and Riham Miqdadi (2019) have been critical of recent participatory projects in Jordan, which they identify as continuing to impose ideas from outside of the region onto local people and local heritage, despite the espoused goals of greater inclusion. This is a potential pitfall of many projects, even if they have good intentions at their core, as their goals and preferences may not always reflect those of the local communities. Even in the West, expert-led decisions concerning which categories of heritage to protect or restore can generate controversy and even outrage in the wider public (e.g., While 2007; La Roche and Blakey 1997).

The chapters of the first section of this book, "Work with Communities," outline a range of methods and ways of thinking about the process of archaeology—particularly public archaeology—but they go beyond simple engagement for the sake of participation. The groups involved in each case study have quite different stakes in the sites being discussed and are affected by the project outcomes in different ways.

Minkoff, Brock, and Reeves, as mentioned in the previous section, strive to create an anti-racist archaeology and archaeological organization in the Montpelier Foundation, Virginia. This anti-racism is targeted at increasing representation, participation, and determination of African Americans in particular. Inspired by Kendi's writing, they note not only historically racist methods and assumptions that have been associated with the practice of archaeology, but also the unfair treatment of African American archaeologists (including continued structural barriers within the archaeological profession) and the continued predominance of white scholars and practitioners within Historical Archaeology. The efforts to become anti-racist that they document in their chapter seem comprehensive, covering aspects of training, social inclusion, archaeological heritage interpretation, and of course participation in public archaeology projects—particularly those working explicitly with African American heritage. Fortunately, too, they are able to differentiate that African Americans are not themselves a homogeneous group, but comprise many aspects. In the context of Montpelier this includes "descendants, local residents, or archaeological practitioners" (p. 25, this volume).

At Montpelier, policy and practice changes are gradually implemented, no mean feat considering the documented difficulties that cultural organizations can experience in trying to alter their operational cultures (e.g., Sandell 2003). Acknowledging their own whiteness and continuing to push for even more change within their organization, the authors nonetheless demonstrate that positive change is possible, and that individuals working within organizational structures can make a lasting difference over time.

Reflecting upon past actions and injustices is a continued theme for the next chapter. In the twentieth-century history of the United States, one shameful episode is the incarceration of Japanese Americans that took place in World War II. Camps set up for internment of these people—men, women and also children, the majority of whom were US citizens—were often deliberately placed in remote, sparsely populated locations (Kamp-Whittaker and Clark 2019: 150). Jeffery Burton and Mary Farrell present community archaeology carried out around one such camp: the Manzanar Relocation Center, located in Owens Valley, California, which was designated a National Historic Site in 1992. Yet the World War II history is not the only aspect of this site, nor are the experiences and views of the survivors and descendants of Japanese American internees the only ones presented and engaged with, although naturally these remain centrally crucial.

A critical public archaeology in this case for the US National Park Service has involved not only including perspectives from descendants of both camp internees and camp guard personnel, but also the local residents of Owens Valley. In addition to this layer of multivocality, the work at the site has been an opportunity to challenge assumptions about the site's wartime history, including the reality of conditions in the camp (assumed by some to be much more luxurious than they actually were), the legal status of the incarcerees as US citizens rather than as aliens, and evidence of acts of resistance. Furthermore, in reaction to local resident wishes—some of whom were afraid of the wartime history putting their valley in a negative light—other aspects of the area's history were also covered. An important acknowledgment coming out of this and other critical public archaeological research on these Japanese American camps of

World War II (e.g., Camp 2016) establishes the role of racism, rather than any realistic threats to national security, in the wholesale deprivation of a particular ethnic group of their property, rights, and freedoms. As with Minkoff, Brock, and Reeves's work, acknowledging a racist past and challenging and disrupting existing power dynamics is a crucial step in critical public archaeology.

The thread of activism is overtly stated in M. Jay Stottman's chapter in which archaeology is framed as a performance; a means of animating a place with potentially significant implications. This positioning of the archaeological process in and of itself as a performance, and not merely a means to an end, recognizes and makes room for the public fascination with archaeological methods—especially excavation—as well as the imprint upon a landscape and upon memories that such activity renders. Recognizing himself and his practice of critical public archaeology as a form of activism, Stottman is both self-reflexive of his own process as well as meticulous in his deployment of critical public archaeology as a "reanimation" of Portland Wharf in Louisville, Kentucky. Stottman reveals that the neighborhood's prosperity and reputation have deteriorated, and that a master plan for developing a Portland Wharf Park included a prominent role for public archaeology interventions. Although relatively small in scale, Stottman is able to evaluate the potential for using consciously critical public archaeology approaches for activism in changing community perceptions of a particular space.

Activism is not a new notion to archaeology—especially that which seeks to redress historical injustices or to support previously marginalized groups (e.g., Atalay et al. 2016). However, Stottman identifies that public archaeology has opportunities to move beyond stewardship and education to more critically activist goals. Such activisms have manifested at different times and may not always directly involve archaeologists themselves at all (see, e.g., Moshenska [2020] for examples of public protest against archaeological works in the UK, including the removal of Seahenge from its site of discovery). That there are unavoidable divergences between community and archaeologist values, needs, and perspectives and even degrees of power is central to critical public archaeology thinking, and captured in Stottman's conclusion thus: "There is much more to being an activist than just marching side by side with the community for their causes. We cannot know or even relate to the struggles and issues of that community because we do not experience their community like they do. In the end, however, we still control the archaeology and the discourse around it."

Advancing Methods: Blending Archaeology with Other Interventions

Like most other activities in the world, archaeological work has been impacted by the COVID-19 pandemic, with many planned in-person activities canceled or postponed, due to the inherent risks of spreading infection connected to group gatherings. However, this has also presented an opportunity for developing other forms of engagement. Digital approaches to public archaeology had already been discussed and even tried out (e.g., Richardson 2013) and projects such as Archaeology in the Community (AITC), based in Washington, DC, were quick to adapt. AITC's Young Archaeologists' Club switched to virtual meetings instead of the planned in-person activities, including providing instructions to parents on activities that they could create and carry out at home (Jones and Pickens 2020). In other parts of the world, archaeological museums and attractions have begun cautiously to reopen, often with social distancing measures and other necessary restrictions in place. In some cases, more violent natural disasters, such as the March 2020 earthquake in Zagreb, Croatia, have had significant impact on archaeological heritage (such as the Archaeological Museum of Zagreb, which as of March 2022 was still closed until further notice due to earthquake damage[3]), and its custodians' abilities to engage with the public.

The other likely outcome of the pandemic, at least in the short term, is a reduction in international travel, both for business and for leisure. This will have an impact on the extent to which archaeological projects involving international teams can occur. This may in turn lead to a greater emphasis on developing archaeological skills locally, including within local communities, and in turn give more autonomy to local communities concerning the management, interpretation and study of archaeological heritage.

The chapters of this book were mostly written before we knew that the coronavirus pandemic was on its way, and their methodological approaches, already touched upon in the earlier section of the book, are a particular focus of the middle section, "Advancing Methods." These include movements toward the digital turn, mentioned by Monika Stobiecka and a particular focus of Adam Fracchia, and present sometimes tried and tested methods within the context of a critical public archaeology approach.

Monika Stobiecka's point of departure for considering the possibility of a critical archaeological museum is the work of art historian and sometime museum director Piotr Piotrowski, whose attempts at creating a critical museum out of the National Museum in Warsaw was at once inspired by the established "new museology" movement while also too radical for the conservative values of museum personnel and visitors alike. According to Stobiecka, "at that time neither the staff working at the museum nor the Polish audience were ready for Piotrowski's experiment" (p. 95, this volume). Connecting Piotrowski's aims to the recent ICOM proposal for a new museum definition,[4] it is worth noting that this definition has itself run into resistance, and that it was not in the end accepted, with a decision for a new definition once more opened for consultation until April 2021. Clearly and perhaps unfortunately, both public and professional expectations and assumptions about the role and form of established institutions such as museums can in themselves be a barrier to change.

Still, Stobiecka outlines a proposal for a critical archaeological museum that requires methodological changes in such a museum's interpretation strategies as well as its management. As she notes, while digital interventions have produced new media for museums to use for audience engagement, the message has often still not greatly changed. With a case study example of the *Heavy Water* artwork by Agnieszka Kalinowska, she highlights how artistic installations are a particularly powerful way of engendering critical engagement between audiences and museum exhibitions. Connecting lessons from the archaeological past to preparedness for possible futures—especially in light of the ongoing and impending global climate crisis (see also Morgan 2021)—has been argued elsewhere as a compelling reason for critical engagement with archaeological heritage and past ways of living (e.g., Rockman 2015). Such structural change as Stobiecka advocates for is daunting, and not always immediately successful, as noted with the Piotrowski example. However, as with Minkoff, Brock, and Reeves's chapter, efforts toward critical and reflexive change at the organizational level are worthwhile, even if it takes time and several false starts.

Working class heritage of court housing is the focus of Kerry Massheder-Rigby's chapter, which reflects upon work at the National Museums Liverpool's *Our Humble Abodes* project and which deployed oral history as a methodology alongside more traditional archaeological methods. As Massheder-Rigby notes, the court housing of Liverpool, as with back-to-back housing in other industrial cities of the UK such as Birmingham, Nottingham, York and Bradford, are still present (although also fading) in the British collective memory and enjoy a resoundingly negative reputation associated with the hardships and suffering endured by the working classes of the nineteenth and early twentieth centuries. My own personal recollection of such housing comes from childhood visits to museums in my home city of Nottingham, in which the images and descriptions of both the houses and living conditions therein filled me with dread and pity in equal measure. As Massheder-Rigby notes, "[T]he generally held impression of the court housing experience is not necessarily incorrect or untrue, but it is limiting" (p. 120, this volume).

Through oral history approaches, a particular subsection of the public—those with living memory and experiences of Liverpool's court housing—are afforded the role of expert as they provide a crucial component of the tangible and intangible elements associated with court housing that archaeologists and other specialists cannot fill in: personal experience. As with Westmont (below), narratives, in this case resulting from oral history sessions with particular individuals, take a central place in the interpretation of this period and social phenomenon. As with Burton and Farrell's work at Manzanar National Historic Site, the approach of the *Our Humble Abodes* project also allowed an opportunity to dispel some of the myths and assumptions that had grown around this particular heritage. Instead of a focus solely on social deprivation and suffering, the project was able to uncover rich stories of the sense of community and belonging, even in an environment in which residents regularly moved on and represented huge diversity in "skills, race, religion, and wages."

V. Camille Westmont's chapter focuses on narrative as a core critical method as well, although in all but one case the narratives used at her case study site, the Lone Rock Stockade in Tennessee, are historical, removing the opportunity for oral history. Rather than data collection, however, Westmont's focus is on the interpretation itself and the use of narratives in order to generate public empathy and ultimately activism in light of forms of forced labor that continue into the present. The third of her case study narratives presented in the chapter brings this powerfully home with the story of an inmate and their unjust treatment—which late into the narrative is revealed to have taken place not in the nineteenth century as with the previous examples, but rather is a story of an individual still enduring forced labor and physical injury as a contemporary prisoner.

Westmont's approach, drawing on the notion of "dark heritage" as a means of fostering activist, critical community archaeology, and a repositioning of local understandings of historical events (also in Westmont 2021), aims to make visitors aware of the continuing corrupt practices that not only take advantage of incarcerated individuals with no agency over their rights, but also circumvents what would otherwise be chances to open up employment opportunities for local communities by instead using cheaper prisoner labor. Although it is not addressed in detail in the current chapter, it will be fascinating and useful to learn in future research the extent to which this approach of deploying narrative based on the data from prisoner records has fulfilled this goal and the ways in which visitor perspectives of both past and present are enhanced as a result. As with the work of Minkoff, Brock, and Reeves, and the work of Burton and Farrell, racism is inevitably at the core of past and present injustices uncovered by Westmont's research. The use of voluntary action to transcribe and eventually digitize the prisoner records from the Lone Rock Stockade offer a tantalizing glimpse into possible future interventions and engagements.

Digitization is the primary focus of Adam Fracchia, who describes the ongoing work to digitize and make publicly available data from the long-running Archaeology in Annapolis project—itself clearly influential in inspiring many of the chapters in this volume with its long history of arguably critical public archaeology work. The goal of creating online databases for public access and consumption is a laudable one, and Fracchia is realistic about the challenges and opportunities that this brings, including difficulties over ownership of different materials, barriers and specifications dictated by funding, and the importance of representing and "voicing" different sections of the local community.

Although the digital turn has been present in public archaeology for some time now, there are continued questions over its goals. As hinted by Fracchia but also addressed elsewhere (e.g., Börjesson, Pettersson, and Huvila 2015), archaeological digital data is very often shaped, even unconsciously, by dominating ideologies and assumptions concerning the organization of archaeological heritage and its management. Critical public archaeology approaches then can also help us to interrogate archaeological data as it appears and is served up in the digital sphere. User experience is also an important consideration, especially for new resources, in order to ensure that potential users are not only aware of the resource but can find the type of information that is useful to them, taking into account that there are likely a wide range of different types of users all with different objectives and interests (e.g., Wessman, Thomas, and Rohiola 2019). It will be fascinating to see how this digital resource evolves over time, as well as to find out, if it is possible to do so, who uses it and for what purposes.

Situating Critical Archaeology:
Heritagization Processes and Audience Perceptions

As Westmont has shown in her introductory chapter to this book, critical public archaeology's relationship to critical theory is not unique within archaeological work. The final two chapters offer reflection for how critical public archaeology may move forward, as well as its limitations. Torgrim Sneve Guttormsen connects public archaeology with "public historiography" in his application of critical theory to the Norwegian Museum of Technology's foundation and development. According to Guttormsen, his study of public archaeology using public historiography as an approach means "when public archaeology, thereby the relationship between archaeology and the public, adequately manage to explain the social problems that exist in society, offer practical solutions for how to respond to them and make changes, and clearly adhere to the norms of criticism established by the field" (p. 181, this volume). In approaching an early twentieth-century museum's foundation (the Norwegian Museum of Technology was founded in 1914), Guttormsen is able to apply critical theory as inspired by Mikhail Mikhailovich Bakhtin, especially drawing upon the concept of dialogism and its use to expose power relations and other social and societal relationships.

In the context of early twentieth-century Norway, important archaeological discoveries such as the Oseberg grave mound were woven into national and European narratives concerning technological progress. When the Norwegian Museum of Technology opened, according to Guttormsen, it was similarly interwoven into a broader narrative of technology as progress and a heritagization process resulting in "technological cultural heritage." As such, Guttormsen argues, the connection of the Museum of Technology with the Viking Ship Museum made perfect sense at the time according to contemporary notions of heritage.

Museum archaeology is central also to the chapter of Chiara Zuanni, who presents another related field of inquiry and methods—visitor studies—through her research at the Manchester Museum's Ancient Worlds Galleries. Like Stobiecka, Zuanni draws on the long and continuing history of new museology to situate her work. Her results, indicating that few museum visitors experience exhibitions in exactly the ways in which curators—applying all kinds of approaches and techniques—intended, is informative for all critical public archaeology interventions.

Zuanni notes that the exhibitions applied a range of "design solutions," from expositions of archaeology and its methodological processes through to presentations of well-known ancient civilizations (namely in this case Ancient Egypt) in dialogue with nearby cultures that are rarely considered in relationship to them, such as Islam, in order to provoke new perspectives in the audience. The approaches shown in the Manchester Museum resonate with many of the chapters in this book, and speak to Stobiecka's proposals for a critical archaeological museum as well as Guttormsen's identification of contemporary messages and concerns communicated within museum settings. As with many chapters here, the exhibitions that Zuanni analyzed also aim to place both novel and established forms of interpretation and public engagement into scenarios in which sometimes hidden power structures are revealed, and the visitors or participants are inspired to update their perspectives on the past and present. Zuanni's work explores methods as well as her experiences working with different communities—in this case specifically people that had visited the Ancient Worlds Galleries. Highlighting the importance of the personal and social contexts of each visitor in shaping the messages that they take home from, or even interpolate into, the exhibitions is a stark reminder that no matter the efforts of public archaeologists and others, much of what the public chooses to engage with and in what ways remains out of our hands.

Final Reflections

The chapters of this volume present ongoing and recently completed research that strives to bring a criticality to public archaeology that arguably has not always been present before. They offer clues as to the future trends in public archaeology discourse and initiatives, at a time when—as Stobiecka notes and Kristian Kristiansen (2014) suggested—archaeology more broadly may be moving toward "scientific" methods.

In a late- and post-COVID world, and with the constant reminder that the climate crisis has not gone anywhere, communities are grappling not only with past traumas and injustices, with which archaeology can potentially help, but also with serious anxieties concerning possible futures. Heritage stewardship has to evolve beyond simple safeguarding for future generations in order to take into account not only likely changes to the environment, but also changing needs that the public will have from the remains of the past. This could be everything from the sustainability lessons that the past might offer through to opportunities to provide sources for stability and fortitude, even if unity is less likely. A critical public archaeology may well prove essential for these challenges.

Suzie Thomas is Professor of Heritage Studies at the University of Antwerp in Belgium. She holds a PhD in Heritage Studies from Newcastle University (UK) and has previously worked at the Universities of Glasgow (UK) and Helsinki (Finland). She is particularly interested in participatory approaches to heritage and was a founding editor of the *Journal of Community Archaeology and Heritage*.

Notes

1. College Fix. 2020. "Academics Call for Cancellation of University-Published Archaeology Book." *College Fix*, 18 December. Retrieved 7 March 2022 from https://www.thecollegefix.com/academics-call-for-cancellation-of-university-published-archaeology-book/.
2 See Abadia and Lewis-Sing (2021) for a discussion of positivist and epistemological theories in the context of public engagement.
3. AMZ. "Announcement about Working Hours." *AMZ*. Retrieved 7 March 2022 from https://www.amz.hr/en/amz-announcements/announcement-about-working-hours-earthquake/.

4. ICOM. 2019. "ICOM Announces the Alternative Museum Definition that Will Be Subject to a Vote." *ICOM*, 25 July. Retrieved 7 March 2022 from https://icom.museum/en/news/icom-announces-the-alternative-museum-definition-that-will-be-subject-to-a-vote/.

References

Abadía, Oscar Moro, and Emma Lewis-Sing. 2021. "The Decline of Epistemology in Archaeology: Comments on an Ongoing Discussion." In *Interdisciplinarity and Archaeology: Scientific Interactions in Nineteenth-and Twentieth-Century Archaeology*, ed. Laura Coltofean-Arizancu and Margarita Díaz-Andreu, 203–23. Oxford: Oxbow Books.

Abu-Khafajah, Shatha, and Riham Miqdadi. 2019. "Prejudice, Military Intelligence, and Neoliberalism: Examining the Local within Archaeology and Heritage Practices in Jordan." *Contemporary Levant* 4(2): 92–106.

Atalay, Sonya, Lee Rains Clauss, Randall H. McGuire, and J. R. Welch, eds. 2016. *Transforming Archaeology: Activist Practices and Prospects*. London: Routledge.

Bollwerk, Elizabeth, Robert Connolly, and Carol McDavid. 2015. "Co-creation and Public Archaeology." *Advances in Archaeological Practice* 3(3): 178–87.

Börjesson, Lisa, Bodil Petersson, and Isto Huvila. 2015. "Information Policy for (Digital) Information in Archaeology: Current State and Suggestions for Development." *Internet Archaeology* 40. https://doi.org/10.11141/ia.40.4.

Byrne, Denis. 1991. "Western Hegemony in Archaeological Heritage Management." *History and Anthropology* 5(2): 269–76.

Camp, Stacey Lynn. 2016. "Landscapes of Japanese American Internment." *Historical Archaeology* 50(1): 169–86.

Chirikure, Shadreck, and Gilbert Pwiti. 2008. "Community Involvement in Archaeology and Cultural Heritage Management: An Assessment from Case Studies in Southern Africa and Elsewhere." *Current Anthropology* 49(3): 467–85.

Díaz-Andreu, Margarita. 2016. "Arqueología, comunidad y valor social: un reto para el patrimonio arqueológico del siglo XXI." In *Arqueología y comunidad: el valor social del patrimonio arqueológico en el siglo XXI*, ed. Margarita Díaz-Andreu, Ana Pastor Pérez, Apen Ruiz Martínez, 69–90. Madrid: JAS Arqueología.

González-Ruibal, Alfredo, Pablo Alonso González, and Felipe Criado-Boado. 2018. "Against Reactionary Populism: Towards a New Public Archaeology." *Antiquity* 92(362): 507–15.

Ichumbaki, Elgidius B., Marco Cherin, Fidelis T. Masao, and Jacopo Moggi-Cecchi. 2019. "Local People's Interpretations of the Hominin Footprints at Laetoli, Tanzania." *Journal of Community Archaeology & Heritage* 6(2): 122–38.

Immonen, Visa, and Jussi-Pekka Taavitsainen. 2011. "Oscillating between National and International: The Case of Finnish Archaeology." In *Comparative Archaeologies: A Sociological View of the Science of the Past*, ed. Ludomir R. Lozny, 137–77. New York: Springer.

Ingold, Tim. 2000. *The Perception of the Environment: Essays on Livelihood, Dwelling and Skill*. London: Routledge.

Jones, Siân. 2017. "Wrestling with the Social Value of Heritage: Problems, Dilemmas and Opportunities." *Journal of Community Archaeology & Heritage* 4(1): 21–37.

Jones, Alexandra, and Sydney Pickens. 2020. "The Power of Community Archaeologists in Uncertain Times." *Journal of Community Archaeology & Heritage* 7(3): 155–57.

Kamp-Whittaker, April, and Bonnie J. Clark. 2019. "10 Social Networks and the Development of Neighborhood Identities in Amache, a WWII Japanese American Internment Camp." *Archeological Papers of the American Anthropological Association* 30(1): 148–58.

Kristiansen, Kristian. 2014. "Towards a New Paradigm? The Third Science Revolution and Its Possible Consequences in Archaeology." *Current Swedish Archaeology* 22: 11–34.

La Roche, Cheryl J., and Michael L. Blakey. 1997. "Seizing Intellectual Power: The Dialogue at the New York African Burial Ground." *Historical Archaeology* 31(3): 84–106.

Mickel, Allison. 2019. "Essential Excavation Experts: Alienation and Agency in the History of Archaeological Labor." *Archaeologies* 15(2): 181–205.

Morgan, Colleen. 2021. "Save the Date for Future Mourning: Prefiguration and Heritage." In *Forum Kritische Archäologie* 10: 1–5.

Moshenska, Gabriel, ed. 2017a. *Key Concepts in Public Archaeology*. London: UCL Press.

———. 2017b. "Introduction: Public Archaeology as Practice and Scholarship Where Archaeology Meets the World." In *Key Concepts in Public Archaeology*, ed. Gabriel Moshenska, 1–13. London: UCL Press.

———. 2020. "Archaeological Excavations as Sites of Public Protest in Twentieth-Century Britain." *Fennoscandia Archaeologica* 37: 181–95.

Richardson, Lorna. 2013. "A Digital Public Archaeology?" *Papers from the Institute of Archaeology* 23(1): 1–12. https://doi.org/10.5334/pia.431.

Rockman, Marcy. 2015. "An NPS Framework for Addressing Climate Change with Cultural Resources." *The George Wright Forum* 32(1): 37–50.

Sandell, Richard. 2003. "Social Inclusion, the Museum and the Dynamics of Sectoral Change." *Museum and Society* 1(1): 45–62.

Schlanger, Nathan. 2017. "Brexit in Betwixt: Some European Conjectures on Its Predictability and Implications." *The Historic Environment: Policy & Practice* 8(3): 212–22.

Shelton, Anthony. 2013. "Critical Museology: A Manifesto." *Museum Worlds* 1(1): 7–23.

Skipper, Jodi. 2014. "Sustaining Visibility? The Quandary of St. Paul and Archaeology in the Long Run." *Journal of Community Archaeology & Heritage* 1(3): 210–27.

Smith, Laurajane. 2006. *Uses of Heritage*. London: Routledge.

Smith, Laurajane, and Gary Campbell. 2017. "The Tautology of "Intangible Values" and the Misrecognition of Intangible Cultural Heritage." *Heritage & Society* 10(1): 26–44.

Seymour, Michael. 2014. "Early Excavations around the Globe." In *Encyclopedia of Global Archaeology*, ed. Claire Smith, 2219–30. Cham: Springer.

Taylor, Brian. 1995. "Amateurs, Professionals and the Knowledge of Archaeology." *British Journal of Sociology* 46(3): 499–508.

Thomas, Suzie. 2014. "Clubs and Societies Promoting Archaeology (National and Local)." In *Encyclopedia of Global Archaeology*, ed. Claire Smith, 1513–18. Cham: Springer.

Trigger, Bruce G. 1989. *A History of Archaeological Thought*. Cambridge: Cambridge University Press.

Wessman, Anna, Suzie Thomas, and Ville Rohiola. 2019. "Digital Archaeology and Citizen Science: Introducing the Goals of FindSampo and the SuALT project." *SKAS* 1(2019): 2–17.

Westmont, V. Camille. 2022. "Dark Heritage in the New South: Remembering Convict Leasing in Southern Middle Tennessee through Community Archaeology." *International Journal of Historical Archaeology* 26(1): 1–21.

While, Aidan. 2007. "The State and the Controversial Demands of Cultural Built Heritage: Modernism, Dirty Concrete, and Postwar Listing in England." *Environment and Planning B: Urban Analytics and City Science* 34(4): 645–63.

Index

Milton Keynes UK
Ingram Content Group UK Ltd.
UKHW022307230424
441636UK00005B/99